Accusatory Practices

Studies in European History from the
Journal of Modern History

John W. Boyer, Sheila Fitzpatrick, and Jan E. Goldstein
Series Editors

Denunciation

in Modern

European

History,

1789-1989

ACCUSATORY
PRACTICES

Edited by

Sheila

Fitzpatrick

and

Robert

Gellately

The University of Chicago Press

Chicago and London

The essays in this volume originally appeared in the *The Journal of Modern History,* Volume 68, Number 4, December 1996.

The University of Chicago Press, Chicago 60637
The University of Chicago Press, Ltd., London
© 1997 by The University of Chicago
All rights reserved. Published 1997
Printed in the United States of America
01 00 99 98 97   5 4 3 2 1

Library of Congress Cataloging-in-Publication Data

Accusatory practices : denunciation in modern European history, 1789–1989 / edited by Sheila Fitzpatrick and Robert Gellately.
    p.   cm.
    Collection of essays originally published in the Journal of modern history, v. 68, no. 4, Dec. 1996: most of the essays were originally presented at a conference held Apr. 1994, University of Chicago.
    Includes bibliographical references and index.
    Contents: Introduction to the practices of denunciation in modern European history / Sheila Fitzpatrick and Robert Gellately—The theory and practice of denunciation in the French Revolution / Colin Lucas—A culture of denunciation : peasant labor migration and religious anathematization in rural Russia, 1860–1905 / Jeffrey Burds—Denunciation as a tool of ecclesiastical control : the case of Roman Catholic Modernism / Gary Lease—Signals from below : Soviet letters of denunciation of the 1930s / Sheila Fitzpatrick—Denunciation and its function in Soviet governance / Vladimir A. Kozlov—The uses of Volksgemeinschaft : letters to the NSDAP Kreisleitung Eisenach, 1939–1940 / John Connelly—Denunciations in twentieth-century Germany : aspects of self-policing in the Third Reich and the German Democratic Republic / Robert Gellately.
    ISBN 0-226-25273-6 (cloth).—ISBN 0-226-25274-4 (pbk.)
    1. Denunciation (Criminal law)—Europe—History.   2. Denunciation (Canon law)—History.   I. Fitzpatrick, Sheila.   II. Gellately, Robert, 1943–   .
KJC9520.A89   1997
363.25'2—dc21   97-10693
                                                                                                    CIP

Contents

1 SHEILA FITZPATRICK and ROBERT GELLATELY
Introduction to the Practices of Denunciation in Modern
European History

22 COLIN LUCAS
The Theory and Practice of Denunciation in the
French Revolution

40 JEFFREY BURDS
A Culture of Denunciation: Peasant Labor Migration and
Religious Anathematization in Rural Russia, 1860–1905

73 GARY LEASE
Denunciation as a Tool of Ecclesiastical Control: The Case
of Roman Catholic Modernism

85 SHEILA FITZPATRICK
Signals from Below: Soviet Letters of Denunciation of the
1930s

121 VLADIMIR A. KOZLOV
Denunciation and Its Functions in Soviet Governance:
A Study of Denunciations and Their Bureaucratic
Handling from Soviet Police Archives, 1944–1953

153 JOHN CONNELLY
The Uses of *Volksgemeinschaft:* Letters to the NSDAP
Kreisleitung Eisenach, 1939–1940

185 ROBERT GELLATELY
Denunciations in Twentieth-Century Germany:
Aspects of Self-Policing in the Third Reich and
the German Democratic Republic

223 INDEX

233 CONTRIBUTORS

Introduction to the Practices of Denunciation in Modern European History*

Sheila Fitzpatrick
University of Chicago

Robert Gellately
Huron College, University of Western Ontario

This collection is a preliminary exploration of a new subject of historical inquiry: the phenomenon of denunciation in modern European history. It is based on a conference on practices of denunciation, focused particularly on the Soviet Union under Stalin and on Nazi Germany, which was organized by Sheila Fitzpatrick and Robert Gellately at the University of Chicago in April 1994. More than half of the papers published here were originally presented at that conference.[1]

We must begin with the question of definition. This is tricky, because the accusatory acts by citizens that we are interested in are not clearly distinguished as a category of everyday behavior in contemporary English. The word "denunciation" comes closest but has the disadvantage of exoticism: an English speaker is more likely to use it in connection with, say, Nazi Germany than in describing the mores of an English village. We should say at the outset that we assume that practices of denunciation may be found close to home as well as far away.

For the purposes of the present project, denunciations may be defined as spontaneous communications from individual citizens to the state (or to another authority such as the church) containing accusations of wrongdoing by other citizens or officials and implicitly or explicitly calling for punishment. Typically, denunciations are written and delivered privately to an addressee rather than published. They are likely to invoke state (or church) values and to disclaim any personal interest on the part of the writer, citing duty to the state (or the public good) as the reason for offering information to the authorities. Denouncing and informing are closely related but not synonymous acts. The term "informer" generally implies a regular, often paid, relationship to the police.

* Robert Gellately is the author of Secs. I, II, and VII of this introduction, and Sheila Fitzpatrick, of Secs. III, IV, V, and VI.

[1] The conference was made possible by the generous support of the National Council for Soviet and East European Research and the University of Chicago.

This essay originally appeared in *The Journal of Modern History* 68 (December 1996).

Denouncing and informing take many guises. Denunciations may be delivered orally to the police, in person, or by telephone. In some societies, like Communist China, denunciations are posted on walls. In others, television viewers and radio listeners phone in their denunciations at the ends of broadcasts on "most wanted" criminals.[2] In addition to the unpublished written denunciations with which this collection of essays is primarily concerned, there are also published denunciations. Newspapers receive many letters from citizens whose avowed aim is publicity for their accusations. While many of these writers may in fact be satisfied if their letters provoke official investigations into their grievances without publication or publicity, others are appealing not so much to the state as to an imagined "court of public opinion" that may act on the state, as in Zola's famous "*J'Accuse*" letter in the Dreyfus case.

The state (or its agent) is typically a recipient of denunciations, not an author. But this is not always or entirely so. Denunciatory statements may be solicited from individuals by police during interrogations (a favorite practice in the Stalinist Great Purges) or by public bodies like Royal Commissions or the notorious U.S. House Committee on Un-American Activities. In revolutionary contexts, public indictment of an "enemy of the people" is often an act of collective outcasting that could be described as denunciation *by* the revolutionary state *to* "the people." In totalitarian states, the stigmatization of individuals and categories of individuals (Jews, kulaks, etc.) and their exposure to public ignominy is another form of "state" denunciation addressed to the public.[3]

While our initial focus on the Soviet Union and Nazi Germany remains central to the present collection, we have also sought to put the phenomenon of denunciation into a broader comparative perspective. As the term "practices" suggests, we are interested not only in the political functions of denunciation but also in its social and anthropological aspects. We do not assume that there is a single practice of denunciation in modern European—or even in twentieth-century European totalitarian—societies. Rather, we start from the premise that there is likely to be a range of practices whose societal and political functions vary greatly. We see these practices as an important but unstudied point of contact between individual citizens and the state, one that embodies a whole set of unarticulated decisions about loyalties to the state, on the one hand, and to family and fellow citizens, on the other. This is a topic that has not previously been systematically investigated or analyzed by scholars, and we are

---

[2] Dieter Mayer-Simeth in Nicole Czechowski and Jacques Hassoun, eds., *La délation: Un archaïsme, une technique* (Paris, 1992), pp. 78–85, on German TV program *Dossier X . . . non résolu,* created by Édoard Zimmermann, running since 1967. *Crime Watchers* in Britain is a knockoff.

[3] Colin Lucas has contributed a great deal to this discussion of state denunciation.

conscious that the present work is just scratching the surface. Our objective in this collection is not to offer definitive conclusions but, rather, to open the discussion.

I. THE IMPACT OF 1989

Our interest in the subject of denunciation was sparked by a particular historiographical conjuncture. Since the end of the Cold War and the collapse of Communist regimes across central and eastern Europe, there has been a significant shift in the study of modern Europe's terroristic regimes—particularly Hitler's Germany and Stalin's Soviet Union. To some extent the shift had already commenced in the 1980s, but it has been reinforced considerably by recent revelations about the "posttotalitarian" terror systems that were established after 1945 across central and eastern Europe. With the end of the eastern dictatorships, symbolized by the dramatic fall of the Berlin Wall in November 1989, came a good deal of rethinking about terror and "totalitarian" regimes from before and after 1945. Witnesses from the old Soviet bloc came forward with testimonies, books and articles were written by liberated dissidents and former victims, and these materials frequently offered telling insights into the everyday terror. (One thinks particularly of the writings of Václav Havel, but there have been important and numerous publications from most of the former Soviet bloc countries.)[4]

In some of these countries, notably in the old German Democratic Republic (GDR), the files of the secret police forces themselves have been made available for study. Discussions of regimes like the ones in the GDR have focused a great deal of attention on informing by "ordinary citizens" who were not actually members of the secret police but who collaborated on a regular basis. Access to declassified materials has made it possible to carry out research, and interest in exploring the Stasi material has been remarkable.[5] For the second time in fifty years a German state's most secret and sensitive files were inherited by a new regime and made available for scrutiny. By May 1995, 1,500 researchers and 3,200 reporters had already applied for permission to examine

---

[4] See, e.g., Václav Havel, "The Power of the Powerless," in *Open Letters,* ed. Paul Wilson (London, 1991), pp. 125–214. For other recent responses of writers, see, e.g., Jürgen Fuchs, "Ich du er sie es wir ihr sie: Eine 'Kontaktierungs' Revue," *Kurzbuch* (March 1994), pp. 41–58; Norman Manea, *On Clowns: The Dictator and the Artist* (New York, 1992), pp. 3–32.

[5] Stasi is short for Staatssicherheit, or also Staatssicherheitsdienst, both of which are short for the Ministerium für Staatssicherheit (abbreviation: MfS). A sense of the complexity of the MfS or Stasi can be gained from the recently published list of initials and oft-used concepts used by the Stasi. This *Abkürzungsverzeichnis* (Berlin, 1993) runs to nearly fifty pages.

these records. In addition, public and private institutions had asked for back-ground checks on about 1.6 million people, so that the new federal institution with jurisdiction over the files (usually termed the "Gauck-Authority" after its administrator, Joachim Gauck) has been faced with an avalanche of work.[6] A sense of how many people were directly affected by the Stasi terror may be gained from the fact that, by May 1995, some 2.7 million requests had been made to the Gauck Authority to see the files—950,000 from private citizens alone.[7] Even five years after its founding, the Gauck Authority continues to receive about one thousand requests per working day from people who wish to examine the information collected about them by the Stasi.[8] Similar though less extreme perturbations have swept the newly de-Sovietized countries of Eastern Europe.[9]

These monumental historical changes have not only led to painful examina-tions by contemporaries of these recently fallen regimes; they have also had an impact on the study of terroristic regimes of the past. New social and political impulses have revitalized the study of the terror in Hitler's Germany and post-war Eastern Europe. Until the end of the 1980s, the Nazi terror was very much seen "from the top down," defined in terms of the main perpetrators and dis-cussed in the context of the Nazi "police or SS state." An associated variety of scholarship focused on state treatment of the victims, especially the Jews and other targeted social groups, but also on political opponents like the Commu-nists and Socialists. As was true also for the study of the Soviet Union, the totalitarian model provided the main theoretical framework for research. How-ever, by 1985–90 and perhaps even earlier, anomalies were beginning to accu-mulate (to paraphrase Thomas Kuhn), and historians, particularly those inter-ested in social history, started to broaden their investigations to study the everyday or routine terror in society at large and to place greater emphasis on the terror as seen "from the bottom up."[10]

Much of this new research has pointed to the importance of denunciation by

[6] By the second half of 1993, 759 research projects on various aspects of the GDR's history were already under way, and there are very likely even more today. Reported in Jürgen Kocka, "Ein deutscher Sonderweg: Überlegungen zur Sozialgeschichte der DDR," in *Aus Politik und Zeitgeschichte,* B40/94 (October 7, 1994), p. 34.

[7] The official title is "Der Bundesbeauftragte für die Unterlagen des Staatssicherheits-dienstes der ehemaligen Deutschen Demokratischen Republic."

[8] *Zweiter Tätigkeitsbericht des Bundesbeauftragten für die Unterlagen des Staats-sicherheitsdienstes der ehemaligen Deutschen Demokratischen Republik 1995* (Berlin, 1995), pp. 4–7.

[9] See Tina Rosenberg, *The Haunted Land: Facing Europe's Ghosts after Communism* (New York, 1995).

[10] For analysis of the historiography see Robert Gellately, "Situating the 'SS-State' in a Social-Historical Context: Recent Histories of the SS, the Police, and the Courts in the Third Reich," *Journal of Modern History* 64 (1992): 338–65.

members of the general population.[11] Denunciations—which occupy a kind of intermediate space between the society "below" and the state or the authorities "above"—evidently constituted a crucial ingredient of both Nazi and Soviet terror. Recent publications have revealed that many people were involved—either "formally" as civilian agents signed up by the secret police or "informally" as occasional denouncers of others for breaking laws, deviating from ideological teachings, or demonstrating some other social or political failings. Informers were not simply—or at least not always—"true believers"; they often had motives of their own. Frequently their motives were mixed, and personal interests could play a significant role in citizens' decisions to turn in friends, neighbors, and even relatives. Nevertheless, their collaboration greatly facilitated the functioning of the terror at the grass roots. The historiographical shift now under way in studies of the terror in Nazi Germany and in the Soviet Union suggests that in both cases it was more multifaceted, dynamic, and complex than has often been supposed. New research is restoring the voices of the men and women who had been silenced by the terror, and this development has dovetailed with the demands for democratic reforms and the insistence on civil rights all across Eastern Europe in the last decade or so. Public outrage in these countries and abroad at the human rights violations of the secret police has greatly heightened interest in the history of terroristic regimes.

Since 1990, there may well have been more publications on various aspects of dictatorship, secret police, and terror than in any comparable period in the half-century since the end of World War II. The newest revelations about terroristic regimes have demanded attention and analysis and call for historians to rethink many of their understandings of such regimes. How did these systems really work? What were the responsibilities and the duties of the "good citizen"? How important were denunciations from the population? What purposes did denunciations serve, besides helping the terror system function smoothly?

II. NAZI GERMANY

In recent scholarship on Nazi terror, there has been something close to a paradigm shift associated with a growing consideration of the role society played in the system, especially at the local level, which is where terror takes place. We have become more aware than ever that the people governed by terroristic

---

[11] Until 1990, besides Robert Gellately's essay ("The Gestapo and German Society: Political Denunciations in the Gestapo Case Files," *Journal of Modern History* 60 [1988]: 654–94), and his book, *The Gestapo and German Society: Enforcing Racial Policy, 1933–1945* (Oxford, 1990), there were only two essays on denunciations in Nazi Germany. One (from 1979) only appeared posthumously; see Reinhard Mann, *Protest und Kontrolle im Dritten Reich: Nationalsozialistische Herrschaft im Alltag einer rheinischen Grossstadt* (Frankfurt am Main, 1987), pp. 287–305. Martin Broszat published

regimes were involved in the everyday terror in countless ways: they were not
just victims who were silenced or driven in retreat to their private spheres. It
is true that certain forms of political participation, such as voting in elections
for the Reichstag, were robbed of real meaning because all opposition parties
were banned and criticism of the government was turned into a crime. But
if participation in formal politics was virtually brought to an end, or at least
made into a hollow exercise in Nazi Germany, certain avenues remained open
through which citizens could express their opinions, articulate their interests,
and seek to satisfy them. One of the ways citizens participated in the Nazi
system was to mail countless letters of supplication, complaint, or accusation
to officials at all levels. These letters were usually efforts to get some "action"
from the state, but some of them were simply expressions of loyalty and even
love for Hitler and Nazism. Denunciations from the general population were
also channeled to various levels of the Nazi Party. In addition, we would be
mistaken to think that the Gestapo—the notorious Secret State Police—was
so murderous and incalculable that it was viewed by ordinary citizens as utterly
unapproachable at the time. Denunciations were in fact often sent directly to
the Gestapo. It could be argued that it was precisely the Gestapo's mythical
powers and its ruthless reputation that made it into a much favored destination
for accusations. Germans could not fail to realize that the Nazi regime would
need more information than the Weimar democracy it had replaced, given its
desire to transform and regulate social life from cradle to grave. Citizens
quickly learned that this great hunger for information could be made to serve
purposes of their own, and thanks to the sympathetic hearing they could expect
if they approached the party or the police with the "right kinds" of information,
they were not shy to come forward. From studying the documentation that
survives on Nazi Germany, it seems clear that this kind of citizen activity, even
if much of it was not motivated by an "idealistic" faith in Nazism, nevertheless
contributed greatly to the enforcement of many of the most repugnant of Hitler's policies. The Nazi "police state" was not merely imposed on society from
above by a ruthless dictator.

A central contribution of research on Hitler's regime in the last five years
has been the rediscovery of the important role of denunciations in the routine
operation of the Gestapo and the terror system. Denunciations represented the
key link in the three-way interaction between the formal terror system, the
German population, and the enforcement of various laws and similar measures.

---

an essay in an obscure archivists' journal; see his "Politische Denunziationen in der
NS-Zeit: Aus Forschungserfahrungen im Staatsarchiv München," *Archivalische Zeit-
schrift* 73 (1977): 221–38. He decided not to include that study in the collection of his
essays; see Martin Broszat, *Nach Hitler: Der schwierige Umgang mit unserer Geschichte* (Munich, 1988), p. 8.

The enforcement of Nazi anti-Semitic policies, to mention a particularly important example, was more dependent than we had suspected on private persons coming forward with information to the Gestapo or other authorities. It was not necessary that Germany as a whole, or even individual informers, become rabidly anti-Semitic—only that information from the population flow to the secret police or to other organizations of the German state or Nazi Party.[12]

In Nazi Germany, a host of factors influenced the propensity of the population to inform. Their willingness to denounce, and even the frequency with which they did so, differed from place to place and over time, as well as according to the various official measures that the regime wanted to enforce. As recent work has shown, however, there is no question that the Nazi regime's most important enforcement organization, the Gestapo, could hardly have operated with such "success" had it been denied the participation of the German population as occasional voluntary denouncers.

III. THE SOVIET UNION UNDER STALIN

Turning from Germany and Eastern Europe to the Soviet Union, both the historical and the historiographical patterns change, despite significant points of similarity. The opening of Soviet archives in the 1990s has been less complete than elsewhere in the former Soviet bloc. In the Soviet Union, most of the former state archives, including their classified sections, have opened, and along with them the former Communist Party archives, which have come under the state archives' jurisdiction for the first time. But the change of regime following the collapse of the Soviet Union was by no means so absolute and unambiguous as elsewhere. Consequently, the present regime still protects part of the secret archives of its Communist predecessor (in the closed Presidential Archive), and the former KGB, now known as the Federal Counter-Intelligence Service (FSK), is still in control of its archives and those of the police agencies that preceded it and allows only the most selective and partial access. There are, to be sure, huge numbers of denunciations in other archives (state, party, military, etc.). But since the issuance in 1992 of new regulations protecting individuals from disclosure of personal data, these archives too have been wary of giving out files that clearly contain denunciations.

Partly because the opening of archives has only been partial, it has not produced the same kind of shocked public reaction to disclosures about police files and denunciations that has occurred in Germany and Eastern Europe. There have been publications of individual denunciations—especially those written about or by well-known political or cultural figures—both in scholarly journals and, with more sensational intent, in the press, causing embarrassment

[12] See Gellately, *The Gestapo and German Society,* p. 259.

to some individuals.[13] There were also some demonstrative repudiations of the famous child denouncer of the Stalin era, Pavlik Morozov, which involved the renaming of kindergartens and the taking down of monuments[14] (although by the time of Gorbachev's perestroika, Pavlik was already an icon of the distant past, whose monuments remained in place only through inertia). Generally, however, things have been comparatively quiet.

This striking contrast with the situation in the GDR and Eastern Europe requires some additional explanation. One factor contributing to the Soviet lack of excitement is undoubtedly that the most extreme practices of the Soviet police state belong to a period now half a century gone, not to the immediate past. To find a sense of outrage and revelation in Russia comparable to that expressed in the early 1990s in Germany and Eastern Europe, we would have to go back to the Twentienth Party Congress and Khrushchev's Secret Speech. Emotionally, this seems to be only a subdued replay of the trauma of 1956 for many Russians. In the decades after de-Stalinization was halted in the mid-1960s, Western Sovietologists often remarked that in the end the Soviet population would have to come to terms with its own past, meaning the Great Purges, the gulag, and the terror system in general. It looks now as if that is just what they did, albeit quietly, passively, and without the anticipated cathartic effect. Sometime in the Brezhnev "era of stagnation," Stalinist terror apparently became old news to Soviet citizens.

This is not to say that there has not been a great accession of knowledge about Stalinist terror, at least in some of its aspects. Quantitative data on numbers of prisoners in the gulag, executions, administrative exiles, and so on have become available for the first time. Of course the interpretation of these data remains a matter of controversy among scholars, but as far as the Western Sovietological community is concerned, some of the earlier estimates of victims of Stalin's terror were so high that the revelation that at the height of the Great Purges gulag camps contained over a million prisoners, more than 40 percent of whom were "politicals," can scarcely come as a shock. The surprises for Western scholars have been the number of straight-out executions during the Great Purges (a figure of well over half a million is quoted, and this is probably based on incomplete data) and the large number of persons living as administrative exiles and deportees or otherwise deprived of full civil

---

[13] See, e.g., the publication by N. Teptsov, "Tainyi agent Iosifa Stalina. Dokumental'naia istoriia o donosakh i donoschike," in *Neizvestnaia Rossiia: XX vek* (Moscow, 1992), pp. 56–128.

[14] See, e.g., I. Prelovskaia, "Mif i sud'ba, ili Pochemu zatianulsia spor o Pavlike Morozove," *Izvestiia* (July 15, 1989), p. 3; V. Kononenko, "Pavlik Morozov: Pravda i vymysel," *Komsomol'skaia pravda* (April 5, 1989), p. 2. The classic debunking work on Pavlik, written in the Brezhnev era and published outside the Soviet Union, is Iurii Druzhnikov's *Voznesenia Pavlika Morozova* (London, 1988).

rights without actually being imprisoned (about 3 million at the end of the 1930s).[15]

Our information on the Stalinist secret police (OGPU, NKVD, MGB/MVD) remains much less complete than that now available on the Nazis' Gestapo. As already noted, the FSK (KGB) archives are still largely inaccessible for systematic study. The NKVD/MVD archive for the period 1944–60 constitutes an exception because it is located in the Russian State Archives (GARF);[16] this was the source base for the article in this collection by the Russian historian Vladimir Kozlov, who is GARF's deputy director. But even GARF's police records for the Stalin period are not yet freely available to Russian and Western scholars. Despite the gaps in our knowledge, however, sufficient data are already available to indicate that the discoveries made by Gellately and others about the remarkably small size of the Gestapo and its informer network are most unlikely to be duplicated in the Soviet case by future researchers. If we compare the latest figures for the German Gestapo cited by Gellately with those for the Soviet NKVD registered in 1939 census materials, the disparity is astonishing: 7,500 persons employed in the Gestapo against 366,000 working for the NKVD (including gulag personnel).[17] That implies a saturation rate of one secret policeman per ten thousand population in the German case and one per *five hundred* of population (twenty times as great!) in the second. Even if later research requires some adjustment of these figures, it is not likely to change the difference in their order of magnitude, which requires us to conceptualize the Nazi "police state" very differently from the Stalinist one.

IV. DENUNCIATION AND TOTALITARIANISM

Among the questions we wanted to address when we undertook this comparative study was what special relationship, if any, the practice of denunciation had to totalitarianism. The notion that denunciation is part of a specifically totalitarian kind of intimidating universal surveillance is shared by many writers on totalitarianism, without being fully developed by any of them. Hannah

[15] On newly available statistics, see J. Arch Getty, Gabor T. Rittersporn, and Viktor N. Zemskov, "Victims of the Soviet Penal System in the Prewar Years: A First Approach on the Basis of Archival Evidence," *American Historical Review* (October 1993); and J. Arch Getty and Roberta T. Manning, eds., *Stalinist Terror: New Perspectives* (New York, 1993), esp. Alec Nove, "Victims of Stalinism—How Many?"

[16] For more detailed information on the NKVD and its archive, see Vladimir A. Kozlov, "Denunciation and Its Functions in Soviet Governance: A Study of Denunciations and Their Bureaucratic Handling from Soviet Police Archives, 1944–1953," in this issue.

[17] For German figures, see Robert Gellately, "Denunciations in Twentieth-Century Germany: Aspects of Self-Policing in the Third Reich and the German Democratic Republic," in this issue. For Soviet figures, see Nove, p. 269.

Arendt alluded to the similarities of Nazi and Soviet denunciations and their importance to the secret police in both regimes, observing that there developed "a system of ubiquitous spying where everybody may be a police agent" (so at least thought Arendt, though Gellately's findings may put this in doubt) and where "each individual feels himself under constant surveillance."[18] Others noted the peculiarly exalted concept of loyalty to the Führer and the Party prevailing among Nazis in Germany and Communists in the Soviet Union, according to which denunciation of one's nearest and dearest was construed as an act of civic virtue. Friedrich and Brzezinski cited the Soviet case of Pavlik Morozov, the Young Pioneer who denounced his own father for offenses against the state, in this connection.[19]

Mutual neighborly surveillance in Nazi Germany and Stalinist Russia is amply documented in the studies by Connelly, Gellately, Fitzpatrick, and Kozlov in this collection. But whether this differs significantly in kind from the intense neighborly scrutiny described in countless studies of ordinary village life[20] (including Jeffrey Burds's essay in this collection on the *pre*revolutionary Russian village) is disputable. Our contributors encountered comparatively few cases where denunciations seemed to be motivated by genuine ideological fervor, and only a minority of the denunciations they cite are even couched in the language of devotion to the national or party cause. Denunciation was too ordinary a practice in these societies to have the exalted quality, the flavor of spiritual dedication, implied in the totalitarian literature. In the most literal sense, it was an *everyday* practice—though, to be sure, this was not the *Alltag* of popular resistance celebrated in much German *Alltagsgeschichte* on the Nazi period, but rather an *Alltag* of popular collaboration.

The internal culture of the Soviet Communist Party—and of its fraternal parties and the Comintern—certainly made mutual denunciation an obligation as well as a virtue. The Bolsheviks' famous notion of "party discipline" required a transparency (to use the French Revolutionary term) that could only by achieved by constant scrutiny of each member; and numerous rituals such as periodic party purges (*chistki* [literally, cleansings]) and public self-criticism fostered denunciation of Communist by Communist, both public and private.[21] Surprisingly, however, the Nazi Party seems not to have developed such prac-

---

[18] Hannah Arendt, *The Origins of Totalitarianism,* new edition (New York, 1973), p. 431.

[19] See, e.g., Carl J. Friedrich and Zbigniew K. Brzezinski, *Totalitarian Dictatorship and Autocracy* (Cambridge, Mass., 1956), p. 244.

[20] On denunciations in village life, see, e.g., David Warren Sabean, *Power in the Blood: Popular Culture and Village Discourse in Early Modern Germany* (Cambridge, 1984).

[21] The best outline of Soviet Communist rituals and mores is Nicholas Werth's *Etre communiste en URSS sous Staline* (Paris, 1981).

tices to any significant degree. The best comparison here would seem to be between the Soviet Communists and the Jacobins of the French Revolution or the seventeenth-century Puritan "communities of saints,"[22] rather than the comparison between Communists and National Socialists that lies at the heart of Arendt's and Friedrich and Brzezinski's totalitarian models.

It was in the Nazi and Soviet youth movements—the Hitlerjugend and the Bund Deutscher Mädel on the German side and the Komsomol and Young Pioneers on the Soviet side—that the most "totalitarian" kind of denunciation was located, namely, denunciation of erring parents by children who recognized a higher duty to the state. Such denunciations are so poorly represented in our contributors' archival sources that one has to wonder about their frequency in real life, but there is no doubt that they figured prominently in Soviet and Nazi propaganda (as well as in the anti-Soviet and anti-Nazi propaganda generated by opponents of those regimes).

Jan Gross has posited a paradoxical kind of special relationship between denunciation and totalitarianism: he suggests that, because of the totalitarian state's exceptional willingness to receive denunciations from its citizens and to act upon them, that state's formidable punitive powers were in effect put at the disposal of individual citizens.[23] If you had a private enemy, why not denounce him to the police as a Jew or a Trotskyite? Then the Gestapo or the NKVD would take him away to a concentration camp, and your problem would be solved. As the contributions on Nazi Germany and the Soviet Union in this collection show, this kind of manipulative denunciation was extremely common in both societies. "Class enemies" were denounced in Stalin's Russia by neighbors who coveted their apartments; Jews were denounced by neighbors in Nazi Germany for the same purpose, and with similar success.

A different kind of special relationship between denunciation and totalitarianism, related to the communitarian, antibureaucratic, and welfare orientations of totalitarian states, might be inferred from John Connelly's contribution in this collection. Disputing the contention of many scholars of Nazism that *Volksgemeinschaft* was a "myth," Connelly analyzes Eisenach citizens' letters of complaint, accusation, and appeal to the Nazi *Kreisleiter,* and the *Kreisleiter*'s responses to them, as part of a process of creation of a real *Volksgemeinschaft,* if not exactly the kind of *Volksgemeinschaft* that the Nazis intended. The paternalist relationship that the *Kreisleiter* strove (with some success) to inculcate in Eisenach through his attentiveness to the letters of individual citizens appears intriguingly similar to relationships and practices in Stalin's Rus-

---

[22] Michael Walzer, *The Revolution of the Saints: A Study in the Origins of Radical Politics* (Cambridge, Mass., 1965).

[23] Jan T. Gross, "A Note on the Nature of Soviet Totalitarianism," *Soviet Studies,* vol. 34, no. 3 (July 1982).

sia that have become more visible to us since the opening of the party archives. Soviet *obkom* (regional party) secretaries, like Nazi *Kreisleiter,* received thousands of citizens' letters of complaint, denunciation, and appeal and answered many of them.[24] They too sought to create a bond with citizens based on their willingness to respond to their appeals, act upon their accusations, investigate their grievances, and arbitrate their quarrels, no matter how trivial.

We have already noted the enormous difference in size of the Nazi Gestapo and the Soviet NKVD. The low figures on Gestapo personnel and informers imply, Gellately argues, that German society in the Nazi period was to a large extent self-policing through popular denunciations and other mechanisms. But it is impossible to regard Stalinist society—under surveillance by a large NKVD and a rapidly growing network of regular informers[25]—as self-policing in a similar sense, despite the prevalence of popular denunciation. This suggests at least one fundamental difference between the two "totalitarian" regimes.

On a scale of intensity of surveillance, the GDR went far beyond the Soviet Union even at the height of Stalinism, let alone Nazi Germany. While German commentators tend to focus on a possible line of descent from the policing practices in Nazi Germany to those in the GDR, the more significant and direct line of succession runs from the Soviet secret police to the Stasi. Nevertheless, the type of surveillance that developed in East Germany was different from that practiced by Stalin's secret police in the Soviet Union. On the one hand, it was less closely linked with repression and punishment; on the other, it was accomplished by massive recruitment of citizens as informers. All those who acted as informers had to see themselves as in some sense collaborators with the regime. At least in post-1989 retrospect, informing was popularly regarded as something odious and shameful.

Regular police informers were also held in low regard by the population in the Soviet Union and Nazi Germany. But citizens who wrote spontaneous denunciations to Nazi or Stalinist authorities fell into a different category. Writing to the authorities with grievances, complaints, and requests was accepted everyday practice, to which (in most circumstances) no particular odium was attached. In most cases, writers would be seeking to achieve some private pur-

---

[24] See Sheila Fitzpatrick's "Signals from Below: Soviet Letters of Denunciation of the 1930s," in this volume, and her article "Supplicants and Citizens: Public Letter-Writing in Soviet Russia in the 1930s," *Slavic Review* 55, no. 1 (Spring 1996): 79–105. The importance of the Soviet "right to petition" was first pointed out by Merle Fainsod in his book *Smolensk under Soviet Rule* (Cambridge, Mass., 1958).

[25] Reliable figures on the number of regular informers (*osvedomiteli, sekretnye sotrudniki*) working for the NKVD are not yet available. The Russian historian Arsenii Roginskii, who has worked extensively in the KGB archives, suggests that the number was around three hundred thousand in 1937. Interview with Roginskii, Moscow, March 1994.

poses of their own through their letters, not writing out of patriotism or loyalty to the regime. They would mentally categorize their communications as "letters" or "complaints," avoiding any pejorative term associated with "denunciation."[26] They were unlikely to feel that such an act was shameful, and the idea that it might make them—or might make them appear—collaborators with the regime probably did not even occur to them.

To sum up: while there are similarities between the practices of denunciation that prevailed in Nazi Germany and Stalinist Russia, and between those that prevailed in Stalinist Russia and the German Democratic Republic, denunciations in the three regimes were also dissimilar in important respects. Moreover, similarities also exist between denunciatory practices in one or more of these "totalitarian" states, on the one hand, and other states with quite different characteristics, on the other (the French Revolutionary state, the "communities of saints," the absolute monarchies of early modern Europe, etc.). The Nazi/Soviet similarities are not so striking or pervasive as to convince us that denunciation is a specifically "totalitarian" phenomenon or that the practice of denunciation in totalitarian societies has to be treated as a separate category. For students of denunciation, it seems, the value of the Nazi and Soviet cases is not qualitative but quantitative: these regimes were relatively (though not uniquely) receptive to denunciations, and large numbers of denunciations were written by their citizens. In order to understand the phenomenon, however, we need to use a broader comparative framework.

V. DENUNCIATION IN COMPARATIVE PERSPECTIVE: AN OVERVIEW

The practice of denunciation exists to some degree in all organized societies. But it is much more widespread in some societies than others, depending on political and cultural traditions, the degree of state encouragement, and so on. Some states have had long traditions of denunciation: the Venetian Republic, for example, where the jaws of the famous Lion of St. Mark's were open to receive the denunciations of citizens, or Russia, whose regimes in the Muscovite and Petrine periods were notorious for the energy with which they imposed a "duty to denounce" on their citizens. In other states, such as modern Britain, societal tradition is more skeptical of state power and more inclined to fear its abuse, and denunciation tends to be discouraged.

State laws or religious decrees may require citizens or the faithful to denounce certain types of offenses against the state or church. In France, for example, the Napoleonic Penal Code of 1810 imposed severe penalties for failure to denounce crimes against the security of the state; these penalties

---

[26] In Russian, the words *donos* (denunciation) and *donoschik* (informer) are clearly pejorative, as is *Denunziant* (informer) in German. The German terms for denunciation, *Anzeige* and *Denunziation,* are more neutral.

were lifted in 1832 but reimposed on the eve of the Second World War.[27] Failure to denounce crimes of varying types and weights has been an offense under many other criminal codes as well.[28] The state may also offer financial rewards for denouncers. This was the case in the Roman Empire at the beginning of the Christian era, as the example of Judas Iscariot and the thirty pieces of silver reminds us. In the Restoration period in England, denunciation of dissenters was frequent and advantageous to the denouncers, since they shared a part of the fine levied by the state. An act of 1692 in England authorized bounties (parliamentary rewards) for those who provided information leading to the prosecution of highwaymen; rewards for informing on other offenses like burglary followed. As a result, "there grew up a class of people who lived by prosecuting offenders."[29]

There is clearly a relationship between the practice of denunciation and the existence of police whose charge includes reporting on dangerous moods and opinions among the population. This characteristic of the absolutist states of early modern Europe has recently received more attention from historians as a result of rising interest in public opinion and popular politics.[30] But all police forces cultivate a network of informers in the criminal milieu and in addition receive information through spontaneous denunciations by members of the public. "Even today," noted a late nineteenth-century edition of Larousse, "the most precious discoveries of the police are due not to overt or secret agents but to anonymous denunciations (*délations*) which arrive every day at Rue de Jérusalem, products of the vengeance of betrayed women and friends or jealous parents."[31] This was still true a century later.[32]

A political police with a network of informers is not a necessary prerequisite for the practice of denunciation, however. Any constituted authority, secular or ecclesiastical, may be the recipient of denunciations. In eighteenth-century France, lettres de cachet sent to the king were a denunciatory instrument whereby individuals could request the state to take custody of (i.e., imprison) their delinquent children or spouses.[33] In the twentieth century, newspapers

[27] *Grande Larousse encyclopédique,* vol. 3 (Paris, 1960), s.v. *délation.*

[28] For example, the Imperial Russian criminal code; see *Entsiklopedicheskii slovar' 'Granat',* 7th ed., vol. 18 (Moscow, n.d. [ca. 1914]), p. 623.

[29] J. J. Tobias, *Crime and Police in England, 1700–1900* (New York, 1979), pp. 119–20.

[30] See, e.g., Arlette Farge, *Subversive Words: Public Opinion in Eighteenth-Century France,* trans. Rosemary Morris (University Park, Pa., 1994).

[31] *Larousse grande dictionnaire universel du XIXe siècle,* vol. 6 (Paris, 1870); s.v. *delateur.*

[32] See Jean-Paul Brunet, *La police de l'ombre: Indicateurs et provocateurs dans la France contemporaine* (Paris, 1990); and Czechowski and Hassoun, eds. (n. 2 above), pp. 59–68.

[33] See Arlette Farge and Michel Foucault, *Le désordre des familles: Lettres de cachet des Archives de la Bastille* (Paris, 1982).

have become major recipients for another type of denunciation, written by people who perceive themselves to be victims of bureaucratic injustice or persecution[34] or who wish to disclose wrongdoing by big corporations and government agencies.[35]

In the medieval and early modern eras, denunciation and the rooting out of heresy and witchcraft were closely connected. Wherever the Inquisition was active, denunciation also flourished.[36] As one historian of the Spanish Inquisition writes, "There was no need to rely on a secret police system, because the population as a whole was encouraged to recognize the enemy within the gates. . . . The majority of denunciations were made . . . by ordinary people—neighbours, acquaintances—in response to appeals made in the edicts of faith or simply as a result of personal conflicts."[37] Denunciation of moral lapses and backsliding was also encouraged and practiced in Protestant "communities of saints" such as Calvin's Geneva.[38] As Gary Lease shows in his article on denunciation to the Vatican in this collection, the practice of denunciation remained firmly embedded in the Catholic Church in the late nineteenth and early twentieth centuries.

Police, revolutionary, and theocratic states and communities—as well as twentieth-century totalitarian states—have been particularly likely to encourage their citizens or members to write denunciations against each other for purposes of maintaining social control, ideological purity, virtue, and so on. The zealous hunt for heretics, witches, counterrevolutionaries, and other deviants periodically reaches a pitch of collective hysteria when waves of denunciation for fantastic offenses flood in to the authorities—as, for example, in the Salem witch craze in seventeenth-century Massachusetts or the Jacobin terror of 1794. The Stalinist Great Purges of the late 1930s had some characteristics of a witch craze, as did the anti-Communist fervor in the United States in the 1950s.

War and occupation by foreign powers have seemed to provide particularly

[34] For an analysis of denunciations sent to the French newspaper *Le monde* in the 1980s, see Luc Boltanski, *L'amour et la justice comme compétences* (Paris, 1990), and Boltanski's article, on which the book is partly based, "La dénonciation," *Actes de la recherche en sciences sociales,* vol. 51 (1984). Letters to Soviet newspapers are discussed in Fitzpatrick's article in this collection, "Signals from Below."

[35] On the practice of "whistle-blowing" in the United States, see Alan F. Westin, ed., *Whistle Blowing! Loyalty and Dissent in the Corporation* (New York, 1981).

[36] Carlo Ginzburg's miller, Menocchio, was called in by the Roman Inquisition in 1583 after a denunciation to the Holy Office that evidently came from a local priest. Carlo Ginzburg, *The Cheese and the Worms: The Cosmos of a Sixteenth-Century Miller,* trans. John Tedeschi and Anne Tedeschi (Harmondsworth, 1986), pp. 2, 4.

[37] Henry Kamen, *Inquisition and Society in Spain in the 16th and 17th Centuries* (Bloomington, Ind., 1985), p. 143.

[38] See William E. Monter, *Enforcing Morality in Early Modern Europe* (London, 1987).

fertile climates for denunciation to flourish in the twentieth century. During the First World War, and again in the Second World War, the new situation of "total" mobilization of society in the belligerent countries produced new patterns of behavior that included widespread denunciation (even in nondenunciatory England) of spies, saboteurs, Germans, suspected Fifth Columnists, and so on. Of course, in wartime all states insist that patriotism—a citizen's allegiance to the nation-state—override all other loyalties. But heightened patriotism does not satisfactorily explain the flood of denunciations that French men and women sent in to German occupiers during the Second World War;[39] or the denunciations those in the Vichy zone sent to Pétain against communists, socialists, and Jews;[40] or the denunciations of their neighbors that Polish peasants sent to Soviet occupiers of Eastern Poland in 1941.[41]

While a late twentieth-century American may have the impression that denunciation plays little role in his everyday world, this is partly a matter of semantics. Incidents of "whistle-blowing" are regularly reported in the U.S. press, as are exhortations to the public to inform the authorities about a range of minor delinquencies by fellow citizens.[42] In the 1980s and early 1990s, the United States even experienced a kind of latter-day witch craze in which large numbers of parents, day-care workers, and priests were accused of incest and child abuse.[43]

Denunciation has many targets. It may be aimed against demonized "enemies of the people"—alleged witches, heretics, Communists, counterrevolutionaries, child abusers, or terrorists. It may focus on persons defined as

[39] See André Halimi, *La délation sous l'Occupation* (Paris, 1983), and "Une certaine France sous l'Occupation," in Czechowski and Hassoun, eds., pp. 138–45. During the Occupation in France, the French wrote between 3 and 5 million letters of denunciation, most of them signed. They were sent to French authorities like the Commissariat Général aux Affaires Juives as well as the Gestapo. Radio-Paris had a program called *Répétez-le* that "consisted only of letters from listeners denouncing their neighbor, their rival in love or in business, even their own families" (Halimi, "Une certaine France," p. 139).

[40] See Marc Ferro, *Pétain* (Paris, 1987), pp. 149–52, 235–41.

[41] See Jan T. Gross, *Revolution from Abroad: The Soviet Conquest of Poland's Western Ukraine and Western Belorussia* (Princeton, N.J., 1988), pp. 145–46.

[42] For example, speeding on the highways, violations of zoning laws, tax evasion, illegal immigrants, and so on. For a more or less random sample, see *Chicago Tribune* (October 16, 1994), sec. 8, p. 1, and (October 21, 1994), pp. 1, 21. (Thanks to Joshua Sanborn for noticing these reports.)

[43] According to the *New York Times* (October 31, 1994), thousands of court cases involving child molestation and sensational press accounts of adults who "rediscovered" hidden memories of incestuous abuse under psychotherapy "have led many people to believe that there is a nationwide network of satanic groups preying upon the young." Out of more than twelve thousand accusations of "group cult sexual abuse based on satanic ritual" investigated in a 1994 survey, not one had been substantiated.

outsiders and pariahs—*Gemeinschaftsfremde* in Nazi usage, "social aliens" (*sotsial'no-chuzhdye*) in that of Soviet Communists—such as Jews, gypsies, homosexuals, religious dissenters, foreigners, or members of stigmatized social groups (e.g., aristocrats and priests in the French Revolution, capitalists and kulaks in the Russian Revolution).

Denunciations are made against big- or small-time criminals, by persons animated by public spirit, malice, or a desire to be taken on as regular police informers. They may be made against powerful people by citizens who seek, from a less powerful position, to exercise what Boltanski calls "the competence of justice." But a very large number of denunciations in most societies are against ordinary people—neighbors, fellow villagers, work colleagues—against whom the denouncer has an everyday grievance. In such cases, the denouncers often do not even bother to stigmatize their targets as witches or *Gemeinschaftsfremde*.

VI. DISCOURSES OF DENUNCIATION

The denouncer is a citizen who is calling on the state or some other superior authority to take disciplinary action against another citizen. In investigating the phenomenon of denunciation, therefore, we find ourselves exploring the core of citizens' commitment of loyalty to the state and their (perhaps incompatible) commitment of solidarity with their fellow citizens. Denunciation is a practice that tests the relative strengths of those fundamental and highly charged commitments. As Colin Lucas puts it, denunciation lies along the fault line dividing those who find themselves in tension with the state and those who see some of their own identity in the state; it marks the division between a state that is "externalized" and one that is "internalized" by the citizens.[44] Small wonder, then, if in many different societies denunciation has been the subject of two opposing discourses, one exalting it as a duty to the state, the other deploring it as a betrayal of fellow human beings.

Nothing about denunciations is more striking than the sharp contradictions of its representation. The contradictions are so acute that in the French language, and earlier in English, a single word was unable to contain them: *dénonciation* is the word for good (public-spirited) denunciation, while *délation* is applied to bad (treacherous, self-interested) denunciation.[45] The problem of *dénonciation/délation* was explored with great intensity during the French Revolution, as Colin Lucas describes in his essay. But the dichotomy was never

[44] Private communication to the editors, January 9, 1996.
[45] With its separate entries for *dénonciation* and *délation,* Diderot's *Encyclopédie ou dictionnaire raisonné des sciences, des arts et des métiers,* vol. 10 (Lausanne/Berne, 1779), set a pattern that has been followed by virtually all French encyclopedias since.

satisfactorily resolved, despite some Jacobin attempts to banish the pejorative connotations of *délation.*

In the discourse of *dénonciation,* denunciation of wrongdoing is an act of civic virtue or religious duty whose performance may involve personal sacrifice or risk for the denouncer. Zola's famous *"J'Accuse!"*—an open letter to President Félix Faure in 1898 denouncing those responsible for Dreyfus's trial and conviction—is a classic example. Dreyfus's treatment was an outrageous injustice that "begrimed" France, Zola wrote. He himself had only the interests of truth and justice at heart, was without malice or hatred toward those he accused, and wrote "in the name of humanity"; his intervention was "only a revolutionary means for hastening the explosion of truth and justice."[46] Equally passionate rhetoric was used during the French Revolution in defense of the necessity of denunciation to protect the purity and transparency of the revolution.[47]

In the United States in the McCarthy period, the film *On the Waterfront* (1954)—whose director, Elia Kazan, had recently named names of former Communists before the House Un-American Activities Committee—presented an implicit justification for informing with its story of a protagonist who struggles with his conscience and the fear of ostracism before gaining the courage to inform against the gang dominating the dock, "achiev[ing] heroic stature as he single-handedly takes on the mob at the risk of his life."[48] A decade earlier, interestingly enough, the Soviet director Sergei Eisenstein had attempted a similar glorification of denunciation in his film *Bezhin Meadow,* based on the Pavlik Morozov story.[49] In the United States more recently, the courage of "whistle-blowers" who risk their own careers or even their lives for the sake of exposing graft and corruption has been similarly represented.

In the opposing discourse of *délation,* denunciation is synonymous with betrayal; its practice tends to corrupt rather than to protect public morals, and denouncers are treated as contemptible, cowardly, and often motivated by malice. This discourse has a classic locus in the genre of Anglo-Saxon Protestant indictments of the iniquities of Rome, particularly with reference to the Inqui-

[46] *Emile Zola's J'Accuse!* trans. and ed. Mark K. Jensen (Soquel, Calif., 1992), pp. 15, 28.

[47] See the essay by Colin Lucas ("The Theory and Practice of Denunciation in the French Revolution") in this volume.

[48] Victor S. Navasky, *Naming Names* (Harmondsworth, 1981), p. 209. For more on McCarthy-period exhortations to denounce Communists to the FBI and popular approval of this practice, see Stephen J. Whitfield, *The Culture of the Cold War* (Baltimore, 1991) pp. 102 and 136–40; and David Caute, *The Great Fear: The Anti-Communist Purge under Truman and Eisenhower* (New York, 1978), p. 121.

[49] The film was criticized for "formalism" and never released. Jay Leyda, *Kino: A History of the Russian and Soviet Film* (London, 1973), pp. 327–34, 338–39.

sition. "No more ingenious device has been invented to subjugate a whole population, to paralyze its intellect and to reduce it to blind obedience," wrote Henry Charles Lea of the Spanish Inquisition. "It elevated delation to the rank of high religious duty, it filled the land with spies and it rendered every man an object of suspicion, not only to his neighbor but to the members of his own family and to the stranger whom he might chance to meet. Continued through generations, this could not fail to leave its impress on the national character."[50]

The terms and tone in which English and American liberal writers indicted totalitarian regimes in the twentieth century bore a strong resemblance to this older rhetoric of indictment against the Inquisition. In the United States in the 1950s, McCarthyism was attacked in similar terms by American Leftists like Arthur Miller, a member of the blacklisted "Hollywood Ten." Miller's play *The Crucible* (1953) dealt with the baseless denunciation of an innocent couple during the Salem witch craze, implying an analogy between the literal witch-hunting of seventeenth-century Massachusetts and the anti-Communist hysteria of his own time. In *A View from the Bridge* (1955), Miller developed the theme of denunciation as betrayal in his story of a waterfront worker who informs on his nephew, an illegal immigrant.[51]

Despite the recurrence in many different social and historical contexts of competing discourses of *dénonciation* and *délation,* this discursive duality is not universal. In closed institutions like prisons and boarding schools, a single *délation* discourse seems to be the rule. Denunciation ("ratting," "squealing," "tale-telling") flourishes in such environments, but it also incurs special odium there. "In the prison the word *rat* or *squealer* carries an emotional significance far greater than that usually encountered in the free community," writes a sociologist in a famous study of such communities. "It represents the most serious accusation that one inmate can level against another, for it implies a betrayal that transcends the specific act of disclosure. The *rat* is a man who has betrayed not just one inmate or several; he has *betrayed inmates in general by denying the cohesion of prisoners as a dominant value when confronting the world of officialdom.*"[52]

This is an important insight whose significance is not limited to closed institutions. For the *délation* discourse always rests on the assumption that there is a community of citizens (subalterns, prisoners) to which the individual citizen

---

[50] Henry Charles Lea, *A History of the Inquisition of Spain in Four Volumes* (London, 1906), 2:91.

[51] See Navasky, pp. 200–222 and passim; and Michel Ciment, "Les aveux les plus durs," in Czechowski and Hassoun, eds. (n. 2, above), pp. 128–37. *A View from the Bridge* was, of course, also a rebuttal of the film *On the Waterfront,* directed by Miller's former friend and colleague, Elia Kazan (see above).

[52] Gresham M. Sykes, *The Society of Captives: A Study of a Maximum Security Prison* (Princeton, N.J., 1958), p. 87; emphasis added.

owes loyalty. This may conflict with the obligation of loyalty to the state that citizens simultaneously recognize; hence the *dénonciation/délation* dichotomy. Prisoners, however, do not accept an obligation of loyalty to their "state" (the prison administration), since they have become its "citizens" involuntarily and without free consent. In this situation, there is no conflict of loyalty. The prisoner's only moral obligation is to the community of prisoners.

Behind the problem of *dénonciation* and *délation* lie the big philosophical problems of loyalty and citizenship. What are our duties, as citizens, to the state? Do we owe loyalty to an imagined community of subalterns (the free-world equivalent of "inmates in general") that is betrayed by giving information to the state? If the loyalties we feel to family, friends, and larger entities such as the nation turn out to be incompatible, what are our priorities? Do we say, with the English novelist E. M. Forster, "If I had to choose between betraying my country and betraying my friend, I hope I should have the guts to betray my country"?[53] Or do we join the American moral philosopher Judith Shklar in rebuking Forster for frivolity and irresponsibility?[54]

According to Shklar, Forster failed to make the necessary distinction between "good" countries (those "with a decent legal system" like the United States or Britain), in which denunciation of wrongdoing is appropriate, and "bad" countries like Soviet Russia and Nazi Germany, in which denunciation is contemptible. Unsatisfactory as this complacent formulation may be, it does tell us something—namely, that the evaluation of any specific act of denunciation is a highly ideological affair. If we disapprove of a regime, church, or party and regard its interests as distinctly separate from and opposed to the interests of its citizens, we are likely to condemn the citizen who voluntarily offers information on another citizen to the authorities and will characterize his action disparagingly as collaboration or betrayal. Conversely, if we approve of the regime, we will tend to minimize the distinction between state and citizen interests, perhaps even regarding "the state" as synonymous with "the community of citizens," and will see the citizen-denouncer as performing a necessary civic duty.[55]

[53] E. M. Forster, *Two Cheers for Democracy* (New York, 1951), pp. 68–69.

[54] Judith N. Shklar, *Ordinary Vices* (Cambridge, Mass., 1984), p. 156.

[55] The judgmental qualities of the main discourses of denunciation since the French Revolution have sometimes found their way into the scholarship (such as it is) relating to practices of denunciation. See, e.g., the curious postwar essay by two French psychologists who, no doubt reacting to the waves of denunciation that swept France during the German occupation in World War II and after liberation, treat the practices of denunciation as a childish behavior that well-adjusted adults ought to have outgrown: L. Jh. Colaneri and G. Gérente, *La dénonciation et les dénonciateurs* (Paris, 1948). Anthropologists have been more successful in escaping the judgmental trap in their studies of one type of denunciation, witchcraft accusations: see, e.g., Mary Douglas, ed., *Witch-*

VII. SUGGESTIONS FOR FUTURE RESEARCH

As this collection goes to press, we are acutely aware that it ignores the experiences of many countries in Europe and neglects important periods and developments. It lacks the consideration of postwar Eastern Europe that could constitute a bridge between the Nazi and Stalinist cases that are most prominent in this collection. We regret the absence of a discussion of collaborationist regimes in Western or Eastern Europe in the Second World War, and a comparison of the nature and extent of denunciations in Fascist Italy and Nazi Germany.[56] Remarkably enough, we still know little even about denunciations in Germany prior to the Nazi era. There is no investigation of the civic tradition in Germany which, at least according to popular mythology, encouraged people to inform the police. Looking beyond twentieth-century totalitarian regimes, we feel the lack of any essay on bureaucratic denunciatory cultures such as that of the prewar Austro-Hungarian Empire. We would have liked to know more about the forms and practices denunciations may have assumed in liberal democracies, such as England, and it would be particularly interesting to know what, if anything, changed there on the home front during the First or Second World War.

These gaps exist either because the work has not yet been done or because we were unable to find a scholar who could write about them within the time frame of this publication. We suspect, however, that such lacunae are inevitable in a collection that sets out to break new ground and pose new problems. It is our hope that bringing the subject to the attention of the profession at this time will stimulate further research and foster debate on the practices, functions, and discourses of denunciation.

---

craft Confessions and Accusations (London, 1970); and Max Marwick, comp., *Witchcraft and Sorcery: Selected Readings,* 2d ed. (Harmondsworth, 1982).

[56] See the remarks of Jonathan Steinberg, *All or Nothing: The Axis and the Holocaust, 1941–1943* (London, 1990), pp. 168 ff.

The Theory and Practice of Denunciation in the French Revolution*

Colin Lucas
Balliol College, Oxford

> Denounce the crimes, denounce the criminals, a double reward awaits you: the voice of your conscience, for denunciation is a virtue; and a legitimate reward, for the National Convention is just and desires that each virtuous act should be a means by which the sans-culotte may improve his lot. . . .
>
> Friends, nothing can, nothing should constrain your ardor here: former servants must not forget that the Motherland is their sole mistress; nor relatives forget that it alone is their mother; nor citizens forget that they owe themselves utterly to this Motherland which rewards their zeal so effectively, but which would sanction without pity their negligence and punish their criminal silence.[1]

This proclamation, issued in December 1793 by the Commission Temporaire (an ad hoc revolutionary authority installed in the city of Lyon after the Federalist revolt) is a fairly standard example of the rhetoric of the radical Terror. Behind its large claims about civic behavior lay a relatively small objective: the discovery of precious objects hidden by the insurrectionists (one-twentieth of whose value was promised to the denouncers). Nonetheless, the proclamation does evoke, either explicitly or implicitly, some of the major themes that must be addressed in a discussion of revolutionary denunciation in France: the notions of citizen and civic act, the sense of critical danger to the Revolution, the typing of the denounced as criminal, the relationship between public and private, the submerged Classical reference, the tension between the defense of liberty and the threat posed to liberty by such defense, and finally the problem of how denunciation was done and how it fitted into a process of destroying threats to the Revolution.

---

* Denunciation, long neglected as a theme of French revolutionary history, has recently been treated by three historians, and this article draws on some of their arguments. They are Lucien Jaume, *Le discours jacobin et la démocratie* (Paris, 1989), pp. 192–215; A. de Baecque, *Le corps de l'histoire* (Paris, 1993), pp. 257–302; and J. Guilhaumou, "Fragments of a Discourse on Denunciation (1789–94)," in *The Terror,* ed. K. M. Baker (Oxford, 1994), pp. 139–55.

[1] *La Commission Temporaire à tous les vrais Sans-culottes* (Commune-affranchie, an II = Lyon, 1793).

This essay originally appeared in *The Journal of Modern History* 68 (December 1996).

The study of denunciation leads us directly both to the concept of the Revolution as process and to the question of how the revolutionaries tried to think the difference between the new society and the Old Regime. These were intensely problematic and divisive issues, and thus it is not surprising that denunciation should have been a problematic and divisive category, which the revolutionaries sought to define carefully. As in so many other aspects of this period, the Jacobin version of denunciation, which appears so emblematic of the Terror, was in fact rooted in dilemmas apparent from the beginning of the Revolution four years earlier. The main lines of the issue were already set in 1789–90.

Both the function and the necessity of denunciation resided in the fragility of a revolution perceived to be surrounded by pervasive and dangerous enemies. That is a banal self-evidence, but it must be stated. The justification for denunciation was the imminent danger to the Revolution. In recent years, historians have much discussed the role of the enemy "Other" in the revolutionary imaginary. It has been argued that the revolutionaries' belief in a single, indivisible, sovereign Nation endowed with a single General Will necessarily entrained a form of Hegelian dialectic that specified all dissent and opposition as inimical, as criminal, as an antithetical Other outside the single, indivisible body of the Nation. It is argued, as a consequence, that the revolutionaries invented a single, indivisible, pervasive enemy and imagined a death struggle with this opposite, whose supposed power and coherence vastly exaggerated the tangible evidence. In reality, this evidence pointed only to a disparate array of dissent ranging from outright militant counterrevolution to grumbling discontent and the rejection of specific revolutionary initiatives. Now, how far one should accept this interpretation is a matter for debate. I will not linger upon that issue here except to say that such radical Manicheism is certainly visible in the Jacobin mind-set and pervades the Terror, but that one should not commit the error of seeing Jacobins as the only—or the only true—revolutionaries.

Nonetheless, it is important for an understanding of revolutionary denunciation to retain the notion that all shades of revolutionary opinion found it very difficult to distinguish between outright counterrevolution, resistances to revolutionary initiatives, and plain ordinary disorder. Revolutionaries were inhabited both by a property owners' sense of order as public peace and by an Enlightenment perception that they were restoring France to a social harmony grounded in Nature's eternal and universal precepts. They always tended, therefore, to understand opposition most readily in terms of unnatural, criminal selfishness and corruption; and they always tended to connect popular disturbances with the hold of such corrupt and selfish people over the ignorant poor. Since the earliest events of the Revolution there was hard, verifiable evidence of plots, resistance, and disorder—a crescendo that I have no need to catalog here, beginning as it did with the resistance of the privileged in the Estates General and the events surrounding July 14, 1789. Moderate and radical revolutionaries did not disagree over the existence of enemies but, rather, over their identity and what to do about them. Moderates and radicals increasingly saw each other as the principals in selfishness, corruption, and counterrevolutionary activity; and, subsequently, radical factions similarly typed each other. In this sense, the triumph of Jacobinism with the Terror (and the appearance of denunciation as a systematized element of government) did not alter the essential character of the revolutionary discourse on its enemies.

Proposing the establishment of a *comité de recherches* in the National Assembly on July 28, 1789, Adrien Duport stated (to hardly a murmur of dissent) that "plots are being mounted against the well-being of public affairs [*la chose publique*], we can be in no doubt of that. There can be no question of deferring this to the law courts. . . . We must acquire ghastly and indispensable knowledge. . . . We will learn terrible but necessary truths. . . . Let our vigilant eye be turned in every direction."[2] Although this committee was intended merely to scrutinize seized correspondence (and it became embroiled in a debate about the sanctity of the mails), the door was already officially opened here to the search for "terrible truths" by means of denunciation. That much was evident in October 1789 when the Commune of Paris set up its own *comité de recherches* specifically to receive denunciations and called upon the "good citizens" to reveal to it all knowledge and information they might possess on plots against the public good. "One of the obstacles to restoring good order and public peace is the mystery with which the authors of plots surround themselves," and "the safety of the State depends upon their discovery."[3] This governmental attitude was made more precise two years later, when in November 1791 the new Legislative Assembly in its turn set up a *comité de recherches* to gather all individual facts known to citizens. "We are," said Basire, introducing the measure, "surrounded by conspirators; everywhere plots are under way and you are continually receiving denunciations of individual facts, which are all connected with the great conspiracy, about whose existence none of us can have any doubt. These facts are all separate and, if they were all put together, they would offer a general body of crime which would finally throw a great light on the intentions of our enemies."[4]

These texts make immediately apparent the function of denunciation in broad outline: it serves to reveal the hidden, to bring together the small knowledge of individuals into a great, general body of understanding, and thus to save the Revolution from its enemies. Such definitions did not change in later years. However, significant though they are of the acceptance of denunciation

[2] *Archives parlementaires,* 8:293.
[3] S. Lacroix, ed., *Actes de la Commune de Paris pendant la Révolution* (Paris, 1895), 2:366 (October 21).
[4] *Archives parlementaires,* 35:361 (November 25, 1791).

by the revolutionary authorities at an early and moderate date, these statements do not get us very far. In these definitions, denunciation was a phenomenon limited by being addressed only to a committee of the National Assembly or of the Commune in Paris and presumably largely confined to great conspiracies against the state. It was, moreover, clearly conceived as a first step in another process: it was a quick indication of where trouble might be lurking, which would lead to an inquiry and ultimately to a body of evidence to be deferred to a law court for trial, even if that law court might be an exceptional tribunal. In the French legal system, it formed therefore an additional part of the procedure of *instruction*. Indeed, the Commune's October 1789 order creating its *comité de recherches* explicitly described its function in those terms.[5] At the same time, the Commune distinguished carefully between denunciations and evidence, charging its committee to receive "dénonciations et dépositions," the latter being the word for evidence given to an inquiring magistrate. The distinction was clear. "Déposition" was a formal legal action, one, indeed, that could be constrained if not given voluntarily; it was an assertion of something presented as known. "Dénonciation," by contrast, was spontaneous, an indication offered voluntarily about something not necessarily known, but suspected, even if not understood. In these terms, therefore, denunciation was a discrete category of action, quite separate from evidence or proof.

Matters were not, however, as simple as this, even in 1789–90. On the one hand, denunciation was extremely controversial; on the other, quite different senses were being accorded to it by the more radical revolutionaries. The *comité de recherches* of the Commune allows us, once again, to enter the controversy. The Commune authorized its committee to arrest and interrogate denounced persons in the course of assembling "a body of *instruction*." This was in fact to conflate procedures, even if it maintained semantic separation. The moderate journalist Loustalot pointed out the dangers. What had been established, he said, was a "civil inquisition"; this was "a means to destroy morals, to destroy all confidence between citizens and all security; this is a means to provoke calumny and to favor informing [délation]. . . . It resembles dictatorship, it is the best shield for tyranny."[6]

Loustalot was in fact airing here a debate that had started in the National Assembly in July 1789 and would continue around the *comités de recherches* of the Assembly and the Commune well into 1790. How, indeed, to prevent the discovery of enemies by means of denunciation from becoming a source of discord and mutual enmity within society, thus weakening the Revolution rather than strengthening it? How to prevent denunciation from being a tool of vengeance and intrigue? How to prevent an opinion from being confused with

[5] Lacroix, ed.
[6] *Révolutions de Paris,* no. 8 (November 14, 1789).

evidence of crime? How to prevent those institutions charged with receiving denunciations from becoming government boards of inquisition, very much in the manner of Venice to which orators tended to refer? In sum, how to prevent revolutionary practices from resembling Old Regime ones, how to prevent the defense of liberty from assassinating liberty? This dilemma was broadly encapsulated in the debate over the difference between *dénonciation* and *délation* (denouncing and informing). It was a debate that was never resolved, any more than the Revolution ever escaped these contradictions.

Revolutionary elites were imbued with the history of Classical Rome through which substantial parts of their education had been conducted. Their Roman authors of reference were, however, most frequently those hostile to the Empire or to the decaying late Republic who looked back to a rather pristine, perhaps mythic period of a virtuous Republic. Such perceptions, often further recycled through eighteenth-century philosophical texts, informed the debate over denunciation. Classical Rome certainly offered models, since it had practically no formal prosecution structure and its standing courts depended upon individuals initiating cases by laying information against others. That is to say, they worked on the basis of denunciation; those who brought information in this way were called *delatores.* However, the revolutionaries were aware above all of the imperial record of *delatores,* when the name became attached to those who secretly informed to the Emperor and whose information was rewarded, when it led to the conviction of a senator, by part of the victim's estate and by his senatorial rank. The revolutionaries were imbued with Tacitus's insistent condemnation of this practice as largely responsible for the degeneration of the Empire.

There was another Classical model: the two *censores,* whose function was to supervise the morality of citizens.[7] These were essentially a feature of the Roman Republic, since they disappeared under the Empire, except when emperors took their powers from time to time. This was, therefore, a more welcome and attractive model, and all the more so since the *censores* were much preoccupied by luxury and extravagance, those great concerns of enlightened opinion in the later Old Regime. In 1790, for example, Pierre Manuel prefaced his long and hostile description of the Old Regime policing of Paris with the proposal that, instead of police, each town should have an official with the duty to inform the administrators of their failings and to teach the citizens the respect they owed to the administrators.[8] Jean-Paul Marat, too, was very much in favor of republican "censors." He wanted them to act as denouncers to a revolutionary tribunal—a considerably more lethal project than that of the original model censors, whose power consisted in awarding black marks.[9]

[7] A. E. Austin, *"Regimen Morum," Journal of Roman Studies* 78 (1988):14–34.
[8] Pierre Manuel, *La police de Paris dévoilée,* 2 vols. (Paris, 1790), 1:ix–x.
[9] J. P. Marat, *Appel à la nation* (February 15, 1790).

The Classical model proved inadequate in this case, as it did in most cases where it was invoked during the Revolution. *Delatores* more closely fitted the Revolution's need for information volunteered from among the people, but they were tarnished in history; the *censores* were untarnished, but the model offered was scrutiny from above by two magistrates who inflicted "hardly more than a blush" upon the persons they named, as Cicero put it. Nonetheless—again as usual in the Revolution—however imperfect the Classical model was, it did influence the way in which revolutionaries tried to think through their difficulties. This is visible in the debate over *délation* (informing) in 1789–90. For a conservative like Stanislas de Clermont-Tonnerre, from the moment a free and constitutional society states that *"the general will is the law,* then it prevents itself from indulging in spying, informing, violence." The general will can only remain pure as long as all opinions are free; truth is to be found in the diversity of opinion and error is not feared. The love of liberty in the society is the guarantee against the success of the enemy.[10] More radical or "patriot" opinion, however, attempted to find a way of incorporating the word into the revolutionary vocabulary in order to meet a perceived need. This was best articulated by Pierre-Jean Agier's report on the activities of the Commune's committee.[11] Noting the reticence of even enlightened people about denunciation even where the safety of the state was at issue, he stated that the time had come to be rid of these "prejudices, which are fit only for Slaves, but are unworthy of a free People." It had been right to hate the informer under the Old Regime, because he delivered often innocent, even virtuous people up to arbitrary authority and to a partial, cruel, and secretive system of justice. Now, however, all had changed. The purpose was to denounce plots threatening the Motherland: the accused would be brought before his peers for immediate examination and would be either exonerated or sent to justice—but "to a humane, public, impartial justice, which can be terrible only to wrongdoers." Thus, "as far as informing is concerned, silence is a virtue under Despotism; it is a crime, yes indeed, a crime under the rule of Liberty."

Agier was not alone in this view. We find it in men as diverse as Mirabeau ("in the perils which surround us, informing . . . must be seen as the most important of our new virtues"), Desmoulins ("I am trying to rehabilitate the word 'informing.' . . . In our present circumstances, we need to see the word honored"), Mercier (denunciation is one of the "heroic virtues"), Marat, and so on. The reference to Rome was often explicit. Mirabeau quoted the celebrated Senatorial decree "Caveant Consules ne respublica quid detrimenti capiat" (The Consuls shall take care that the state shall suffer no harm); Des-

---

[10] Stanislas de Clermont-Tonnerre, *Nouvelles observations sur les comités de recherches* (Paris, n.d.).

[11] P.-J. Agier, *Compte-rendu à l'Assemblée générale des représentants de la Commune, au nom du Comité de Recherches, le 30 novembre 1789* (Paris, n.d.).

moulins quoted Cicero's phrase "Accusatores multos esse in civitate utile est" (It is useful to have many accusers among us) and concluded, with Cicero, that half-proof is enough to speak, for "in the night all faithful dogs may bark at passers-by, because of thieves."[12]

The belief in the need for such a mechanism emerges clearly from these early "patriot" attitudes. However, the struggle with the word *délation* reflects the difficulty they had in incorporating the mechanism into the new society. Informers were simply too closely bound up with the universally hated police spies of the Old Regime; the perception that informing was essentially corrupt snooping and settling of private scores was too intimately connected with the definition of Old Regime government as tyranny (and there was a strong Classical heritage attached to that word as well).[13] Pierre Manuel's examination of Old Regime policing began with precisely this point: it was, he said, the multitude of petty police agents that had fashioned the population to slavery.[14] Revolutionary conceptions quickly moved, therefore, toward a different word, *dénonciation,* defined as a different and revolutionary practice. Nonetheless, any reader of the *Encyclopédie* would already have been familiar with the weakness in such an endeavor. The *Encyclopédie* had tried to separate Classical notions from contemporary ones, and it had sought specifically to distinguish between denouncing and informing. However, it had to admit that "the condition of being an informer and that of being a denouncer are at root the same."[15]

In order to capture better the revolutionary definition of denunciation as it emerged in the years before the fall of the king in mid-1792, let us dwell for a moment on two fundamental elements in the extracts I have quoted so far from revolutionary statements. These are virtue and publicity. Indeed, these two attributes constituted the essential difference between informing and revolutionary denunciation. We have seen the birth of the notion that denunciation was a civic act; if one looks back to the quotation with which I began this essay, one will realize that this definition remained central right through to the Terror. In radical conceptions, denunciation was secured as a critical act of citizenship. In one sense, this was just an updated version of the Classical conception of civic virtue: the concern with and active care for public affairs, for the res publica. Denunciation was the civic duty of the citizen, expressive of his vigilance in caring for public affairs, one of his individual actions to defend and promote the Revolution and to secure its successful transition from tyranny to

---

[12] A. de Baecque, *Le corps de l'histoire* (Paris, 1993), p. 272; C. Labrosse and P. Rétat, *Naissance de journal révolutionnaire: 1789* (Lyon, 1989), pp. 201–2.

[13] On the hatred of police spies and its significance in the early Revolution, see David Andress, "Social Prejudice and Political Fears in the Policing of Paris," *French History* 9 (1995): 202–26.

[14] Manuel.

[15] *Encyclopédie ou dictionnaire raisonné des sciences, des arts et des métiers,* 4:777.

liberty and equality. As the symbiotic growth of counterrevolutionary threat and radical suspicion led the Revolution into the Terror, this definition of denunciation intensified and rendered denunciation an imperative—as our opening quotation suggests. More important, the notion of virtue here was related to the disinterestedness (or in Jacobin phraseology, increasingly, the "purity") of the denouncer. Virtue was the guarantee against the misuse of denunciation, against its slippage toward informing. Jean-Paul Marat led the way, but all Jacobins followed him, in ceaselessly proclaiming the purity of his intentions and his devotion to the cause of the People.

Marat, however, extended this perception by converting denunciation from a duty into a right. In the course of a single passage, he mutated his argument from a declaration that, the salvation of the state being the supreme law, its defense is therefore the first duty of the citizen into a declaration that "the denunciation to the Motherland as traitors of all those who attack the people's rights and threaten public liberty is . . . the right of every individual."[16] This position, adopted very early by Marat and followed only later by conventional Jacobin thinking, introduced two distinctive new notions: that denunciation was an act of sovereignty, and that, made by a member of the sovereign people, it was essentially addressed to the sovereign people. This leads to our second fundamental element: publicity.

All those who debated the question of denunciation before 1793 insisted on the central importance of publicity. Denunciation was a public act, denouncers had to sign their denunciations, and (with many references to Roman prescriptions against false denunciation) proposals were made to post the names of false denouncers alongside the lists of enemies of the People. It was this publicity that was seen as the guarantee against calumny and the settling of private scores.[17] However, the notion of publicity necessarily contained another notion: it evoked the presence of public opinion as arbiter and thus overflowed irrevocably the confined space within which early official projects sought to contain it. Keith Baker and others have taught us a great deal about the significance of public opinion in the prerevolutionary contestation of absolute monarchy.[18] Within the Revolution, the notion of public opinion was one of the primary sites for the debate between radicals and moderates over the question of where the sovereign people was to be found and how it expressed itself. The issue of denunciation (as Marat unerringly saw) exposed the weakness of a moderate position that sought to confine sovereignty to the National Assembly.

---

[16] *Le Publiciste Parisien,* no. 5 (September 15, 1789).

[17] See, e.g., J.-P. Brissot, *Lettres à Monsieur le Chevalier de Pange sur sa brochure* (Paris, 1790): "The means of removing the danger of *délations* is to force their conversion into public accusations."

[18] K. M. Baker, *Inventing the French Revolution* (Cambridge, 1990), esp. pp. 167–99.

Publicity necessarily raised the question of who was denouncing to whom. Seen as a mechanism for preventing abuse, publicity also involved soliciting the people as a tribunal (the oft-cited "tribunal of public opinion") and invoked this public ultimately as the voice of the sovereign people, the impartial and supreme dispenser of justice. "Publicity can never harm innocence," stated Jean-Pierre Brissot (in his pre-Girondin phase); "sooner or later, innocence will triumph because the public is an impartial judge."[19] Such definitions entirely suited radicals in their struggles to subvert National Assembly power by harnessing an arena of politics outside it.

In reality, however, all these polemics were contained within a much more general practice of public politics born with the Revolution of 1789. The explosion of the press in the revolutionary crisis produced a sudden invasion of the public space by an unregulated maelstrom of printed commentary, information, and exhortation. Indeed, the press largely created public politics in the Revolution and, from the very beginning, it did so in the double terms of both the threats to the newborn Revolution and the threats to social coherence offered by the Revolution itself. Very soon, the radical press (at both ends of the spectrum) expressed itself essentially as the vigilant eye of the People, denouncing to it the dangers and the hidden maneuvers of its enemies. The very titles of many pamphlets and newspapers reveal this phenomenon: publications abound whose titles contain the words *Sentinelle, Observateur, Spectateur, Vérités, Secrets dévoilés, Véridique, Amis, Censeur, Dénonciateur.*[20] In important senses, the press became public opinion; it became a forum in which denunciation and self-defense were played out. The revolutionary mind-set of suspicion and fear of secret enemies was endlessly exercised there—most violently by Marat and Hébert, but by many others, too. Public denunciation in the press existed separately from the kind of denunciation envisaged by decrees and orders such as those setting up the *comités de recherches.* Whereas the latter was seen as a step in a process of justice defined in recognizably legal and procedural terms, the former was quite different: it involved accusations launched to a general, unspecified public against which there could be only a counterappeal to the same public. While on one level press denunciation could arguably be presented as a stimulus to legal proceedings, in reality the justice it invoked too easily became a popular summary justice. Marat's *Ami du peuple,* each number of which was a denunciation, certainly moved explicitly in that direction.

The debate on press freedom turned precisely on these issues of denunciation. To those who defended press freedom, journalists were indeed the vigilant eye of the People; they were the very palladium of liberty, and their denun-

[19] *Réplique de J-P. Brissot à Stanislas Tonnerre* (Paris, 1790).
[20] Labrosse and Rétat, pp. 193–97. This is echoed by J. Guilhaumou, "Fragments of a Discourse on Denunciation (1789–94)," in *The Terror,* ed. K. M. Baker (Oxford, 1994), pp. 139–55; and by de Baecque.

ciations were rays of light shining into the darkness of evil. To those who opposed it, public opinion was incapable of making sound judgments on complex matters and was too easily swayed by rhetoric; to them, journalists were in effect *délateurs,* purveyors of calumny, and, thus, generators of fatal discord.[21] Ultimately, the issue of press freedom was resolved in practice by the Jacobin designation of all rival presses as counterrevolutionary and by their forced closure in 1793. The Jacobin press itself, however, continued to practice this form of denunciation.

Although the broad character of revolutionary denunciation and the dilemmas it posed were settled early, the victory of radicalism after the fall of the king in 1792 and more particularly the victory of Jacobinism in 1793 led to some distinctive changes. Certainly, in some senses, these were changes of degree. The combined crises of the economy, military defeat, the Vendée peasant rebellion, and the anti-Jacobin urban rebellion called Federalism served to intensify the pervasive sense of danger and betrayal. The 1793 crises served, therefore, to intensify and broaden the practice of denunciation. Certainly, too, we see an ever more direct assertion of the centrality of the civic act: Felix Lepeletier's funeral oration for the murdered Marat in July 1793 proclaimed that "Denunciation is the mother of virtues just as vigilance is the surest safeguard of the people and of liberty."[22] However, the Terror saw the culmination of three progressive transformations in the practice of denunciation.

First, although the denunciation of enemies continued in the Jacobin press, and although the great oratorical denunciations of factional rivals as agents of counterrevolution continued in the Convention, individual denunciations became less and less public. Recent historians have paid some attention to the ideas of Etienne Barry on political denunciation presented on July 25, 1793.[23] Barry's speech coincided with an exhortation by the Parisian Jacobin Club to make denunciation a general practice throughout France. He made three new claims about what that generalized denunciation should be. The first was that individual denunciation was to be seen as an act by a member of the sovereign people on behalf of that people. It was, therefore, properly seen as a collective act although it was undertaken by an individual. From this he appeared to derive his second claim: the notion that denunciation could perfectly well be anonymous and did not have to engage the responsibility of the denouncer. Third, he asserted that a major function of denunciation as an act of citizenship was to discipline those who did not behave as integral members of the collectivity; denunciation was in a real sense disciplinary and educative as much as it was a weapon against treason.

[21] See esp. Chevalier de Pange, *Réflexions sur la délation et sur le comité de recherches* (Paris, 1790).

[22] Lucien Jaume, *Le discours jacobin et la démocratie* (Paris, 1989), p. 204.

[23] Ibid., p. 203. Analysis repeated by Guilhaumou.

Revealing though Barry is of a burgeoning Jacobin mentality, it is not clear to me that we need to take him quite as seriously as recent historians have done. One does not encounter much anonymous denunciation during the Terror. Nonetheless, inasmuch as anonymity is a reduction of publicity, Barry's analysis does point to another, though different, phenomenon: the growing secrecy of individual denunciation that arrived with the Terror. Denunciations were now made to the vigilance committees (*comités de surveillance*), which had been established by decree in March 1793 as a response to the growing emergency. Certainly denunciations had to be written down and signed, or at least explicitly authored; but they were now made to a small group of men in a private environment.

This was, of course, a major change. As we have seen, in the early Revolution publicity had been one of the central characteristics that separated revolutionary denunciation from informing. This was not merely because it prevented calumny and self-seeking, though that was certainly essential. Above all, publicity testified to the fact that the denouncer spoke to the public—to the People—revealing knowledge that it ought to have for the defense of its liberty. In its original conception, therefore, denunciation was a part of revolutionary democracy. Revolutionary democracy was, however, an unstable idea. Radical revolutionaries in particular faced considerable dilemmas with the notion of the sovereign people, especially when they were confronted with popular agitation capable of both majestic insurrection against the enemies of liberty and riotous and undiscriminating attacks on persons and property.[24] Although Jacobins were always ready to use "public opinion" as an expression of the sovereign people when it suited them, they also recognized the fallibility of the opinion of a people whom they saw as easily misled. Publicity was therefore potentially dangerous. Listen to Pierre-Gaspard Chaumette (soon to be swept up in a factional purge himself) speaking about the trial of the Girondins in October 1793: "The men now before the Revolutionary Tribunal have a plan; the sessions are held in public, and ten thousand people can attest to this fact: they have tried to justify themselves to the people and to pass as innocent, at the very least in the eyes of posterity. They have relied upon their eloquence."[25]

The obvious solution to this particular problem was the one that the Terror government adopted, beginning with the silencing of Georges Danton at his trial in April 1794 and culminating in the Law of 22 Prairial Year II (June 10, 1794), which deprived all the accused of defense lawyers on the grounds that

[24] For an exploration of this dilemma and how radicals coped with it, see C. Lucas, "Revolutionary Violence, the People and the Terror," in Baker, ed., pp. 57–79.

[25] F.-A. Aulard, *La société des Jacobins*, 6 vols. (Paris, 1889–97), 5:482. As evidence of the uncertainty of Jacobin discourse in this domain, see how in the same debate Hébert states that "public opinion has already made up its mind about the crimes of this atrocious faction" and that the trial should therefore be hurried to its conclusion.

innocence needs no defender and crime deserves none. More generally, the Jacobins tried to solve the dilemma over the location of the sovereign people by rooting the Terror in the assumption that, with the expulsion of the Girondins the Convention (unlike all previous National Assemblies) was now purified of traitors and that, thus, it truly enshrined the sovereign people. The multiplication of vigilance committees, therefore, adapted the earlier definitions of revolutionary denunciation to new ideas and circumstances. It was possible to say that the provision of a local institution close to the population generalized and facilitated its opportunity to inform the People, embodied as the Convention, by bringing denunciations to its appointed agents. The reality of the matter was, however, that denunciation was harnessed as an instrument of state power.

The harnessing of denunciation in this way was the second of the three major changes we are examining. These vigilance committees of local patriots had precisely the attributes that Loustalot had deplored as tyrannical in the Commune's *comité de recherches:* they were endowed with arrest powers and became the lowest rung on the ladder of revolutionary repression that led through prison to revolutionary tribunal and up the steps of the guillotine. In its character as a coercive government of combat in circumstances of extreme emergency, the Terror regime systematized the endemic suspicion of earlier revolutionary years into a Law of Suspects (September 17, 1793), which enjoined the summary arrest of anyone deemed suspect. Denunciation was the indispensable twin of the Law of Suspects, for denunciation was indeed primarily the articulation of suspicion without proof. Vigilance committee, denunciation, and arrest were the building blocks of state Terror. Moreover, the pervasiveness that I mentioned was incarnated in these committees: they were not omnipresent, but they were to be found in every city and town down to most small bourgs, as well as in significant numbers of villages in some areas. In these circumstances, denunciation (without the safeguard of publicity) became the first step in an *instruction* that led not to the due process of the regular law courts, but to the summary inquiry and trial of revolutionary justice. One could plausibly argue—and those who overthrew the Terror in 1794 did so—that the bloody inquisitorial regimes of the Venetian Republic had returned, that the Roman Imperial *delatores* had been reinvented. If one inquires into the background of the victims of the anti-Jacobin violence during the Thermidorian Reaction in 1795, it becomes apparent that no one was more hated than the denouncer.[26]

The third major change to culminate with the Terror can be found in the nature of the denunciatory text itself. Essentially, denunciation had had two

[26] C. Lucas, "Themes in Southern Violence after 9 Thermidor," in *Beyond the Terror,* ed. G. Lewis and C. Lucas (Cambridge, 1973), pp. 152–94.

objects in the early Revolution. The one was formed by the most obvious candidates for counterrevolutionary leanings—that is, the evident or self-proclaimed losers created by the Revolution: former ministers, princes of the blood, aristocrats, *parlementaires,* nonjuror priests, and so on. The other was government itself, over which denunciation (particularly that by journalists) acted as a kind of censuring agency. With the crisis of 1792, however, and the ever-widening radical fears of plot and betrayal that accompanied it, this narrow focus could not be sustained. The arrival of the Terror in later 1793 marked a substantial shift in the objects of denunciation. Most obviously, after the victory of Jacobinism denunciation became very much less a censuring watchdog on government. Certainly in high politics denunciation continued to be a weapon of factions inside Jacobinism. Moreover, given the Jacobins' fear that counterrevolutionaries were hidden among the officials and agents of government, denunciation continued to operate in this area. However, this sort of denunciation became a dangerous activity, and very often it was a symptom of either local factional strife or resistance to the Terror. In fact, the principal arena of denunciation shifted elsewhere. The intensification of the sense of a pervasive plot and the systematization of control through vigilance committees transported denunciation down into local communities and installed a mosaic of local surveillance and suspicion that was aimed at qualitatively different objects of denunciation from those of earlier years. In reality, denunciation essentially became a tool of government; instead of the People supervising the government, the population was set to supervise itself.

The regimen of denunciation that emerged with the Terror was, then, a multilayered phenomenon. In its most spectacular and visible forms, denunciation constituted part of the revolutionary attempt to invent the harmonious and virtuous society of the future by reading its antithesis in the catalog of crimes of specified enemies. Denunciation undergirded the show trials by asserting the self-evidence of improbable connections and webs of complicity. For example, the trial of Danton and his friends was based on Saint-Just's denunciation of them in the Convention on 11 Germinal Year II (March 31, 1794). Saint-Just began with a hopelessly tangled skein of intertwined references to the permanence of subversion, the existence of conspiratorial factions, the maneuvers of foreign powers, plots for an Orleanist monarchy, and a list of previously identified traitors. From this he pulled out one thread that, through a series of assertions and associations, identified Danton as an integral part of all that had gone before. The speech rose to a series of accusatory peaks: "Danton, you have served tyranny"; "Could you really be that blind to the general interest?"; "Danton, you were thus the accomplice of Mirabeau, d'Orleans, Dumouriez, Brissot"; "Bad citizen, you are a conspirator."[27] Nonetheless, the patent absurd-

---

[27] *Oeuvres de Saint-Just* (Paris, 1946), pp. 221–36.

ities of these show trials should not blind us to the fact that elsewhere denunciation did perform the function for which it was designed: that is, to neutralize real counterrevolutionaries as well as those whose revulsion from Jacobinism threatened the Jacobin version of the republic.

Beyond that, however, denunciation within the community (and especially the small community) is hard to read. In part this is due to the stereotyped language, borrowed from official discourse, in which it was so often written. It can be hard to discern authentic voices there. In smaller communities, denunciations tended to reflect local preoccupations—problems of food supply, the memory of seigneurial exaction, tensions over nonresident landlords, and so on. It is clear too that genuine conviction about the reality of pervasive threats and commitment to the revolutionary cause were present—visible, for example, in the denunciations of nonjuror priests and secret Catholic rites. At the same time, it is undeniable that denunciation was used as a form of communal protection against revolutionary pressure from outside. In such cases, denunciations tended to be made (often by the vigilance committee itself) against stock characters (nobles or priests) who were often conveniently absent and against whom no hard evidence was ever discovered. Indeed, denunciation and vigilance committees could also be used as communal protection in ways that had nothing to do with the Revolution—for instance, as a means of removing from a village a perpetual troublemaker or petty thief. Of course, it is also true that vigilance committees fell into the natural structure of power relations in small communities and thus reflected the complicities and conflicts built into those communities. Inevitably, denunciations belonged within a continuum of such rivalries and their often partisan character cannot be dismissed. At the same time, it seems to me that, with the exception of the bitterly factionalized small towns of the southeast, revolutionary committees in smaller communities did usually seek to ignore or downplay denunciations that were too overtly motivated by personal interests and emotions. It is only in some larger towns that one sees real cases of cynical, greedy, and polemical denunciation in conjunction with frankly criminal behavior. The most glaring case was that of the revolutionary committee and the "Compagnie Marat" of Nantes, who brutalized prisoners, stole from them, and finally systematically drowned a number of them in the Loire.[28]

Denunciation was the spouse of suspicion. "Suspicion," said Robespierre, "is the guardian of the rights of the People; it is to the profound feeling for liberty what jealousy is to love."[29] But denunciation was always more than just a statement of suspicion. Like jealousy, denunciation was an interpretation, a process of giving meaning to behavior, gestures, and appearances. Thus, for

---

[28] R. C. Cobb, *Les armées révolutionnaires,* 2 vols. (Paris, 1961–63), 1:576–87.
[29] *Oeuvres de Maximilien Robespierre* (Paris, 1961), 8:76.

example, when Huard came under pressure in the Paris Jacobin Club, the most convincing denouncer was the one who invited people to see "how he has listened to the discussion. Just by looking at him, I would pronounce him guilty."[30] Even in the early moments of the Revolution, revolutionary denunciation rarely involved the straightforward announcement of a counterrevolutionary event or action. Denunciation was always descriptive, but it also interpreted that description either by associating it with extraneous considerations or by imputing a meaning on the basis of supposed general truths. Thus, a man's journey out of town might become suspect if he were a noble; a banging door at night might become suspect if the door were that of a bakery; a woman carrying a large basket at an unusual hour might be suspect if she were the servant of a rich person; a wealthy merchant was more likely to be hostile to the Revolution than a shopkeeper; prostitutes were more likely to regret the fall of the Old Regime than pregnant, unwed servant girls (however reprehensible); and so on and on.

Louis-Pierre Dufourny's denunciation of François Chabot in the Jacobin Club in November 1793, which began the latter's journey to the guillotine, offers a prime example of the weaving of fact, assertion, and implication that comprised denunciation.[31] Dufourny began by stating that Chabot had said that there ought to be an opposition in the Convention. Discussion about the public good is doubtless necessary, said Dufourny; but we are not like England (a first damningly charged reference), where there is a ministerial party and therefore necessarily the party of the people as an opposition. Is there, he asked, an opposition party, a party of the right, in the Jacobin Club (damningly associating Chabot's notion with the anathema of "party" and "right," and thereby opposing him to the Jacobin Club)? With hardly a transition, Dufourny went on to Chabot's recent marriage to the sister of the brothers Frey, wealthy Austrian-Jewish bankers. His wife, he said, had apparently brought a large dowry, but a deputy should not run after wealth (implying that this was Chabot's motive). And what time did he choose for his marriage to an Austrian? The very moment when (the Austrian) Marie-Antoinette was before the Revolutionary Tribunal, when the nation was "at the *height* of its execration of foreigners," and when "our brothers" at the frontiers (facing the Austrian troops) are leaving widows and families for us to console and sustain. He really ought to have enquired more carefully into her background. What is more, he had an affair with a French woman who had a baby by him—and he has abandoned them for a foreigner.

Dufourny's denunciation amalgamated a political opinion with an error of judgment in private life; it tainted both by associating them with the country's

[30] Aulard, 5:489.
[31] Ibid., p. 518.

wartime enemies; it contrasted the wealth of the bride with the poverty of the widows, victims of the patriotism of their husbands; it then proceeded to suggest Chabot's personal immorality by making an unverified assertion about a previous liaison; and, finally, it managed to represent the ending of the liaison as being as immoral as the beginning of it and, what is more, decidedly unpatriotic. In terms of the art of denunciation, this is an exceptionally elegant specimen. It achieves its full resonance when one understands, as the audience would have, that Chabot was a self-defrocked priest and a hot radical. He had fallen afoul of the Girondins and the so-called Austrian Committee in 1792; he had been a leader of the August 10 insurrection to overthrow the King; he affected the negligent dress of radical sympathizers with the poor; and he was a tireless denouncer of enemies of the people. Dufourny's denunciation suggested that some of Chabot's behavior could be read as a demonstration that his republicanism was a mask for counterrevolution. The denunciation offered no proof—only a series of observations arranged in such a way as to imply proof. From this beginning, much was embroidered in the next few months.[32]

Indeed, the fundamental point about suspicion is that, like jealousy, it imagines what it cannot prove. In the revolutionary imaginary, plots and subversion were always hidden: that was what made them so dangerous and the ramifications of their conspiracies potentially so endless. The function of denunciation was to reveal the hidden. The denouncer served to "discover" crime in the sense of "uncover" (*découvrir* has this double sense in equal measure). The art of denunciation was, therefore, to remove the mask, to penetrate the disguise, to see into the dark, to make the secret public—hence the revolutionary coupling of denunciation and vigilance. Denunciation was the weapon with which radicalism pursued its goal of social and individual transparency;[33] thus it became an art of reading signs, an exercise in semiotics. It was based on the premise that appearances were deceiving and that a person's speech, looks, clothes, habits, relationships, and so on all had to be scrutinized for clues to an inner, secret, real self. Thus, denunciation elicited a very distinctive counterdiscourse of defense that, more than denouncing the hidden motives of the denouncer, tended to present a counterdescription of one's own patriotic record—a counterinterpretation that claimed a greater degree of transparency than the version of the denouncer. As the first denunciations against him began to emerge, Danton stood up in the Jacobin Club and asked, "Have I, then, lost those features that mark the face of a free man? Am I no longer that same man who stood beside you in moments of crisis? Am I not he whom you have so often embraced as your friend and who shall die with you? Am I not the man

[32] See N. Hampson, "François Chabot and His Plot," *Transactions of the Royal Historical Society,* 5th ser., 26 (1976): 1–14.

[33] On this, see de Baecque (n. 12 above).

who has been weighed down by persecution? I was one of Marat's most fearless defenders. . . . You will be astounded when I make known my private behaviour. . . . I defy the malicious to provide any proof of crime against me."[34]

The defense against the denouncer was, therefore, to demonstrate that he or she had mistaken reality for a mask.[35] It would be wrong to think that denunciations were taken at face value in the Terror and that no attempts were made to verify them, even though the Terror was more efficient at locking people up than it was at releasing them. However, this defense was by no means easy. François Chabot stood up at the end of Dufourny's speech and said: "I deny categorically all these facts" (thereby unconsciously saluting Dufourny's brilliance at passing off implication as fact). "I call on all good citizens to help me to unmask the calumniators." "That," rejoined another Jacobin, "is the kind of thing conspirators always say."[36] In this case, the mask that had fallen was Chabot's. As both Chabot and Danton and still others discovered, a good record was no good defense. When Jacques-Alexis Thuriot listed at length his revolutionary conduct, Jacques-René Hébert snapped, "What is proved by services rendered to the Revolution? Conspirators always adopt this method. In order to deceive the people, one has to have served it; one has to gain its confidence the better to abuse it."[37] More than mere assertion or patriotic behavior was required to persuade people that a denunciation was wrong. Petit was lucky when he was denounced in the Jacobin Club: "Roussel points out that Petit's son is crying in a corner of the hall. Young Petit, aged twelve, rushes forward to the rostrum and declares that his father is a good patriot and has raised him in the purest principles of the Revolution. The Society applauds this child with enthusiasm and the Chairman embraces him. The father is admitted to membership and the child is given an entry ticket to the Society's meetings."[38] There could be no better testimony than that given from the purity of childhood.

The triumph of Jacobinism marked the culmination of an evolution away from scrutinizing likely categories (such as nobles and nonjuror priests) and noting visibly suspect behavior. What emerged now was the complete sense that counterrevolutionary corruption could be lodged everywhere. The corollary of this sense was an increasingly fine scrutiny of ordinary appearance.[39] Above all, the Jacobin form of denunciation was ultimately concerned to penetrate that most hidden of all areas, human intention. This was a move initiated

[34] Aulard, 5:542.
[35] Some interesting examples and discussion in Sylvie Garnier, *Les conduites politiques en l'an II,* 2 vols. (doctoral diss., Université de Paris X-Nanterre, 1992).
[36] Aulard (n. 25 above), 5:519.
[37] Ibid., p. 512.
[38] Ibid., p. 545.
[39] This argument makes it evident that I disagree with Jaume's (n. 22 above) perception that Jacobin denunciation involved the deindividualization of the suspect (p. 205).

by Robespierre in January 1792 when, in opposing the war demands of his Brissotin rivals, he queried, "I ask myself who proposes it [the war], how, in what circumstances, and why?"[40] This was precisely to raise the question of intention and to impute ill intention on the basis of interpreted circumstantial evidence. When posed, as this question was, about certified patriots, it meant that no one was safe. Virtue itself could be a mask that denunciation should penetrate. It was on this issue, indeed, that the Jacobins tore themselves apart under the Terror.

The core problem of revolutionary denunciation was precisely the one speakers saw in the very first Assembly debate on the subject in July 1789. "I ask you," said one, "what will be the limits on the powers that we shall exercise? Who will be able to judge us? Who will be able to remind us of our principles?"[41] This was to repeat the maxim of those Romans dear to the revolutionaries: "Quis custodiet ipsos custodes?" If denunciation was supposed to be the guardian of liberty, who would guard liberty against the denouncer? Etienne Barry's notion that the denouncer was simply the expression of the vigilance of the sovereign (and therefore just) People was self-evident nonsense. Rather, the Jacobins saw the guarantee in virtue—in the virtue of the People's friends. Thus, the funeral monument for Marat was inscribed, "The virtues dear to patriots are probity, justice, and humanity"—justice thus guaranteed by the other two.[42] It was the purity of heart of the patriot denouncer that alone could guarantee the vigilant precision of the denunciation. Yet if appearances were a mask, and true virtue only verifiable by looking into the heart, then there could be no certainty that the intentions of the denouncer were any purer than the intentions of the denounced. The notion of virtuous denunciation simply did not hold up. *Délation* and *dénonciation* were not different, just as the great *Encyclopédie* had said they were not. This was precisely what the Convention was asserting when it reacted to Robespierre's denunciation in Thermidor (his statement that there were still enemies in the Assembly to be eliminated) by sending him to the guillotine as a traitor intending to be a tyrant. It is no wonder that one of the earliest acts of the Thermidorian Convention was to introduce into the revolutionary tribunal the *question intentionnelle,* which specified that counterrevolutionary acts committed without counterrevolutionary intention were not criminal.

[40] *Oeuvres de Maximilien Robespierre,* 8:76 (January 2, 1792).

[41] *Archives parlementaires,* 8:294 (comte de Virieu).

[42] Musée de la Révolution Française, Vizille. In fact, the inscription was never completed and ends at "probity."

A Culture of Denunciation: Peasant Labor Migration and Religious Anathematization in Rural Russia, 1860–1905*

Jeffrey Burds
University of Rochester

In early October 1872 the peasant worker Iakov Poliakov from Kolomna District in southeastern Moscow Province was working at the machine construction mill of the Struve brothers in Moscow city. In horror at a scene he had witnessed in the factory, he wrote a denunciation to the Moscow District superintendent of police against two other peasants from his district, the metalworkers Vasilii Iakushev and Vasilii Kukushkin. On October 7, Poliakov later testified in Moscow circuit court, he had witnessed these two commit an abhorrent act of blasphemy before the icon of the Mother of God and in plain sight of other workers.

Upon investigation, the Moscow police learned that Iakushev, a thirty-five-year-old skilled craftsman, and Kukushkin, a twenty-one-year-old timekeeper, were on their lunch break when they happened upon a discarded axle box from a railway car in the skilled workmen's shed. For reasons that are never made clear in the report—either drunkenness, or boredom, or simple tomfoolery (intentions were never considered relevant by either the police or the Church authorities)—the two workers decided to conduct a "funeral service" (*otpevanie*) for the dear, departed axle box. "In plain view of the holy image," as the report emphasized repeatedly, the two blasphemers took their unholy charade to greater and greater lengths. They dressed themselves in mock priests' clothes, wrapping their torsos in bast mats to create the impression of vestments.

* I wish to thank V. P. Ivanova of the State Museum of Ethnography in St. Petersburg for her assistance with materials in the Tenishev collection. I am also indebted to L. V. Vaintraub for his invaluable guidance in the labyrinth of the Moscow Spiritual Consistory archives at the Central State Historical Archive for Moscow City. Much of the research for this article was completed with grant support from the International Research and Exchanges Board, the Fulbright-Hays Commission, and a postdoctoral fellowship from the Social Science Research Council. I am grateful to several readers for their comments and suggestions: Sheila Fitzpatrick, Gregory L. Freeze, Tom Gibson, Irene Kuzel, Boris Litvak, Elias Mandala, Brenda Meehan, Timothy Mixter, James Scott, Vera Shevtsov, Andrei Sokolov, and Lynne Viola. Throughout the notes, I use the standard notations for Russian archival materials, which are as follows: *fond* (f.), *opis'* (op.), *razdel* (r.), *god* (g.), *otdelenie* (otd.), *stol* (st.), *delo* (d.), *dela* (dd.), *list* (l.), *listy* (ll.), *oborot* (ob.).

This essay originally appeared in *The Journal of Modern History* 68 (December 1996).

A cross was made from iron bars. A teapot was transformed into a make-shift incense burner. Tallow candles that they had placed before the "casket" burned brightly throughout the blasphemous ritual as Iakushev "the priest" and Kukushkin "the deacon" sang bawdy street songs in sacrilegious mock bereavement. At the end of the "service," Iakushev, removing his trousers and baring his naked rear, bowed to several workers and proclaimed: "The mass is ended."[1]

For this blatant act of hooliganism, the two unfortunate peasants were exiled from the capital and escorted in chains and leg shackles under police guard to their native villages. There they were probably imprisoned for a few days, pub-licly whipped, fined, and anathematized by the local priest and fellow villagers alike. Three factors in particular influenced the severity of their sentence. First, the key witness and denouncer in the events was considered an unimpeachable source: Iakov Poliakov was the *starosta,* or elder, of his own artel of *zemliaki*—neighboring peasants from his region—and was so offended by the display that he appealed to the police to bring the miscreants to justice. Second, the entire blasphemy was far more serious because it was carried out in the pres-ence of the icon of the Mother of God, which hung on the wall of the room where the sacrilege took place and before which workers had placed an icon lamp. Third, the public nature of the offense, the "pernicious moral influence" it exerted on the other workers, was clearly a factor: by their sacrilege, Iaku-shev and Kukushkin not only damned themselves but also threatened to en-snare fellow workers.

Rural Russia during the last three generations of the Old Regime was a soci-ety in flux, a peripatetic world in which traditional relationships and traditional ways of doing things were profoundly transformed. This was observable not just in myriad individual relationships but also in the totality of village social relations. Russia's rapid transition to a commodity economy generated a pow-erful impetus toward the search for nonlocal sources of peasant income, resulting in the last half of the nineteenth century in sky-rocketing rates of peasant labor migration for side earnings. In the Central Industrial Region—Moscow and a surrounding radius of roughly three hundred kilometers—by the 1890s, more than a third of all adult peasant males (at least one member of every peasant household) were involved in some form of work that took them away from their villages for extended periods each year.[2]

---

[1] See the full text of the report from the Moscow Governor's office to the Metropoli-tan of Moscow for October 23, 1872, in Tsentral'nyi gosudarstvennyi istoricheskii arkhiv goroda Moskvy, Moscow (hereafter cited as TsGIAgM), f. 203, op. 341, d. 124, ll. 1–2.

[2] On the rapid growth of peasant labor migration in the Moscow region, see Jeffrey Burds, "The Social Control of Peasant Labor in Russia: The Responses of Village Com-munities to Labor Migration in the Central Industrial Region, 1861–1905," in *Peasant*

This study traces the development of a distinct culture of denunciation in village parishes as the growth in peasant migration for side earnings threatened to destroy the ties that bound rural Russia together. It should not be surprising that it was through the prism of their religious beliefs that Russian peasants handled the tensions of their daily lives. In practice, the religious dimension was pervasive, defining every aspect of the everyday life of the community, overlaying and forming the language of rivalry between clans or socioeconomic groups. In this context, peasant denunciations nearly always took the form of impugning the reputations of fellow villagers.

The discussion below is drawn from over three hundred cases of religious denunciations in village parishes that were recorded in the archives of the Moscow Spiritual Consistory throughout the nineteenth and early twentieth centuries.[3] I have devoted particular attention to cases of religious deviation involving the rejection (*uklonenie*) of Russian Orthodoxy for the Old Belief or for sectarian faiths.[4] The most remarkable feature of this material, and the factor that unifies nearly all of these cases, is that over 90 percent of the three hundred cases of religious denunciations reviewed were directed against peasant workers who migrated for side earnings.

Economy, Culture, and Politics in European Russia, 1800–1921, ed. Esther Kingston-Mann and Timothy Mixter, with the assistance of Jeffrey Burds (Princeton, N.J., 1991), pp. 52–100. For a focus on peasant women's migration, see Barbara Alpern Engel, *Between the Field and the City: Women, Work, and Family in Russia, 1861–1914* (Cambridge, 1994).

[3] These cases are preserved in TsGIAgM, f. 203, "*Moskovskaia dukhovnaia konsistoriia.*" The typical file contains either a peasant's written denunciation (in rare cases) or a written summary of such denunciations prepared by a parish priest or the local superintendent. In addition, I have relied on unpublished ethnographic collections, most notably: Gosudarstvennyi Muzei Etnografii Narodov SSSR. Sektsiia Rukopisei, St. Petersburg (hereafter cited as GME), f. 7, "Materialy 'Etnograficheskogo Biuro' V. N. Tenisheva, 1897–1901," a remarkable collection of over eighteen hundred files, with original reports from three hundred correspondents, who responded to over four hundred questions. I have also used police files of the Russian Ministry of Internal Affairs in Rossiiskii gosudarstvennyi istoricheskii arkhiv, St. Petersburg (hereafter cited as RGIA), f. 1284, "Department Obshchikh Del Ministerstva Vnutrennykh Del"; and in local village police and court records preserved in TsGIAgM.

[4] In the pages below I draw no distinction between various forms of religious sectarianism in Russia. This is to a large degree merely a reflection of the popular and official belief among Orthodox believers, for whom all forms of heresy were equally repugnant. For a more nuanced treatment, see A. I. Klibanov, *History of Religious Sectarianism in Russia, 1860s–1917* (Oxford, 1982).

PEASANT LABOR MIGRATION AND MORAL CORRUPTION

> What's shameful in your own village won't be seen [if it's done]
> somewhere else. (PEASANT SAYING IN KALUGA PROVINCE, 1890s)[5]

Few popular attitudes of the peasantry were so widely accepted as the general agreement that life outside the village corrupted peasants. There was a broad consensus that *otkhodniki,* or peasant labor migrants, were "spoiled" in two very Russian meanings of the term. First, they were spoiled in the Russian sense of *izbalóvannyi:* they were deluded and enticed by expectations of imminent prosperity, by the wealth of consumer goods, by the comparatively easy life of nonvillage labor, by the absence of the guiding hand of strict patriarchal authority in their lives. An excellent illustration of this pervasive attitude was provided by the *zemstvo* correspondent Nedokhodovskii writing from Il'inskaia *volost,* in Kaluga in 1896: "The earnings of dyers, metal workers, caretakers, and others are decent enough, but very little ends up at home. Much is spent on fancy dress: topcoats, jackets, trousers, waistcoats, highboots with galoshes, and so on; and for women, [town-style] dresses, cosmetics. . . . In general, there is among factory workers an extreme disgust toward the village: only children are held back by women between the factory and the village."[6] Another report from a village priest in 1896 repeated the general anxiety: "The people of our village have grown lazy: they are careless toward agriculture and yearn for Moscow, where they have grown accustomed to living freely and showing off. . . . They have good jobs, but . . . the people spend a lot on wine, on good appearances, on luxurious clothing and footwear, . . . as a consequence of which little money makes its way home."[7]

Young migrant workers were thought to be particularly vulnerable to the seductions of life away from the village. In 1888, a peasant correspondent in Podol'sk District, Moscow, wrote disparagingly:

Many of these so-called [peasant workers] . . . have become attracted to the excessive use of strong drink. This is especially [true] of the young generation, which in former times was ashamed of [such behavior], but now has come to be proud of it. Let's take for example the holidays, when the youth come home. No longer evident are those innocent and decent village amusements of an earlier generation, popular songs and dances of a proper kind. . . . The songs which are sung are more indecent. In round dances it is evident that a large number of the village lads are drunk, affected and with cigarettes in their teeth. Today's youth stroll along the streets, brazen in their drunken state, with harmonicas and indecent songs, ashamed neither [in front of members of

---

[5] *Statisticheskii obzor Kaluzhskoi gubernii za 1896 god* (Kaluga, 1897), pt. 2:49.
[6] Ibid., p. 38.
[7] Ibid., pp. 38–39.

the opposite] sex nor [in front of their] elders. Obedience to parents and elders has almost completely fallen away. Drunkenness, luxurious attire and willfulness are everywhere taking root deeper and deeper.[8]

It was popularly believed that the "free atmosphere [and] the easy, high-paying work" in the town or factory enticed all peasant labor migrants, but especially the youth, and made it all too easy for them to neglect their responsibilities to religion and family. While most young migrants were generally thought to be spoiled in this first sense, there were also a few in every village who were generally believed to suffer from a far more insidious form of moral decadence: a condition usually described by the Russian word *ispórchennyi*, meaning corrupted or immoral. Charges of spiritual laxness, decadence, and immorality were inseparably linked in popular perceptions of peasant labor migrants. A village priest from Iur'ev-Pol'skii District, Vladimir, complained at the end of the 1890s:

Migration to the factory exerts a corrupting influence on the workers and their families. A departing youth, lacking any of the supervision of family elders and having for himself a steady flow of money and free time, does not concern himself with the household, gets into the habit of undesirable vices, debauchery, a loss of morality, indifference to religion and to the rites of the Church. On Good Friday, a worker thinks nothing about duty until [he is] disgracefully drunk, gorging himself with sausage, playing the accordion, dancing and singing various songs.
    . . . For several years they do not go to confession and do not partake of the Blessed Sacraments; nineteen-, twenty-, twenty-two-year-olds refuse to get married, but instead prefer to live together conjugally outside the law.[9]

Labor migrants were identified as potentially more corrupted members of the community in every way: they were considered to be more likely to neglect religious duties; they showed a greater propensity toward celebration and rabble-rousing and were thought to be wastrels of vitally needed family resources; and they were considered to be more sexually profligate.

The profoundly distinct moral universe of peasant workers was revealed in a written confession mailed to a village priest by one peasant woman who lived and worked in Moscow during the mid-nineteenth century. The confession survived because it was intercepted by the Moscow police. While for the modern reader the woman's litany of sins is a lesson in the profound distance that separates our moral universe from that of the nineteenth-century Russian peasant, for contemporaries the list was just one example of the decadent moral universe of a corrupted peasant worker. Her list of sins included, among other

---

[8] *Statisticheskii ezhegodnik Moskovskoi gubernii za 1889 g.* (Moscow, 1889), sec. 3, pp. 21–22.
    [9] Quoted by Burds, pp. 58–62.

things, admissions of breast-feeding another woman's child, as well as a kitten; playing kissing games with men and kissing men at *khorovody* (round dances); seducing a priest and surreptitiously kissing a priest; wearing men's clothes; swinging on a swing; telling fortunes; despairing and asking God for death; gazing at the sacred image while thinking fornicatious thoughts; and smearing herself with badger fat, probably with incantations in a popular ritual for inducing abortion.[10]

Regardless of one's perspective or social position, the "Russian peasant *away* from the village, . . . the peasant decontextualized, severed from his native cultural milieu" was a potential threat to all: in various ways, the entire system in Old Regime Russia worked to uphold the imperatives of maintaining the peasant migrant's link to his native village and regulating the behavior of peasants who worked away from their families and villages.[11]

"THE SLIPPERY PATH OF EVIL": *Otkhodniki* AND PARISH PRIESTS

Ostensibly, the extension of controls over peasant labor migrants began in the village parish and, in particular, with the village priests. As the official arbiters of morality in Russian Orthodox villages, all priests were encouraged to denounce to Church authorities or the police anyone who was deemed a threat to the spiritual or civil order. The notorious *Ecclesiastical Regulation,* promulgated at Peter the Great's initiative in the spring of 1722, explicitly required Orthodox priests to honor a "higher moral code" as an act of their Christian duty and even to violate the sanctity of confession when information thereby obtained threatened the interests of the state.[12] Until the very end of the Old Regime, all new parish priests—as a prerequisite of appointment—were required to make an oral and written oath (*prisiaga*) of loyalty to the reigning tsar, which explicitly placed civil authority on a higher plane than that of the Church and which made a virtue of denunciations against parishioners.[13]

The question of whether parish priests actually fulfilled their oaths is extremely controversial. The dual roles of parish priests as agents of state author-

[10] See the tendentious summary in F. V. Livanov, *Raskol'niki i ostorozhniki: Ocherki i rasskazy,* 4th ed. (St. Petersburg, 1872), 1:356–57.

[11] The quote is taken from Reginald E. Zelnik, "'To the Unaccustomed Eye': Religion and Irreligion in the Experience of St. Petersburg Workers in the 1870s," *Russian History/Histoire Russe* 16, nos. 2–4 (1989): 302.

[12] See James Cracraft, "Opposition to Peter the Great," in *Imperial Russia, 1700–1917: State, Society, Opposition: Essays in Honor of Marc Raeff,* ed. Ezra Mendelsohn and Marshall S. Shatz (Dekalb, Ill., 1988), pp. 29–30, and *The Church Reform of Peter the Great* (Stanford, Calif., 1971), pp. 238–40.

[13] For an example of the standard oath, see "Prisiaga proizvodimym v sviashchenniki stavlennikam," TsGIAgM (n. 1 above), f. 206, op. 1, d. 163, ll. 6–7.

ity and spiritual pastors certainly generated confusion and considerable conjecture. To be sure, until the very end of the Old Regime official edicts were
announced from the priestly pulpit, lending a distinct aura of officialdom to
even the most recalcitrant parish priest. The important issue here, however, is
not whether priests actually fulfilled their oaths in practice but, rather, that
they were perceived to do so: priests were widely seen as channels to higher
authorities. As we shall see, this perception set the stage for a popular culture
of denunciation in rural Russia: imparting information against a fellow villager
to a parish priest was the primary channel for denouncing neighbors.

The Church hierarchy's position on the threat to parish life posed by labor
migration was unequivocal: in numerous ways village priests were called upon
to battle vigorously against the disintegration of religious belief that was engendered by migration. In official correspondence and in the ecclesiastical
press, priests received a barrage of communications and reminders about their
social and spiritual roles. A particularly comprehensive and articulate program
appeared in 1894 in *The Helmsman* (Kormchii) and was subsequently reprinted in religious journals throughout Russia under the rather innocuous title
"One Subject Deserving the Particular Attention of Village Pastors."[14] The article was a manifesto against the nefarious influence of the outside world on the
social and spiritual life of the village parish: "Our task consists above all . . . in
turning the attention of village pastors to the *necessity* of struggling against the
corrupting influence on the simple people of those who live outside of their
parishes: in the towns, at the factories, in the mills, [among workers in] hired
agricultural labor and various forms of outside employment."[15] A particular
threat to village spirituality and cohesion was perceived in the growing prevalence of peasant out-work, especially among unmarried men and women:

A long way from their families and homes, free from any restraining moral authority
and, not infrequently, deprived for a more or less prolonged period . . . of an opportunity to satisfy their religious needs, these people naturally display insecurity and irreso-
lution in their moral conceptions. Moreover, the temptations—particularly in the
towns—are too great for them; and the comradeship in which they are thrown by
chance, in which they will always find evil and corrupted elements, set an infectious

[14] See the version in *Kostromskiia eparkhialnyia vedomosti*, g. 8, no. 13 (July 1894):
273–76 (hereafter cited as *Kostromskiia eparkhialnyia vedomosti*). The Russian title
was "Odin iz predmetov, zasluzhivaiushchikh osobennogo vnimaniia sel'skikh
pastyrei." The same theme was heard in the Church's survey of the causes of hooliganism in Russian society: the vast majority of Russian Orthodox bishops identified a
direct relationship between hooliganism and peasant migration for side earnings. See
the collected reports in RGIA, f. 796, op. 195, d. 3223, passim. A partial and incomplete
summary of the reports was published in P. A. Blagoveshchenskii, *O bor'be s khuligans-
tvom: Iz eparkhial'noi zhizni* (St. Petersburg, 1914).
[15] *Kostromskiia eparkhialnyia vedomosti*, p. 276.

example and not infrequently push them along the same slippery path of evil. . . . Drunkenness, moral dissoluteness, disrespect toward elders, the absence of religious piety, the inclination toward various kinds of luxury, wild living and revelry, and many other undesirable habits and tastes are introduced into the healthy peasant environment by this means.[16]

In response to this challenge, the author proposed an ambitious social program that promoted greater spiritual regulation of migrants. Pastors were exhorted to pay special attention to the salvation of those "lost souls" who had been particularly corrupted by outside life.[17] Rehabilitation and reintegration of *otkhodniki* were closely tied to village rituals—the collective worship and celebration of births, weddings, deaths, saints' days, and numerous religious holidays, as well as religious processions and annual pilgrimages.[18] Noting that "regular annual performance of the Christian duty of Confession and Holy Communion has a great importance for each person and is a wholesome influence on his spiritual life," *The Helmsman* commended the practice observed in several villages whereby "some of the parishioners who are away from the parish for several years unfailingly send their priest every year written statements about their attendance at Confession and Holy Communion" and sometimes even "appear in person in their parish during the Lenten season for fasting."[19]

At least once each year, and often more than once, priests would visit each household individually to bless the home and farmstead, pray with the family, test the children's knowledge of basic prayers, and in general affirm the relationship between priest and parishioner. These visits were not just celebrations of spiritual renewal but also the primary means by which a vigilant parish priest tested the faith of parishioners and discovered if any of them had grown reluctant to take part in sacred rituals of the Church. As in Catholic Medieval Europe, the "refusal to take communion was tantamount . . . to an admission of guilt."[20] A typical case was reported in mid-July 1872 in Klin District, northwest of Moscow. The parish priest in Selinskoe village, Father Dmitrii Sokolov, was going from house to house in an annual visit, blessing peasants' homes

---

[16] Ibid., p. 273.

[17] Ibid., p. 275.

[18] On ritual integration of *otkhodniki* into community life, see T. A. Bernshtam, *Molodezh'v obriadovoi zhizni russkoi obshchiny XIX-nachala XX v.: Polovozrastnoi aspekt traditsionnoi kul'tury* (Leningrad, 1988), pp. 210–11.

[19] *Kostromskiia eparkhialnyia vedomosti,* pp. 275–76. For other priests' calls for such integration of peasant workers into the village ritual process, see the discussion in Blagoveshchenskii, pp. 6–7, 10–11.

[20] R. I. Moore, "Popular Violence and Popular Heresy in Western Europe, c1000–1179," in *Persecution and Toleration,* ed. W. J. Sheils, Papers of the Ecclesiastical Historical Society (London, 1984), p. 49.

and praying with the families. The recurring ritual went ahead without interruption until the priest reached the home of one peasant worker, Fedor Petrov, who happened to be home from his usual work in Moscow. The priest, "having finished prayers in [Petrov's] home, bid [Petrov] to bow down before the Icon, the cross, and the Evangelist," but Petrov refused. The refusal caused a scandal, and the parish priest convened a meeting of the communal assembly where he vehemently denounced Petrov for religious apostasy. A heated public discussion followed in which "the entire community of peasants began to reproach" Petrov for "deviating from the Orthodox faith." The tension grew, but when threatened with physical punishment Petrov refused to conform: "You can cut me to pieces," he cried in a dramatic confrontation with fellow villagers, "but I will not give up my faith."

In the police inquiry that followed, at least twelve witnesses were interviewed. All of the signs of a fall from faith were discovered: Petrov had not partaken of the Blessed Sacraments for two years; he had frequently been absent for long periods working in Moscow. When interrogated, the recusant peasant Petrov revealed that he had lived in Moscow each winter for five consecutive years, working at the factory of the peasant Timofei Ermolov Sergeev, who belonged to the Old Believer sect at the Rogozhskii cemetery. "At this factory there lived many workers, natives of Kaluga Province, schismatics, from whom I learned to read and obtained Holy books. Having read [these books] and having listened to the workers' discussions about church matters, I came to the conviction that one should not bow before either icons or priests." Even worse, several parishioners testified that Petrov had openly defied the true faith in the fateful communal assembly where he had been summoned to explain his blasphemy. In open defiance of the community, he had ardently proclaimed: "You have been baptized with an accursed cross! You bow down to accursed icons, made with your own accursed hands!" One fellow villager, Lev Ivanov, testified that when he had visited the blasphemer's home Petrov had read to him from a book that "proved that Orthodox Christians do not make the sign of the cross as they should." Even more damning was evidence that Petrov had actually succeeded in converting a fellow villager, the peasant woman Dar'ia Fedorova.

Petrov was found guilty on three counts of criminal conspiracy. First, he was proven to be a recusant religious dissenter who had fallen away from the true faith and had cursed holy images. Second, and much more seriously, he was deemed to be a danger to his community, as demonstrated by his efforts to attract others to his renunciation of faith. For this he was found guilty of violating articles 72 and 134 of the Russian criminal code, which prohibited missionizing efforts to convert others to the schismatic faith and to deny Orthodoxy. Third, Petrov was likewise found guilty of open slander (*khula*) against the Orthodox faith. His case was transferred from the ecclesiastical court to the jurisdiction of the civil authorities, and Petrov was ordered to stand trial before the prosecutor of the Moscow Circuit Court.[21]

Elsewhere the same pattern was followed: a peasant's refusal to take part in local religious rituals drew the attention of the parish priest and fellow villagers alike. In another typical case, the parish priest, Father Viktor Gur'ev, denounced a negligent peasant woman to his local superintendent in December 1886: "The widow Florova does not permit discussions [with the priest] about faith at home with her children. Likewise she [resists] prayer services [at home] on Holy Days. . . . She always avoids discussions about faith."[22]

The imposition of ritual obligations was the chief means by which priests, acting on their own, could root out religious nonconformists. The annual duty was considered so important that all parish priests were required to file annual reports—confession and communion registers (*ispovednye vedomosti*)—in which religious attendance was discussed and deviants were singled out. These reports were one of the only means by which the Holy Synod could monitor parish religious life, and they were treated with the utmost seriousness. Repeated failure to submit an annual report led to severe reprimands and even the loss of one's parish. Reports that revealed declines in religious attendance in one's parish provoked investigations, usually performed by representatives of the central Church administration—the local superintendents (*blagochinye*).[23]

The authority of priests in a village community was not generally limited, however, to the powers granted them by law. In traditional society, as in Third World villages today, outsiders seeking information often worked through references provided by local priests, which lent priests enormous authority and influence. Finding work outside the village often depended on a good relationship with one's parish priest, as did passport issuing and renewal; securing a loan or a cash deal; and receipt of packages, letters, and cash transfers. When the police intervened, they often followed the lead of the parish priest to estab-

---

[21] TsGIAgM, f. 203, op. 342, d. 31, ll. 11–14, passim (1872). The file is a full summary of the judicial and Church proceedings against Petrov. For a detailed inventory of Petrov's books, see the report on ll. 21–22. The possession of a prohibited book aggravated Petrov's case; he was found guilty of violating article 550 of the criminal code.

[22] TsGIAgM, f. 203, op. 371, g. 1886, d. 10, l. 1 ob. (Moscow District).

[23] Different researchers have found conflicting evidence on this point. While in theory a close watch was kept on confession and communion registers, the practice varied considerably. In my work in the Moscow Consistory I have found numerous cases in which nonreporting, or reports that reflected a marked decline in parish attendance, provoked investigation by the local superintendent. In her work in Vologda Province, in contrast, Vera Shevtsov (personal communication, May 1993) has found that the local consistory was more or less indifferent to such annual reports and intervened only in particularly egregious cases when the recusant's conduct had drawn the attention of others. Compare I. S. Belliustin, *Description of the Clergy in Rural Russia: The Memoir of a Nineteenth-Century Parish Priest* (Ithaca, N.Y., 1985), pp. 173–78.

lish the reputation and reliability (or unreliability) of locals.[24] In short, priests played an essential role in sustaining a peasant's good reputation with local peasant officials, as well as with outsiders.

Besides reporting a parishioner's failure to fulfill ritual obligations, priests also actively denounced peasants for immoral behavior in two other types of cases: noncanonical marriages and the failure of families to baptize newborn infants. The parish priest wielded enormous power to regulate marriages. At the end of January 1887, for instance, the parish priest Aleksei Zhuravlev of Nativity Church in Dmitrov District filed a denunciation against the Old Believers who had led astray the nineteen-year-old son of one of his parishioners. The young peasant worker, Vasilii Nikolaev, had been a faithful servant of Orthodoxy: "Every Sunday and Holiday he attended matins and the Liturgy without omission." Then, charged the priest, he was lured away by false promises of personal gain to follow from his blasphemous marriage to a young girl of the priestly sect: "I am convinced that the . . . peasant [son] went astray to the *raskol* [schism, or sectarianism] not according to the desire of his heart, but from [the seduction of] worldly personal advantages, fearing he might let this notorious [wealthy] bride-*raskol'nitsa* slip away. I consider the behavior of the young bachelor to be brazen blasphemy and insulting to the Orthodox Christian Church."[25] Father Zhuravlev turned to the police, and with their help he presented the young recusant with an ultimatum: he must either marry the girl in the Church or leave her. The Church considered such noncanonical marriages as *nezakonnoe* or *liubodeiannoe sozhitel'stvo*—illegal or adulterous cohabitation—and priests were instructed to do everything in their power to restore the deviant to proper Orthodox rites.

And that power was considerable. If the priest or local ecclesiastical superintendent could demonstrate (1) that the case involved the "falling away" of a former Orthodox Christian and (2) that "undue influence" was used to delude the peasant or to force him to act against his "true will," then priests could call upon the police to separate the married couple. This was true even in cases where the couple had lived together as husband and wife for several years, and even when they had children. To prevent reunification of the pair, local police, officials, and even neighbors were required to sign sworn oaths promising they would help to keep the couple apart.

Because the parish priests maintained the parish registers, upon which all future documentation rested—everything from military service to passports, loans, arrests, and state tax obligations—every peasant, Orthodox or Old Be-

---

[24] For a description of the powerful role of parish priests in *svidetel'stva* or affidavits, see the report of I. Shchelgov, the village elder from Liakhakh village in Melenki District, Vladimir Province (GME [n. 3 above], f. 7, op. 1, d. 41, l. 4).

[25] TsGIAgM (n. 1 above), f. 203, op. 371, d. 18, l. 1.

liever, had to reach some sort of understanding with the local parish priest. The effectiveness of religious controls was dependent largely, but not exclusively, on their vigilance. But several factors severely undermined their ability to monitor the moral activities of their parishioners. First, most parishes were far too large. The number of parishioners in Russia as a whole expanded far more rapidly than the number of available priests: by 1904, the ratio of parish priests to parishioners was 1:1,844, and even if all clerical staff were included, the ratio would still be a discouraging 1:826.[26] Second, Orthodox parish priests were overburdened by a surfeit of rituals and practices. As the leading historian of Russian parish priests, Gregory L. Freeze has observed, "The Russian parish priest had to perform a plethora of rites and sacraments, often in the parishioner's home, and it was just physically impossible to minister to the ritual needs of overly large parishes. . . . And the task in Russia was further complicated by the low population density; often a parish consisted of many hamlets scattered all over the surrounding countryside."[27] Third, the turnover of priests was too high to allow them to develop intimate acquaintances with members of their parishes. Far more than in the West, Russian Orthodox parish priests depended directly upon parishioners' contributions and on the fees they collected for the performance of rites in order to make ends meet. The high rate of parish turnovers was directly associated with the extreme disparities between parishes and parish incomes, as well as the career patterns of the clergy, who competed to win and retain berths in wealthier parishes.[28]

The priest's task was particularly difficult in parishes with high rates of out-migration for side earnings. It was in fact quite easy for a recusant to avoid the parish priest for long stretches. Out-migration presented a very special set of circumstances that undermined the parish priest's ability to supervise parishioners and facilitated tactical escape by wily apostates. The peasant recusant Iakov Grigor'ev, for instance, managed to use his migrant status as a means to escape detection for several years. It was only when he was denounced to the Moscow police—probably by his own father—that Grigor'ev was brought to justice. As the local superintendent's report indicated,

This falling away [*otpadenie*] was completed in secret, so that Grigor'ev's father did not immediately notice it. But it was never discovered either by the parish priest at St. Sergei's Church [in Moscow], nor by the parish priest in Domodedovo village, the parish to which [Iakov] belonged [from birth]. The former did not notice Grigor'ev's turning away [*uklonenie*] because he [the recusant] lived at St. Sergei's parish only temporarily and could have gone to church at a nearby monastery . . . where many pa-

[26] Gregory L. Freeze, *The Parish Clergy in Nineteenth-Century Russia: Crisis, Reform, Counter-Reform* (Princeton, N.J., 1983), pp. 459–60.
[27] Ibid., pp. 64–65.
[28] Ibid., pp. 58–59.

rishioners of St. Sergei's Church confess and partake of the Blessed Sacraments. Nor did the latter notice because he [Grigor'ev] lived constantly in Moscow.[29]

To guard against such lying and evasion, more vigilant priests increasingly demanded that peasant workers unable to fulfill religious obligations in their native parishes should be required to bring certificates (*svidetel'stva*) signed by the priests in the parishes near their workplaces verifying their religious attendance.[30] In one case, three peasant women of the same family from Moscow District lived and worked not far from their native village sewing gloves at a local workshop. After a fellow villager denounced them, their parish priest invited them to fulfill their religious obligations, to which they responded "that they had fasted while on religious pilgrimage." On his insistence, the women promised to present the proper documentation. "But in spite of their promises and my requests," Father Smirnov later wrote in his formal denunciation to the ecclesiastical superintendent, "the Skundova women have hitherto presented no evidence either of their attendance at Confession or Holy Communion or of their preparation for Communion at [another] church. Moreover, it was rumored in the parish that the Skundova [women] had turned away from Orthodoxy." In order to verify the rumors, Smirnov confronted the women, who eventually admitted that they had left the Church.[31]

As long as there was no denunciation, a peasant's lapse from Orthodoxy might go undetected for quite some time. For instance, the peasant Boris Martynov was fifty-six years old before his long-standing Old Believer status was discovered and investigated. Born in a village in Kolomna District, Moscow, in 1839, Martynov was baptized the day after his birth into the Orthodox Church. In the confession registers for 1848, the eight-year-old Martynov attended confession and communion—the one and only time in his life. In 1849 Martynov's father died, and with him ended his young son's only tie to the Orthodox Church. Martynov was raised by his mother, who immediately lapsed back into Old Belief. Upon questioning in 1895, the elder Martynov

[29] TsGIAgM, f. 203, op. 342, d. 106, l. 1 ob. For similar cases of evasion or deception, see the following documents in TsGIAgM: f. 203, op. 347, g. 1876, d. 49, l. 6 (Vereia); op. 349, g. 1877, d. 53 (Serpukhov); op. 364, g. 1882, d. 25, l. 10 (Volokolamsk); op. 393, g. 1896, d. 42, l. 2 ob. (Bronnitsy).

[30] Two young brothers who were accused of deviation successfully defended themselves against the charges by presenting such evidence. See TsGIAgM, f. 203, op. 371, g. 1887, d. 10, ll. 1, 3 (Moscow District). For similar cases, see TsGIAgM, f. 203, op. 341, g. 1871, d. 25, ll. 8–9, 15 ob. (Vereia District). The certificates were routinely used for prewedding investigations and were generally required in all marriages taking place outside of the native parish of either the bride or the groom. For an excellent illustration of the difficulty of marrying without such documentation, see the case in TsGIAgM, f. 203, op. 349, g. 1874, d. 85 (Moscow District).

[31] TsGIAgM, f. 203, op. 347, g. 1875, d. 20, l. 1 (Moscow District).

claimed, probably truthfully, that he did not even know he was Orthodox—a credible remark given the forty-eight years that separated him from his last affirmation of Orthodoxy. In the confession registers for 1849, Martynov was cited as not attending confession out of spiritual negligence (*neradenie*). But this was the only year of his life in which this Orthodox Christian turned Old Believer was identified as recusant. Between 1850 and 1860, and for the rest of his life as a peasant worker in Moscow, he was listed in confession registers as a nonparticipant due to his absence (*za otluchku*) from his native parish. In this case, the parish priests in Martynov's native village had for the greater part of his life turned a blind eye to his apostasy. In the end, a disgruntled fellow worker denounced him—but to the police, not to the ecclesiastical authorities.[32]

The sheer overload of cases discouraged even the most vigilant and conscientious parish priests. As the Duma's clerical deputies complained in 1915, "The authority of spiritual pastors is steadily falling, so that even the best, most energetic of them sometimes are powerless and, as if in despair, give up."[33] The inevitable vacuum in the regulation of spiritual life was filled by the development of a distinct culture of denunciation in rural parishes: unable to perform the duty of moral vigilance on their own, priests depended enormously on denunciations from within their parish communities to root out deviants. This was especially true in parishes marked by high rates of out-migration for side earnings. Ultimately, the extensive powers wielded by parish priests to regulate the behavior of fellow villagers were increasingly co-opted by the village community. The crucial issue was the transformation of religious controls into secularized, community-based norms—not village mores founded on Church law but, rather, Church law whose enforcement depended on village norms. This is more than just a semantic transformation: what it meant was that peasants could utilize the power of the Church to root out "deviants" of their own. As we shall see, this gave villagers a powerful weapon in the effort to regulate the behavior of *otkhodniki*.

---

[32] See the Kolomna District Police report on Martynov's activities, TsGIAgM, f. 203, op. 393, d. 8, ll. 1, 3, 5. In defense of his own failure to report Martynov's conversion, his parish priest argued that Martynov had deviated to the *raskol* only at age fifty and now refused to return to the Church out of "stubbornness" (l. 7). For a similar case, see TsGIAgM, f. 203, op. 366, g. 1885, d. 76.

[33] Freeze, p. 461.

The Culture of Denunciation: The Community's Role in Rooting Out Deviants

Rites of denunciation, like all culturally embedded codes, follow distinct procedures and patterns.[34] Historical research in the West has repeatedly demonstrated that heretics themselves—the victims of denunciations—were rarely guilty of heresy; or, at the very least, it was not usually for heretical acts alone that they were singled out for anathematization by members of their own communities. A corollary of this notion is that even when heretics were heretical, special local conditions beyond the act of heresy alone accounted for the singling out of some, while other "heretics" often were not only tolerated but even allowed to flourish. Numerous studies in Western Europe have emphasized "the crucial role of the village community in regulating the identification and persecution of . . . deviants."[35]

A spoken denunciation, delivered in secret to the parish priest, was usually the trigger for proceedings against deviants. Family members, concerned neighbors, or even the police would inform a parish priest, who would proceed according to the law. The seriousness with which family members perceived a turning away from Orthodoxy was revealed in the high frequency of denunciations of recusants by members of their own families—representing nearly 60 percent of the three hundred cases studied. An example will illustrate the usual pattern. Grigorii Fedorov's adolescent son Iakov left his father's farm in Podol'sk District to work in Moscow during the first half of the 1860s. Raised in Orthodoxy, he upheld his faith during his first years in the city. However, not long after he began to work for an Old Believer merchant named Karasev in 1866, Iakov threw aside both Orthodoxy and his family. Without notifying his parents he married Karasev's niece Arafima Rylova, in July 1869, "and through her help became completely lost in the delusion of the Old Belief."[36] Having exhausted himself in various schemes to reclaim his son, the elder Fedorov petitioned the Moscow Metropolitan for help in 1873, in the process denouncing both his son and the evil-doers who had led him astray:

My son Iakov . . . already for seven years has not partaken of the Blessed Sacraments. He has, moreover, married a girl of the priestless sect, which has still more deeply

---

[34] For a survey of relevant literature, see Suzanne Desan, "Crowds, Community and Ritual in the Work of E. P. Thompson and Natalie Davis," in *The New Cultural History,* ed. Lynn Hunt (Berkeley and Los Angeles, 1989), pp. 47–71. More recently, see Pierre Bourdieu, "Rites as Acts of Institution," in *Honor and Grace in Anthropology,* ed. J. G. Perestiany and Julian Pitt-Rivers (Cambridge, 1992), pp. 79–90.

[35] Robin Briggs, *Communities of Belief: Cultural and Social Tension in Early Modern France* (Oxford, 1989), p. 3.

[36] From the report of the local Ecclesiastical Superintendent, TsGIAgM (n. 1 above), f. 203, op. 342, d. 106, ll. 1 ob., 9.

rooted [him in the *raskol*]. [Unable to break] my son of his fanatical conviction, I turn to Your Excellency as to the Father and Head of the Church to heed me, an aged and old man, [and to] return him to the Christian Faith. I hope that as an adherent and Head of the Church You will direct Your Gracious attention to a 67-year-old man for whom it is painful to see his own son living in such delusions.[37]

The degree of the breakdown in relations between Iakov and his family was soberly evaluated by the superintendent's report: "Contrary to the will of his parents, [the younger] Grigor'ev took his share from his parents' home in the village and settled in Moscow, probably depending on the help of a rich relative of his boss, the merchant Karasev. He does not conceal his enmity toward his father and brothers."[38]

Following a police investigation, and on the basis of his father's grief-stricken petition, Iakov Grigor'ev was subjected to a forced separation (*razluchenie*) from his "illegal wife" Arafima: Iakov and his wife were bound by their signatures on a written oath to separate, with compulsory relocation to different residences. Arafima Rylova was issued a separate passport by the Moscow authorities and moved in with her mother. Iakov remained in their former home. Their infant son Mikhail was transferred to Fedorov's passport alone and was registered in his native village in Podol'sk District, where he was raised by members of Fedorov's extended family.[39] In addition to forced separation, the recalcitrant Iakov was charged in his *volost* court with "marrying without the consent of his father."[40]

Heads of households often used denunciations to Church or secular authorities as a means of exercising control over subordinate household members. Wives often employed the same method to free themselves from the repressed and often arbitrary atmosphere of the peasant patriarchal household, denouncing the immoral characters of their spouses in petitions for annulment or for separate passports, which were typically dictated for a fee to scribes who specialized in this service at village markets and annual fairs. As the peasant woman Marfa Iartseva from Volokolamsk District, Moscow complained in 1905: "From the day of our wedding, my husband drank and lived a depraved way of life. Having endured for three years all possible torments and suffering, I am not strong enough to live with him any longer."[41] Likewise, from Ekaterina Sablina, a peasant woman from Bronnitsy District living in dire poverty

---

[37] See the grieving letters of fathers of recusants in TsGIAgM, f. 203, op. 342, d. 106, ll. 3–3 ob., and f. 203, op. 347, d. 21, ll. 1–2.

[38] TsGIAgM, f. 203, op. 342, d. 106, l. 2.

[39] TsGIAgM, f. 203, op. 342, d. 106, l. 24 (police report from December 20, 1873).

[40] TsGIAgM, f. 203, op. 342, d. 106, l. 25 ob.

[41] Petition for annulment on the grounds of her husband's adultery, dated April 28, 1905 (TsGIAgM, f. 203, op. 412, d. 16, ll. 1–1 ob.). Literally thousands of such cases appear in the secret section of each provincial governor's collection. See, e.g., the four hundred cases uncovered by me in TsGIAgM, f. 17, "Kantseliariia Moskovskogo Gu-

on the streets of Moscow in 1896: "My husband, Stepan Andreev Sablin, for several years now has led an impossibly drunken life, and for the past five years he has completely abandoned me with three young children. He shows up only to beat me, and then takes away any valuables I have, only to drink them away in the nearest saloon. . . . A week ago he made off with my last pair of shoes. . . . In the recent past, the children and I have frequently been left hungry, and now he has driven us from our apartment."[42]

Similarly, Luker'ia Guseva, a peasant woman from Riazan Province, was forced to live and work on her own in Moscow because of her husband's abandonment. Despite her anguish, Guseva waited almost eleven years before she filed for an annulment on the grounds of her husband's adulterous behavior. Adultery seemed the least of her worries. "My husband Aleksei Gusev showed no concern for me from the first day of our marriage. He abandoned me to the whim of fate. I have been deprived of my last piece of bread since he has no base in the village [*net krest'ianskoi osedlosti*] and he takes away from me side earnings with which I might support myself." Guseva was desperately afraid of being stalked by her husband and begged the Moscow Spiritual Consistory for an annulment.

My husband . . . leads an extremely debauched way of life. He wanders everywhere around Khitrovo market and does not have a constant place of residence. Nothing can be done to correct either his nasty behavior or his unruly character in general. For almost two years we have not lived together, since he lives only God knows where. I live here [in Moscow] and earn a piece of daily bread for myself with my own personal labor. If my husband finds out that I am living here, then he will come to this house and make all sorts of trouble: he will revile me with insulting words and deeds, and [he will] also make threats that if the owners keep me he will commit murder or write anonymous letters.

Such had already been the case more than once, when Guseva was forced to move by her husband's harassment and threats. Even though she filed for and won restraining orders from the police, and even though her husband had been condemned for his abusiveness by both the village assembly and the *volost* court, he refused to heed the orders and often had appeared at her residence, issuing every kind of threat and swearing he would kill her.[43]

---

bernatora," op. 66 [*tainyi otdel*]. The cases represent a vast, unexplored channel into the horrors of Russian domestic violence: each file includes a statement in the aggrieved wife's own words, followed up by police investigation and testimony of witnesses.

[42] TsGIAgM, f. 17, op. 66, d. 632, ll. 1–2 (woman's written denunciation, dated July 15, 1896, as dictated to a third person). Sablina's petition for a legal separation and separate passport from her husband was granted in September 1896.

[43] TsGIAgM, f. 203, op. 412, d. 36, ll. 1, 8–8 ob. (October–November 1905). Although she paid several rubles in fees and special stamps, Guseva's case was eventually

Morals charges were also an effective means by which husbands could regulate wives. A particularly detailed written denunciation was filed by the peasant worker Ivan Lavrov against his wife Evdokeia in the spring of 1905: "I accuse my wife," wrote the disaffected Lavrov to their parish priest, "of drunkenness and infidelity. . . . I . . . do not desire to live with [her] . . . in Christian wedlock, and want . . . a divorce."[44] Lavrov was a peasant worker from Pokrov District, Vladimir Province, who married a peasant girl from Dmitrov District, Moscow, whom he had met in factory work. The couple was married at the end of June 1898. The newlyweds then moved to a large industrial settlement in Bogorodsk District, east of Moscow, so that Lavrov could work at a local textile factory. But, as the unhappy husband reported, "I did not enjoy marital happiness for long. Shortly after our marriage, my wife said that she was not accustomed to such a monotonous life as they live [in the village], but that she loved 'society' and 'amusement.'" Only after the wedding did Lavrov learn that

before marrying me, she had lived four years in a Moscow brothel. You can be completely sure that after such a debauched and wild life . . . this [worker's] life for her really would be torture. There were many times when, after I left for work, my wife brought young men into my own apartment in my absence and remained alone with them until my return from work. And there were times that upon my return from work, I did not find her at home in the apartment. She appeared after such absences the next day, or the day after, always smelling of vodka. All my [attempts] to make her understand, all my exhortations, she stubbornly answered with silence, and at the present time she has renounced married life.

What made this case particularly striking were the identities of witnesses whom Lavrov named as persons able to verify his story: four of five of these witnesses were fellow peasant workers from his factory who had themselves had "adulterous relations" with his wife.[45]

---

rejected almost eight months later on technical grounds, since she was from a district outside of the jurisdiction of the Moscow Spiritual Consistory.

[44] TsGIAgM, f. 203, op. 412, d. 26, l. 1–1 ob., 16.

[45] Ibid. The sympathetic reader will be interested to learn that the couple eventually reunited. Following strict procedures, the Moscow Spiritual Consistory ordered that the unhappy pair live together for two months, at the end of which they still remained unreconciled. However, the priest handling the case pressed for reconciliation after he learned the following in a sworn statement from Evdokeia, given in Lavrov's presence: "I want to live in Christian wedlock with my husband Ivan Lavrov. I promise to reform my behavior—I will neither fornicate nor drink [vodka]. I first sinned with him, Ivan Lavrov, when I was 12 or 13 or 14 years old. In this way, I consider him the culprit for my degradation, and he knows this. (Evdokeia said this in the presence of Ivan.) Later when he was married to his first wife he also sinned with me" (l. 17). Despite repeated written appeals for over a year by the angry Lavrov, the Spiritual Consistory dragged out the case. Just when an annulment was about to be granted, Lavrov informed the

Beyond the family circle, fellow villagers also exerted considerable influence on the social behavior of their neighbors. In comparative studies of village life, historians have consistently noted "the tyranny of local opinion and the lack of tolerance displayed towards nonconformity and social deviation," the "high value set on social conformity by this tightly-knit, intolerant world."[46] In this, Russia was no exception. The noted historian of the Russian peasantry Boris Mironov has described how the peasant commune exercised "the strictest social control" over the behavior of locals, "a censorship of morals, from which in practice it was impossible to escape."[47] "Attendance at church and appropriate performance of all religious prescriptions played a major role in the formation of individual reputations," the Russian historical ethnographer M. M. Gromyko has observed. "Not only the elders in a family but the entire community would watch to see that youngsters did not miss especially important church services. The neighbors would tell a mother if her son was 'lazy' in going to mass."[48]

Usually such information was passed on informally, anonymously, or as hearsay. Such oblique denunciations were part of the rich oral tradition of the Russian village, where "reputation [among Russian peasants] was attributed to families and could be passed on from generation to generation."[49] The village's "little community" had numerous ways of censuring the behavior of nonconformist fellow villagers: "Slander, character assassination, gossip, rumor, public gestures of contempt, shunning, cursing, backbiting, outcasting" were all sanctions that could be wielded effectively.[50] Almost a third of the cases of deviancy reviewed from the records of the Moscow Spiritual Consistory became known to parish priests through rumors: essentially, angry fellow villag-

---

authorities that he and Evdokeia had been reconciled and withdrew the petition for annulment.

[46] Keith Thomas, *Religion and the Decline of Magic* (New York, 1971), pp. 527, 530.

[47] Boris N. Mironov, "Traditsionnoe demograficheskoe povedenie krest'ian v XIX—nachale XX v.," in *Brachnost', rozhdaemost', smertnost' v Rossii i v SSSR. (Sbornik statei),* ed. A. G. Vishnevskii (Moscow, 1977), p. 84. For a similar notion, see A. F. Kistiakovskii, "K voprosu o tsenzure nravov u naroda," *Zapiski Imperatorskogo Russkogo Geograficheskogo Obshchestva po otdeleniiu etnografii,* vol. 8 (St. Petersburg, 1878).

[48] M. M. Gromyko, "Traditional Norms of Behavior and Forms of Interaction of Nineteenth-Century Russian Peasants," *Soviet Anthropology and Archeology* 30, no. 1 (Summer 1991): 76.

[49] Corinne Gaudin, "Governing the Village: Peasant Culture and the Problem of Social Transformation in Russia, 1906–1914" (Ph.D. diss., University of Michigan, 1993), p. 162. Compare the discussion of the social role of peasant reputations in F. G. Bailey, "Gifts and Poison," in *Gifts and Poison: The Politics of Reputation,* ed. F. G. Bailey (Oxford, 1971), p. 4.

[50] James C. Scott, *Domination and the Arts of Resistance: Hidden Transcripts* (New Haven, Conn., 1990), p. 131.

ers "let it be known" that a certain peasant was living improperly.[51] This allowed the villagers to censure the behavior of their neighbors without actually taking it upon themselves to effect a breach—for to begin a feud within one's commune was to invite disaster.[52] As the parish priest Father Mikhail Sokolov observed in village Petrovka, Vladimir Province, in 1899, "Peasants in general are people who are very self-respecting and proud. Endeavor to offend a peasant . . . with a word [expressing] some unflattering opinion about him—and he will remember it until he is presented with the chance to avenge [the offense]."[53] Open denunciations by a lone fellow villager against a neighbor were extremely rare: covert, behind-the-back attacks were far safer than open breaches.

Nevertheless, open condemnation of behavior that violated general norms was tolerated when backed up by support from other community members. Community opinion often acted as a force unto itself, restraining and—to a certain degree—directing the initiative of village priests. A powerful illustration of a community-based denunciation is the case of the literate thirty-four-year-old peasant tradesman Vasilii Skvortsov, who had converted to a priestless sect of the Old Belief some ten years before his confrontation with his community. Although Skvortsov refused to reveal the agent of his conversion, "it was rumored that he had been seduced" by the ex-*volost* clerk, who had been removed from his official position for his nonconformist religious beliefs. As the local superintendent reported, Skvortsov had been subjected frequently to concerted entreaties by his parish priest, several fellow villagers, and even some monks who were brought in from a nearby monastery. Despite their imprecations, Skvortsov remained stubborn in his faith, declaring before witnesses to the parish priest, "I do not want to speak with you, nor hear your words and attempts to persuade me. I do not wish to be a follower of your faith, [since] I recognize it to be unjust. Think what you want of me, and report me to your authorities [if you must]."[54]

Throughout the discussions and meetings that followed—"educational discussions" that civil and religious authorities forced Skvortsov to attend—Skvortsov met with the parish priest Mikhail Parusnikov as members of his family and community looked on. The community was duly mesmerized and scandalized as Skvortsov laid before them in intricate detail the content of his

---

[51] On rumors, see examples in TsGIAgM (n. 1 above), f. 203, op. 347, g. 1875, d. 20, l. 1, and f. 203, op. 349, g. 1877, d. 53, l. 1–1 ob. The priest would investigate and then file a formal complaint to the appropriate authorities.

[52] For an invaluable perspective on oblique forms of denunciation in village life, see Max Gluckman, "Gossip and Scandal," *Current Anthropology* 4, no. 3 (June 1963): 308, 312.

[53] GME (n. 3 above), f. 7, op. 1, d. 11, ll. 5 ob–6 ob.

[54] TsGIAgM, f. 203, op. 349, g. 1877, d. 53, l. 1 (Serpukhov).

beliefs: his admission that he had in fact for some time "stood aloof from the Orthodox Church and [now] belonged to another community [*obshchina*]"; his Sunday services without priests, instead run by so-called Elders or spiritual advisers (*Startsy*); his two-fingered sign of the cross (versus the post-Nikonian Orthodox three-fingered sign). After the first few meetings, where Skvortsov's family sat silently and listened, they stopped coming altogether. On the evening of June 14, 1877, Skvortsov's wife was notably absent. The next day, "despite his promise" to the parish priest, Skvortsov himself failed to show up for the meeting, leaving word simply that he had gone to Moscow. Outraged, the parish priest summoned Skvortsov officially through the *volost* administration, "in order to advise him again to return to Orthodoxy." On June 18, 1877, three days after Skvortsov stopped showing up for religious education, his commune passed a condemning resolution, which anathematized him for his defiance of local norms:

We . . . the peasants of Serpukhov District, . . . Belopesotskii settlement . . . respectfully submit: Our neighbor the peasant Vasilii Filipov Skvortsov really did convert from Orthodoxy to the *raskol* some ten years ago. We have confirmed this directly. It is demonstrated by the fact that all this time Skvortsov has neither confessed nor taken part [in the spiritual life of the community]. . . . The wife of Vasilii Skvortsov . . . has also converted to the *raskol*. This is demonstrated by the fact that she too began to go to Church rarely. Their children, as a result, will undoubtedly convert to the *raskol*. There have never been *raskol'niki* in our village, and if [Skvortsov] does not return to Orthodoxy, then we with all the peasants will try to throw him out of the commune. We will not tolerate the *raskol*.[55]

Against his will, Skvortsov was returned to his village on July 5, when he had another long exchange with Father Parusnikov.[56] At this time, Parusnikov demanded a written and signed account of Skvortsov's beliefs, and Skvortsov put him off by saying that "perhaps I will again start going to Church." From that time on, Skvortsov refused to meet with any priests, and he continued to defy the community's attempts to force him to desist. Eventually, his fellow villagers were true to their promise: Skvortsov was expelled from the commune altogether.

Such sober, openly defiant confrontations, though common, occurred far less frequently than the insidious, everyday forms of antagonism between Or-

---

[55] TsGIAgM, f. 203, op. 349, g. 1877, d. 53, l. 8. In a resolution of March 12, 1877, the commune confirmed the basic facts of the case: that Skvortsov and his family had been born and raised in Orthodoxy and that Skvortsov had left the faith (l. 4). The preceding discussion was drawn from the description in the local superintendent's report (ll. 6–7).

[56] Until the end of the Old Regime, village communes retained the right to order the forced return of villagers. See the discussion in Burds (n. 2 above), pp. 79–80.

thodox and Old Believer peasants. Such confrontations, denunciations, and counterdenunciations often led to violent skirmishes during the holiday season, when peasant labor migrants were home for winter holidays and when alcohol exacerbated the tensions and led to eruptions above the surface of official calm and toleration.[57]

Inevitably, the interests of priests and parishioners did not always coincide in the social regulation of morals. Sometimes, frustrated or disappointed with the inactivity of overburdened or negligent priests, communities would take matters into their own hands. This was especially facilitated by the fact that the Church hierarchy, always driven by the imperative of keeping its priests in line, readily took heed of the opinions of parishioners communicated outside official channels. In 1871, for instance, the peasant Nikofor Matveev—parish elder of the Church of Our Savior in the village of Arkhangel, Vereia District, Moscow Province—sent a petition of concern to the Moscow Spiritual Consistory on behalf of his fellow parishioners. The gist of Matveev's complaint was the alarming incidence of religious nonparticipation in his parish, where, owing to high rates of out-migration for side earnings, "up to 400 persons have not attended confession in the past year." Matveev charged that the negligence of the parish priest, Matvei Vinogradov, had allowed more than half the parish to fall away from Orthodoxy. Upon investigation, the negligent priest was removed from his post.[58]

Numerous sources indicate that vigilante justice was often applied in cases where the parish priest either neglected or refused to heed denunciations. One particularly vivid case powerfully illustrates the role of *samosud*—peasant self-justice—in community control over peasant workers who blatantly violated community norms.[59] In the village of Gridkina—a few kilometers from Shuiia—in 1897, a young female peasant factory worker named Elena had begun to flout community norms: at the age of sixteen, she began to take lovers openly. As the recusant's parish priest reported: "Working at the factory, living on her own without any sort of family supervision, this girl began 'to roam about' [*shatat'sia*]—that is, to have lovers, of which she had several." Frus-

---

[57] TsGIAgM, f. 142, "Moskovskii okruzhnyi sud," g. 1890, op. 1, d. 162, ll. 2–2 ob., 28, 42–43, 47–49. See also the examples in *Stanovlenie revoliutsionnykh traditsii piterskogo proletariata: Poreformennyi period, 1861–1883 gg.* (Leningrad, 1987). For other examples, see TsGIAgM, f. 203, op. 368, g. 1886, d. 6, ll. 1–1 ob., 3–6, f. 203, op. 364, g. 1884, d. 80; and f. 203, op. 352, g. 1878, d. 11, l. 1. On communal banishment in rural Russia, see the pathbreaking work by Gaudin (n. 49 above), pp. 150–83.

[58] TsGIAgM, f. 203, op. 341, d. 25, l. 1.

[59] *Samosud* as a weapon to impose community control over peasants is discussed in Stephen P. Frank, "Popular Justice, Community and Culture among the Russian Peasantry, 1870–1900," *Russian Review* 46, no. 3 (July 1987): 239–65; and Cathy Frierson, "Crime and Criminality in the Russian Village: Rural Concepts of Criminality at the End of the Nineteenth Century," *Slavic Review* 46, no. 1 (Spring 1987): 55–69.

trated at the failure of the local priest to take the decadent woman in hand despite numerous denunciations of her immoral behavior, fellow workers gossiped bitterly. Eventually, some lads from her village instigated a plot to humiliate the recusant for her misdeeds. "They lay in waiting for Elena . . . while she walked from her factory in the town to her home in the village. As soon as she came alongside a cemetery along her route, the plotters seized her, raised her dress [above her waist], and tied the ends over her head with a noose and secured her in this way to one of the crosses [in the cemetery]. Here she hung until she was seen by others coming from the factory, who freed her from the ignominy" of her position.[60]

POLICE AND PEOPLE

As skyrocketing rates of peasant labor migration seriously challenged the skills of even vigilant parish priests, disgruntled peasant workers and fellow villagers increasingly turned to state agents outside the village as channels for denunciations. Urban police archives are filled with written denunciations (usually anonymous) of fellow workers accused of religious profligacy or of interfering in the religious life of the other workers.[61] For instance, a peasant worker from Vladimir District, Grigorii Tarasov, had come to Moscow in 1867, when he was twenty-seven. He lived and worked in Moscow for almost six years. For the entire period he had identified himself as Orthodox on his passport. On his return from a two-month visit to his native village in August 1873, Tarasov presented a one-year passport in which he and his wife and young daughter were all listed as Old Believers of the Rogozhskii sect. A suspicious Moscow policeman—apparently tipped off by a denunciation from an unidentified source—noted the discrepancy and filed a secret report, which eventually made its way through the office of the chief of police to the Moscow Spiritual Consistory. The chief of police sent an inquiry to the Vladimir District police chief, asking whether Tarasov had in fact thrown aside Orthodoxy. The answer was as expected: "Having lived without interruption for 7 or 8 years in Moscow, where he married, [his] creed was Orthodoxy." His family, consist-

[60] The report comes from Ioakimanskaia *volost,* Shuia District, Vladimir (GME, f. 7, op. 1, d. 58, l. 11). The source of the account, the shamed woman's parish priest (Father Kazanskii), added: "Only such girls who are not at all afraid of people's gibes and condemnation, and who freely 'carouse' [*guliat'*] with several 'playmates' [*igral'-shchiki*] at the same time undergo public condemnation or punishment from the boys." Elena later married, but even then continued to "lead her former life, in spite of the frequent beatings [she suffered] from her husband."

[61] See the sample of an anonymous denunciation written in pencil on a torn piece of paper of a fellow worker and Old Believer denounced for interfering in the religious life of other workers at RGIA (n. 3 above), f. 1284, op. 208, g. 1853, d. 465. Also, TsGIAgM (n. 1 above), f. 203, op. 368, g. 1886, d. 6, ll. 1–1 ob., 3–6, and f. 203, op. 352, g. 1878, d. 11, l. 1.

ing of a father and four brothers, were likewise Orthodox. It was clear, therefore, that Tarasov's "seduction [*sovrashchenie*] to the *raskol* had occurred in
Moscow."[62]

The Moscow police moved quickly on the case, working jointly with the
Moscow Consistory, which reconstructed Tarasov's life before and after his
apostasy. They painted the following scenario: "Seventeen years from birth,
arriving in Moscow, [Tarasov] started working for a schismatic, a furniture
dealer, the Moscow petty merchant Aleksei Akimov (now deceased). After six
years of living in the home of the schismatic Akimov, persuaded by his boss
and with the blessing of his parents, who were themselves not steadfast Orthodox [believers, but were] inclined toward the *raskol,* he turned aside to
the *raskol*."[63] In 1862, the twenty-three-year-old Tarasov married Praskov'ia
Fedorova, a girl from a priestly sect.

Following the decree of the Holy Synod of August 14, 1808, regarding marriages of persons who had deviated to the *raskol,* the Consistory ruled the
marriage invalid and the couple's state "adulterous." The husband and wife
were forced to separate after almost twelve years together; this ruling was carried out on December 24, 1874, almost sixteen months from the time Tarasov's
profligacy was first discovered. Tarasov remained in his Moscow apartment,
while his wife Praskov'ia was forced to relocate to her former residence. Local
officials were instructed to be vigilant and were made to sign oaths in which
they swore to observe the couple's activities and to prevent a renewal of adulterous relations.[64]

It was standard operating procedure in city police stations to investigate
cases of religious deviation and to report the results to Church officials.[65] The
sheer effort expended in this and other cases illustrates the degree to which
recusants and *uklonenie* were taken seriously. The documents reflect a close,
friendly relationship between priests and police—although they were not as
close as generations of Soviet historians have suggested by treating clerics and
police as a reactionary monolith. Nonetheless, the style and language of police
denunciations make it clear that priests often wielded considerable authority.
It is as if the policemen, by upholding Orthodoxy, were paving their own paths
to salvation.[66]

---

[62] TsGIAgM, f. 203, op. 346, d. 11, ll. 1–1 ob. (1873).

[63] TsGIAgM, f. 203, op. 346, d. 11, l. 10.

[64] See the police report to the local superintendent on January 9, 1875 (TsGIAgM,
f. 203, op. 346, d. 11, l. 19).

[65] The text of the tsarist gendarme's oath explicitly required Russian policemen to
track religious dissidents. See the sample on permanent display in the Muzei Ministerstva Vnutrennykh Del (Moscow).

[66] Typical were these reminiscences written by Ivan Golyshev, a peasant lithographer
from Vladimir Province: his father, a *volost* elder, was "a zealous upholder of Orthodoxy, persecutor of the *raskol,* who lived in great numbers in [our village]. He at every

When policemen took the initiative as brutal saviors of souls, however, this did not always meet with the approval of local priests. A prime illustration was a denunciation filed by the parish priest Mikhail Sareevskii against the local constable Kamenskii in the industrial village Ivanovskoe, in the Church of Predtechevskaia in early December 1886.

On the 26th of November, on the feast day of the Great Martyr Saint George in our Predtechevskaia Church, at the time of the Sacred Liturgy, the following event took place: the cossack's wife, Evdokia Pestova, who lives at the factory of the Reutovskaia Manufacturing Company, attended mass together with her friend, a peasant woman from Tver Province, Staritsa District, Blaginna village, Evdokeia Semenova, who also lives there [at the factory]. During the submersion of the Cross in holy water, before the Liturgy, Pestova suffered a fit: she cried out and fell lifelessly to the ground. In that condition she lay for some time, cared for by her friend throughout the service, at the end of which the local constable Kamenskii entered the Church. He stood near the prostrate Pestova and as soon as he saw her . . . lying there, he took her for a drunk and began to shake her, during which he uttered indecent and insulting words, summoned the deputy . . . , threatened to send her to the *Iusupov dom* [a mental hospital], pounded her about the head and face and kicked her in the side; but Pestova still lay there without moving, lifeless.

Pestova's friend Semenova and others standing near the woman pleaded with Kamenskii not to disturb her, since they knew that she was a woman subject to seizures. But Kamenskii, cursing Pestova with words like "you pig" and other more indecent and insulting expressions, said that she was only pretending to be ill and that he would cure her.

All this Kamenskii said so loudly that it could be heard not only in the refectory but even at the altar, so that Kamenskii "with his conduct drew glances and the attention of everyone in the Church." Hearing the noise, Father Sareevskii had to send two ushers, one after another—the unfortunate Piatnit-skii and Zaitsev—in order to get the constable to stop interrupting the service. But Kamenskii only answered that he knew well enough what to do without their advice, and continued with his disturbance, and with renewed vigor took violent reprisals on the poor woman's lifeless body.

The priest, only halfway through the reading of the prayer for the tsar, had to stop and wait until the noise in the church subsided in order to proceed. Not wishing to interrupt the mass, Father Sareevskii again set about reading the prayer. Beside himself with rage, Kamenskii made another peasant, a certain Kolobov, aided by the hapless usher Zaitsev, carry the still-unconscious Pestova outside of the church. Kamenskii accompanied the pair, pushing Pestova all the way to the church porch.

moment of his official service was concerned about the defense of Orthodoxy, and about the persecution of the *raskol*" (I. A. Golyshev, "Vospominaniia Ivana Aleksandrovicha Golysheva [1838–1878]," *Russkaia starina*, no. 24 [1879], p. 755).

And when they had brought her to the jail and laid her down there, Kamenskii again began to stomp on the unconscious woman with his feet, screaming all the while in a rage expressions like: "You drunken bitch!" [*pianuiu stervoiu*]. Later, when Pestova had come to, Kamenskii ordered her to go home and refused to admit her into the Church, even when she fell before him on her knees and begged forgiveness, [asking] for his permission to reenter the Church in order to pray. The usher Zaitsev, returning from the jail to the Church, grew afraid that Kamenskii might do something horrible to the poor woman, so he soon started back to the jail. Along the way, he met with Kamenskii, who told him: "I healed her and took her home." Having taken her home, Kamenskii again appeared in Church after the cherubic song.

Turning to the Church elder, Kamenskii was quoted as saying: "I have the power to heal and to resurrect the dead" but was restrained from further conversation during the mass by the ever more vigilant Zaitsev. Father Sareevskii concluded his denunciation with a strong indictment: "I consider this transgression of the constable Kamenskii to have been an offense against the spiritual atmosphere and an insult to the moral sensibility of everyone present in the Church."[67]

CONCLUSION

In this study, I have surveyed religious denunciations in the Russian countryside in the Moscow region during the last half of the nineteenth century. But it is quite clear that many of these denunciations were not motivated by religious issues alone: the language of the confrontations suggests that the denunciations were often a kind of popular theater that overlay tensions that were far more profound. For example, in one dispute a peasant migrant husband denounced his estranged wife in the terms of religious anathematization. But he also mentioned a host of other factors: "I am suffering enormous deprivation from my

[67] Events reconstructed from the denunciation, investigation, and testimony in TsGIAgM, f. 203, op. 371, g. 1886–87, d. 8, ll. 1–2, 5. The complaint was signed by Father Mikhail Sareevskii, Ivanovskoe village, in the Church of Predtechevskaia. The lesson of this case is also telling. Soon after a formal investigation began, it became clear that Kamenskii managed to intimidate the key witnesses, who, apparently out of fear, refused to verify the testimony they had initially given. The chain of events was, of course, completely different from Kamenskii's point of view: Kamenskii argued that before acting he had consulted yet another peasant woman known to him, a certain Evdokeia Kuzvlina, who worked at the nearby Mazurin factory. Allegedly, Kuzvlina told Kamenskii that Pestova was drunk. In May 1887, the prosecutor in Moscow Circuit Court dismissed the case, which by this time relied only on hearsay evidence (since none of the principal witnesses would support Father Sareevskii's charges). Even Pestova testified that she had heard nothing about having been beaten that day while she lay unconscious and implied that this had been Father Sareevskii's idea a few days later. The nervous friend Semenova was even more forthright: she absolutely refused to testify that constable Kamenskii had been excessive in any way. Several witnesses, even the church guard Zaitsev, likewise retracted their initial testimony in the court.

schismatic wife Matrena Nikolaeva, who with the help of her brothers—[also] schismatics—are taking all of my property away from me. [She] says that it is all hers and not mine. I have turned to the police with a petition, but received no help."[68] For this peasant, religious denunciation against his wife and her family was a last desperate attempt to block his own economic marginalization. He was like a drowning man clutching at a straw, using a religious denunciation only when other more direct tactics had failed.

Similarly, when Orthodox parishioners in the village of Ignatovo, Bogorodsk District, collectively signed a resolution denouncing their village elder in July 1884, they did so using the language of religious anathematization to argue for a resolution in their favor of a dispute about economic exploitation.

The elder—the schismatic Ivan Arkhipov—is himself also a long-standing malevolent enemy of the Church. In order to get revenge on us . . . , he tries to hurt us in every possible way. He, both as a rich man and as a factory owner who has on his side many schismatic accomplices among his fellow villagers, makes things up and accuses us of crimes we never committed. Some of us he drags into court. Others—using his wealth—he puts under arrest. Still others he threatens with alienation from the commune and exile to some distant province. Others he threatens with the most horrible misfortunes. And others he entices with money—so that from our elder there is neither a life nor a livelihood for us Orthodox peasants of Ignatovo village.[69]

The villagers in this case appealed for the "heretic" elder's removal on the basis of a law of March 9, 1839, which prohibited election of non-Orthodox officials in areas where a large number of Orthodox Christians resided.[70] This tactic could sometimes be relied upon to upset the normal order of communal self-management through appeal to an outside agency that could settle local feuds and vendettas in favor of the weaker party. In short, where direct challenges failed, religious anathematization could often be relied upon to confuse issues and possibly tilt ongoing disputes toward a more favorable resolution.[71]

[68] TsGIAgM, f. 203, op. 347, d. 21, l. 22 (May 1876).

[69] TsGIAgM, f. 203, op. 364, g. 1884, d. 80, ll. 1–2 (July 1884). The letter was signed by twenty-one male adults, who represented twelve clans in the village. Almost half the "signatories" were illiterate, so that signatures were placed by others next to each illiterate petitioner's mark ("X").

[70] As the text of the petition reveals, the law had been successfully applied at other times in the history of this mixed Orthodox and Old Believer village (TsGIAgM, f. 203, op. 364, g. 1884, d. 80, ll. 1–2). In a similar case in 1874, a village elder of the Old Belief was removed from his position after a formerly Orthodox peasant failed to baptize his newborn son and refused to return to Orthodoxy or even to sign an affidavit in which he recognized the blasphemous act. See TsGIAgM, f. 203, op. 346, d. 29, ll. 14–15, 18 ob. (1874).

[71] There is an enormous and fascinating comparative literature on religious denunciations as a means by which to gain the upper hand in nonreligious conflicts. Carol F.

The anthropologist Basil Sanson identified such accusations as a tactical strategy, a means of modifying the relationship between the perpetrator and his denouncer. Religious denunciations often served as a convenient method to degrade the status of the accused, to profoundly alter the nature of social relationships in the village, to radically invert village hierarchies.[72] Understood in this way, denunciations were assuredly an integral part of the mechanisms of rural power and control, where kinship and religious factors were equally if not more important than economic and social stratification. In everyday village life, it was not structural forces such as wealth, class, and power that determined status but, rather, popular conceptions of reputation and popular, locally grounded definitions of morality. In village society, an individual's "good name" was his "most vital social possession," yet—paradoxically—also his most vulnerable one, since a good name was not held but conferred by other members of the community.[73]

As we have seen, a peasant's reputation in village society had consequences beyond the religious sphere. As James Scott has argued, "Reputation in any small, closely knit community has very practical consequences. A peasant household held in contempt by their fellow villagers will find it impossible to exchange harvest labor, to borrow a draft animal, to raise a small loan, to marry their children off, to prevent petty thefts of their grain or livestock, or even to bury their dead with any dignity."[74] In Russia, as elsewhere, to flout community norms was to risk not just one's reputation but also, inevitably, one's livelihood. Conversely, to impugn a peasant's reputation was to challenge directly his or her ability to make ends meet, for the social milieu of the Russian peasantry before the Revolution was indeed "a context fraught with need, and a disproportionate reliance on patronage and personal contacts, or *znakomstvo*, to survive from one season to the next."[75] In the universe of the Russian peasant, reputation and opportunity were inextricably fused.

Denunciation as an act of impugning reputations was not exclusively the

---

Karlsen has demonstrated that the women who were most vulnerable to anathematization for witchcraft in colonial New England were "those women [who] were aberrations in a society with an inheritance system designed to keep property in the hands of men" (*The Devil in the Shape of a Woman: Witchcraft in Colonial New England* [New York, 1987], p. 101).

[72] Basil Sanson, "When Witches Are Not Named," in *The Allocation of Responsibility,* ed. Max Gluckman (Manchester, 1972), pp. 193–226.

[73] Peter J. Wilson, "Filcher of Good Names: An Enquiry into Anthropology and Gossip," *Man* 9 (1974): 93–102, quote on 100. Also, see Bailey (n. 49 above); and Thomas (n. 46 above), pp. 526–34.

[74] Scott (n. 50 above), p. 131.

[75] Burds (n. 2 above), p. 99. See also N. A. Minenko, "The Living Past: Daily Life and Holidays of the Siberian Village in the Eighteenth and First Half of the Nineteenth Centuries," *Soviet Anthropology and Archeology* 30, no. 1 (Summer 1991): 6–71.

weapon of peasants against fellow peasants. Other social groups also seized on reputation as a means of social control. It is common, for instance, to find reports that village officials had willfully and arbitrarily (*proizvol'no*) abused their authority by compromising the reputation of a successful local: insiders who threatened local hierarchies by their very success (measured by the attention they received from outsiders) were denounced as politically and morally suspect. As a peasant lithographer in Vladimir Province, Ivan Golyshev, recalled with indignation, the *volost* courts often ordered "punish[ment] with lashes, in order to completely discredit and besmirch a person."[76] Local village officials had their own ways of dealing with upstarts: they were secretly denounced; they were harassed, jailed, even whipped; they were sent off for military service. Here too, acts of denunciation or repression were not ends in themselves but, rather, became part of the paper trail that followed (and haunted) "political unreliables" in the tsarist system.[77]

Employers also tried to impugn the moral character of peasant workers in order to subordinate them and to isolate troublemakers. In 1888, to take just one of myriad examples, Vladimir N. Suvirov, a merchant of the first guild and owner of a cloth factory in Moscow District, withheld wages that were due a peasant worker, Osipov, because Osipov had left for field work prior to the end of his contracted period (September 1, 1888). Osipov filed a countercomplaint against his employer with the local police in an attempt to recover the unpaid wages. Eventually, both Osipov and his wife (who worked together at the factory for a mere 18 rubles per month) were deprived of passports and exiled to their village because Osipov posed "a most evil [*durnoi*] example . . . for the rest of those working at the factory." The "nefarious influence" was their "willful disrespect" (*svoevolnoe bezobrazie*) and, alleged Suvirov (probably slanderously), Osipov's drunken behavior.[78]

In the three hundred cases of denunciation reviewed here, I have found that the overwhelming majority of village "heretics"—by my reckoning nearly 90 percent of those whose occupations were recorded—were peasant workers who migrated for earnings outside the village. Why did peasant workers con-

[76] Golyshev (n. 66 above), p. 354, with cases following.

[77] In Russian provincial police files, there is always a special secret section containing investigations regarding "political reliability" of locals, usually peasants. For examples, see TsGIAgM (n. 1 above), f. 479, "Dmitrovskoe uezdnoe politseiskoe upravlenie," op. 3, g. 1886, d. 28, "Predpisaniia Moskovskogo gubernatora o sbore svedenii o nravstvennykh kachestvakh, ob obraze zhizni i politicheskoi blagodezhnosti otdel'nykh lits" (Instructions of the Moscow governor regarding the collection of information about the moral qualities, about the way of life and political reliability of individuals).

[78] TsGIAgM, f. 17, op. 66, d. 12, ll. 11 ob.–12 (October 14, 1888). The real issue seems to have been the poor living conditions for workers and Suvirov's failure to fulfill explicit promises made to Osipov and his family.

stitute the vast majority of persons denounced on religious and moral grounds? Ultimately, the answer lies in the popular culture of denunciation: the peasants' use of religious denunciations to settle personal scores. Local squabbles between feuding clans were fought within peasant "little communities" by drawing on the language and rhetoric of the official struggle against religious sectarianism that the Russian Orthodox Church had waged since the mid-seventeenth century. Essentially, rival local forces used the language of religious anathematization as a means to isolate, undermine, or destroy opponents. To adapt a phrase from Evans-Pritchard's work on witchcraft, it is in the idiom of religious denunciations that Russian peasants expressed moral rules that lay mostly outside of criminal and civil law.[79]

The evidence from the Moscow Consistory supports the notion that the distinguishing characteristic of the overwhelming majority of "heretics" was their link to migration for side earnings. Village communities worked to protect themselves from the nefarious influence of nonconformity conveyed by the stories, habits, and style of peasants who had experienced life outside their villages. Even when peasant workers wandered far beyond the village boundaries they remained subject to village norms. A typical case was that of the fifty-five-year-old peasant worker Spiridonov, who was denounced as a heretic collectively by fellow villagers in a communal resolution addressed to the district chief of police.[80] The report of the police constable in Vereia made it very clear that Spiridonov's principal "moral" offense lay in his refusal to abide by his community's rules: "Spiridonov's family is not well provided for materially and has accumulated nearly 170 rubles in unpaid fiscal dues. Members of the family receive a means of subsistence from day work, but in view of the limited [availability of such work] they suffer extreme hardship. . . . Spiridonov, as his fellow villagers explained, roams [*skitaetsia*] in Moscow without any fixed occupation or residence. . . . No earnings are sent to his family. No one can say anything definite about Spiridonov's behavior and morals, since for quite some time he has not appeared for work and no one keeps up a correspondence with him."[81] In this case, the mere absence of reliable information regarding Spiridonov's behavior, combined with the relatively low standard of living of his dependents in the village, were sufficient grounds to excoriate him. Subsequently banished from his commune in 1895 "because he cannot be a wholesome member of the commune," Spiridonov learned the hard way the fruitlessness of flagrantly ignoring communal opinion: judged to be a "grave threat"

---

[79] E. E. Evans-Pritchard, *Witchcraft, Oracles and Magic among the Azande* (Oxford, 1937), p. 110.

[80] From the text of a review of the case in the Moscow circuit court (TsGIAgM, f. 17, op. 66, g. 1895, d. 617, l. 4).

[81] TsGIAgM, f. 17, op. 66, g. 1895, d. 617, ll. 3–4.

(*ves'ma vrednyi*) to his commune, he was prohibited from living or working in Moscow Province.[82]

None of this discussion is intended to deny, however, that those branded "heretics" may in fact have been nonconformists. Indeed, there is considerable evidence to support the argument that peasant labor migrants as a social group showed a higher propensity to rebel against village traditions and to challenge village norms. The real question here is why peasant labor migrants in particular were singled out for their heresy, even as others were not. We must recognize the fact that the declining insularity of communal life reflected in the staggering growth of peasant labor migration did pose a serious threat to traditional village hierarchies. A powerful illustration is the way in which peasant workers who had become "politically conscious" through contact with "reds" or labor organizers were anathematized as religious heretics. Fëdor Samoilov, who grew up to become a Bolshevik peasant worker from northeast Vladimir Province, described an event that took place following a major strike among textile workers in Ivanovo-Voznesensk in 1905:

In the beginning of September in my village, with which I then still had a connection, a characteristic event took place that vividly illustrated the attitude of the clergy of that time toward the strike and revolutionary movement. My father came to the town and, in an agitated manner, told my brother and me that our parish priest Dmitrii from the village of Lezhnevo, after a religious procession that took place in the village every year at this time, had at the end of the service delivered before the peasants a reactionary sermon [*pogromnaia propoved'*] in which he unequivocally summoned them to deal with all strikers and revolutionaries, mentioning my brother and me by name, which—so it seemed to my father—made the peasants very hostile to us.[83]

It was inevitable that the scapegoats in the popular culture of denunciation would be selected representatives from the very channel through which change had been introduced into the village: the peasant labor migrants.

What is perhaps most fascinating is that the migrants themselves often refused to accept anathematization at face value but, instead, counterposed an alternative social vision that was itself deeply rooted in the language and traditions of the Schism: consciously or unconsciously, many peasant workers found in the Old Belief a support for their own rebellion against the binding ties of their villages. For instance, battling the powerful forces favoring endogamy that would anchor the peasant laborer to his native community by forcing him to marry a local village girl, a peasant worker "fell away" from the Church

[82] From the memo of the minister of internal affairs to the Moscow governor-general, December 9, 1895 (TsGIAgM, f. 17, op. 66, g. 1895, d. 617, ll. 7–8).
[83] Fedor Samoilov, *Vospominaniia ob Ivanovo-Voznesenskom rabochem dvizhenii* (Moscow, 1921), 1:73.

simply by taking a wife of his own choosing. The language and practice of religious dissent became the source from which opponents to traditional forms of social control drew their strength. They refused to bow down to authority, because "according to the sacred books, one should not bow down before icons or priests." They became indifferent to the rites of the Church, but retained their Christian and religious identities by insisting on their own right to stand before God alone, "without your damned icons, without your accursed priests, without your bloody Evangelists!"[84]

As dramatic and forceful as were these cases of religious anathematization of peasant labor migrants under the Old Regime, they paled in comparison to the attacks that marked the Soviet era, most notably during the early years of collectivization. Peasant denunciations from the period 1927–32 substantiate that peasant labor migrants were often singled out by nonmigrating fellow villagers as pernicious enemies of Soviet power and active opponents to socialized agriculture. Provoking widespread envy among less fortunate fellow villagers, and self-marginalized by their very absence from village meetings, *otkhodniki* were often ruthlessly attacked in dekulakization campaigns.[85] For instance, the peasant Pavel Vasil'evich Belov in Tver District—a self-styled spokesman for the real, "pure-blooded peasants" (*chistokrovnye krest'iane*)— passionately denounced all peasant labor migrants as vicious enemies of collectivization: "The *otkhodnik* . . . , having earned decent money 'on the side,' comes home with quite a purse, and copes well with taxes, [while] he clothes and provides for his family and even has enough left over for drinking. This is an indisputable fact, and no decrees or other incentives will persuade him to join the collective."[86] In Belov's village, any peasant worker who had labored more than a year outside the village was stripped of his land, largely to protect the collective from so-called *kulaki-otkhodniki*—rich and greedy peasant labor

[84] Observations on the basic relationship between religious dissent and popular protest are not new. For related works, see Michael Cherniavsky's classic "The Old Believers and the New Religion," in *The Structure of Russian History,* ed. Michael Cherniavsky (New York, 1971), pp. 140–88; A. I. Klibanov, "Problems of the Ideology of Peasant Movements (1850s–1860s)," *Russian History* 11, nos. 2–3 (1984): 168–208; and V. G. Kartsov, *Religioznyi raskol kak forma antifeodal'nogo protesta v istorii Rossii* (Kalinin, 1971), pts. 1–2. For comparative perspectives, see Christopher Hill, *Antichrist in Seventeenth-Century England* (Oxford, 1971).

[85] Lynne Viola has identified peasant workers as a particularly high-risk group for denunciation and dekulakization after 1927. See her excellent article "The Second Coming: Class Enemies in the Soviet Countryside, 1927–1935," in *Stalinist Terror: New Perspectives,* ed. J. Arch Getty and Roberta Manning (Cambridge, 1993), pp. 65–98.

[86] Autograph letter of March 6, 1928, Rossiisskii gosudarstvennyi arkhiv ekonomiki (hereafter, cited as RGAE), f. 396, op. 6, d. 61, ll. 155–56. For a similar case, see f. 7486, op. 37, d. 65, l. 37.

migrants.[87] This apparent continuity illustrates one very important and remarkable point: while the language and content of peasant denunciations in Russia changed according to context and opportunity, the pool of heretics seems to have remained more or less the same. The primary victims of village religious denunciation during the last generations of the Old Regime, the peasant labor migrants were likewise prime candidates for the label of "enemies of the people" in villages during the early years of Soviet power.[88]

[87] See also the denunciation of selected fellow villagers by M. N. Kozlov in Tula Province (RGAE, f. 7486, op. 37, d. 65, ll. 78–80). Compare RGAE, f. 7486, op. 37, d. 65, ll. 87–88.

[88] Note, however, that Sheila Fitzpatrick's study of peasant denunciations in the late 1930s suggests that labor migrants were no longer a major target. See Fitzpatrick's article in this volume, "Signals from Below: Soviet Letters of Denunciation of the 1930s," and her book *Stalin's Peasants: Resistance and Survival in the Russian Village after Collectivization* (Oxford, 1994), pp. 233–61.

Denunciation as a Tool of Ecclesiastical Control: The Case of Roman Catholic Modernism

Gary Lease
University of California, Santa Cruz

"Few movements among men are so subversive as a change in government or reformation in religion."[1] As a result, religious communities, especially those with an institutionalized structure, have invariably sought control over both the actions and the thoughts of their members. The reasons are not far to seek: any religious system is based at least partially on a commonality of beliefs, ritual performance, and ethical conduct among its adherents. Deviation from these norms and expectations is never simply a failure to conform but also a dangerous threat to the continued existence of the system and its community. Since the "truth" of such a religious system is vital to its thriving, indeed to its very survival, constant monitoring for the presence of such deviations is essential. The entire community becomes responsible for this act of self-protection. Wherever and whenever such deviational threats are perceived, they must be proclaimed, or at the very least the leadership of the community must be alerted. In other words, in religious systems and communities, denunciation becomes a duty.[2]

Though by no means isolated in its practices, the Christian churches have long been associated with denunciation practices of varying rigor.[3] At the very roots of the Christian story lies the betrayal of Jesus by Judas, a betrayal that consisted of denouncing the rabbinic teacher to the authorities.[4] By the second and third centuries, rivalries within Christian communities led to denunciations

---

[1] E. K. Chatterton's succinct commentary in *England's Greatest Statesman: A Life of William Pitt* (Indianapolis, 1930), p. 18.

[2] See my essay "The History of 'Religious' Consciousness and the Diffusion of Culture: Strategies for Surviving Dissolution," *Historical Reflections* 20 (1994): 453–79, esp. 464–75.

[3] One need only refer to the recent Cairo controversy surrounding the delation of a literature professor to a local Islamic court and the consequent imposed divorce of the professor from his wife, even though neither party desired the dissolution of the marriage bonds. Compare the initial report in the *Herald International Tribune* (July 23, 1993), pp. 1, 4; an ongoing account in the *San Jose Mercury* (January 28, 1994), p. A-14; and the final success of the denunciation (*San Jose Mercury* [June 15, 1995], p. A-24).

[4] A tradition reported in all four canonical gospels.

This essay originally appeared in *The Journal of Modern History* 68 (December 1996).

first to non-Christian government authorities and later, at the end of the fourth century, to Christian authorities with secular power. The Donatist controversies in Northern Africa, the struggle with various Gnostic communities in Egypt, and the continuing battles in Syria are prominent examples.[5] During the Middle Ages the rise of institutionalized inquisitorial practices led to systematic encouragement of denunciation and its codification in the laws of the Christian Church.[6] In fact, the final expression of this codification (1918) made it clear that every Christian believer had not only the right but also the duty to denounce crimes against the faith or the church; equally clear was the duty to denounce people, acts, or utterances if they represented a "danger to the faith or religion" (c. 1935). At the same time provision was made for denunciation in order to achieve satisfaction for an injustice done against the denouncer.

It was in the Roman Catholic Church's internal struggle over the so-called Modernist Movement of the late nineteenth and early twentieth centuries, however, that these practices reached a fever pitch. The development of systematic tools and practices of denunciation was preceded by a number of police activities and individual cases of delation to Rome that laid the groundwork for later abuse. For example, Luigi Cardinal Lambruschini, the notorious secretary of state under Pope Gregory XVI (1836–46), was wryly noted to be "liberal chiefly in his employment of spies and prisons."[7] Most common were the imprisonment policies in the Church State's Roman jails. Here were to be found not only murderers, thieves, and other criminals but also blasphemers, drunks, and neighborhood disturbers. The bulk of this latter group had been denounced by local informers—personal enemies or neighborhood gossips.[8] A concrete

[5] For the first, see Peter Brown, *Religion and Society in the Age of St. Augustine* (London, 1972). For the second and third, see Walter Bauer, *Rechtgläubigkeit und Ketzerei im ältesten Christentum,* 2d ed. (Tübingen, 1964).

[6] For the first, see e.g., Emanuel Le Roy Ladurie's *Montaillou: Cathars and Catholics in a French Village, 1294–1324* (London, 1978); also the new, exhaustive study by Benzion Netanyahu, *The Origins of the Inquisition in Fifteenth Century Spain* (New York, 1995). For the second, see Peter J. Marx, *De denunciatione iuris canonici* (Scafhusi, 1859). In the Roman *Codex Iuris Canonici* of 1918 the particular canons were c. 1935–37.

[7] W. W. Rockwell, "Gregory XVI," in *Encyclopaedia Britannica,* 11th ed. (New York, 1910), 12:575–76. Not content to let his enforcement policies stand alone, Luigi Cardinal Lambruschini (1776–1854) was also well known for his opposition to the introduction of railways and gas lighting into the Papal States.

[8] As an example, see the "List of the Incarcerated," a semiannual printed report from the Church State Municipal Police, from August 29, 1851: ninety-six women prisoners (thirty-five at large), well over half of whom were convicted and/or in prison due to local denunciations; and 354 men (128 at large). Compare the Collected Papers (*Spogli*) of Giacomo Cardinal Antonelli (1806–76, secretary of state to Pius IX from 1848 to his death), to be found in the Vatican Secret Archives, case 2, no. 54 (hereafter cited as

example is the imprisonment of Giovanni Favella, denounced in a letter to Giacomo Cardinal Antonelli by Facchini della Dogana di Ripagrande during the war over Rome (1869–70). Another is to be found in a letter from Cardinal Snipe to Cardinal Sabina (April 11, 1869) detailing the case of one Francesco Ciapponi from Palombara; depositions from the witnesses and denunciators are attached to the letter. Ciapponi had run afoul of his neighbors' sensitivity to blasphemy ("heretical cursing"); it seems that he had become drunk quite early in the morning on the day in question and had delivered the pungent interjections "per Cristaccio" and "per la Madonnaccia."[9]

Pius IX had begun his reign on a much different note. Soon after his elevation to the papal throne he had issued a letter to all bishops around the world granting them a dispensation to be used by confessors (November 25, 1846). This relaxation was intended to release all church members, of both sexes, from the obligation of denunciation except in those cases dealing with heretics, or those soliciting opposition to the orders of Pius's predecessors, Gregory XV and Benedict XIV, or those concerning authorities and teachers of Protestant sects. Pius offered this dispensation in conjunction with a jubilee year and in celebration of his election as pope.[10] But the revolution of 1848, accompanied by the assassination of the pope's minister president in the parliamentary chambers and the pope's subsequent flight to Naples, put him in a much different mood. In 1850, upon being restored to his throne by French and Austrian forces, he immediately set about reforming and redesigning the police of the Papal State (November 25, 1850): dividing the jurisdictions into urban and rural, he promulgated harsh rules and regulations governing crimes and procedures surrounding the use of denunciation.[11] As we saw, this led to many general denunciations at the community level, producing a large number of imprisonments for blasphemy and other offensive use of language. It is difficult to avoid the impression that many of these cases were, in fact, ways of "getting even" veiled under the cloak of "danger to religion."

More public, and in many ways more scandalous, was the case of Edgar Mortara, similar in the scope of its European uproar to the Dreyfus affair some decades later. Pius had, of course, kept Rome's Jewish community restricted to its traditional ghetto, but his treatment of the respected and well-off Jewish

---

Antonelli Papers). For others, cf. the files of the secretariat of state, rubrics 95 ("Jails, Prisoners, Guards"), 98 ("Criminal Tribunal"), 155 ("General Police Administration and Ministry of the Interior"), and 204 ("Prisoners and Condemned, 1829–1850," case 354).

[9] For the first case, cf. Antonelli Papers, above, case 2, A-31; for the second, case 2, B-69.

[10] Ibid., case 1, 36.

[11] Ibid., case 2, B-14.

family of Mortara from Bologna overstepped all bounds. Young Edgar Mortara, born in 1851, had been cared for from birth by a teenage Christian girl from Bologna. During his first year he had become quite sick; worried that he might die still an infidel Jew, the young nurse, Anna Morisi, baptized him while the parents were absent. The boy survived the illness and several years elapsed. In 1858 Edgar's younger brother also became ill and then died before Anna could baptize him as she had Edgar. The ensuing guilt made her worry about Edgar's fate: unlike his younger brother he had been delivered from the danger of dying without salvation, yet he did not even know it. Conversations with neighbors made their way to the local priest; from there it was only a short step to the archbishop of Bologna. Despite careful investigation and several court actions, it is still unclear who said what to whom—a clear sign of denunciation at work. What is clear, though, is that on June 24, 1858, the police, under order of the Inquisition, came to the Mortara household, took young Edgar, and disappeared with him. By the next morning he was on his way to Rome.[12]

The European and North American publics were outraged. Appeals were made from throughout the two continents to the Vatican, but Pius IX made it clear that this was a spiritual case outside his temporal jurisdiction. He was bound, he maintained, by an earlier ruling from Benedict XIV (1740–58) according to which Jewish children, even if illicitly baptized, were to be separated from their families and educated as Christians.[13] In any case, conflicting reports very soon circulated: some had him crying for his parents and family and begging for a mezuzzah, while others had him adopting his new faith with warmth and adapting easily to his new residence in the Roman Home for Cate-

---

[12] See first the older, unsigned account in the *Encyclopaedia Britannica,* 11th ed. (New York, 1910), 18:877. Bertram Wallace Korn offers judicious corrections of both the event itself and its public aftermaths in his *The American Reaction to the Mortara Case: 1858–1859* (Cincinnati, 1957); mention is also made in Sam Waagenaar's *The Pope's Jews* (LaSalle, Ill., 1974), pp. 208–13. Many of the contemporary relevant documents are to be found in the pamphlet *Roma e la opinione pubblica d'europa nel fatta Mortara* (Turin, 1859). For the official church file, see the Vatican Secret Archives, Secretariat of State, rubric 66 (Jews, Schismatics, Non-Catholics), year 1864 (1858–64: Posizione relativa al neofito fanciullo Edgardo Mortara. Battesimo).

[13] In his rule "On Baptism of Hebrews, Children and Adults" from 1747. Benedict XIV (Lambertini), a famous canon lawyer, based his opinion on the well-known canon 60 from the Council of Toledo held in 633. It is worth noting that throughout the nineteenth century the old *Corpus Iuris Canonici* remained in force; thus "Sicut Iudeis" (*Decretals* 5.6) specifically prohibited the forced baptism of Jews. The letter was a privilege first issued by Calixtus II and then reissued by Eugenius III, Alexander III, and Clemens III. Although attitudes toward the Jews shifted in the late twelfth century, the provisions of "Sicut" were never overturned or seriously restricted. Lambertini certainly recognized this, as did also Pius IX; the rub was, of course, the status of a forced (and thus illicit) baptism after it had occurred. And here the situation was clear to Pius: illicit or not, it was still valid.

chumens. While declining to take any action to release the child to his parents, Pius did make young Edgar his personal ward.[14]

Finally, in 1861, the Mortara family did persuade the Italian government to demand that at least the nurse should be prosecuted for kidnapping. Pius IX replied that this was impossible since the young woman in question had already entered a nunnery. Indeed, during the traditional New Year's audience granted by the pope to the Jewish community, the Mortara family appeared and appealed to the pope for the release of their son; but Pius replied that he had no intention of paying attention to the general uproar caused by his actions and praised the Mortaras for having given Europe such a wonderful example of obedience to higher authority. Two years later young Edgar was presented to the Jewish community in the robes of a seminarian.[15]

Upon the fall of Rome in 1870, Mortara was given the chance to revert to Judaism, but he chose instead to remain a Catholic and entered the Augustinian order, studying at way stations in Brixen (Tyrol) and Poitiers (France), where he was ordained a priest in 1873. He worked hard in support of the poor, achieving an excellent reputation as a preacher in the many countries in which he served (Italy, Austria, Belgium, France, Spain, England, America). The subject of such intense scrutiny as a child, Mortara died almost unnoticed at the age of eighty-eight in 1940.

Also of far-reaching impact was the infamous case of John Henry Newman (1801–90), the prominent Anglican theologian and leading figure of the Oxford Movement who later converted to the Roman Catholic Church and in his last years was named a cardinal by Leo XIII. His delation to Rome by another bishop caused his career and service within the Roman Church to be severely limited, and he often spoke of the "cloud" under which he had labored. The facts are brief but tragic. In 1859 Newman assumed the editorship of the English periodical *Rambler*, a journal that had already led to agitation among the Roman hierarchy in England, and published his essay "On Consulting the Faithful in Matters of Doctrine."[16] A local theologian, John Gillow from Ushaw, immediately took umbrage and complained to Newman. Not receiving from him the retraction he sought, Gillow alerted Bishop Brown of Newport to the whole affair; Brown, in turn, without informing Newman of his actions, denounced him and the article to Rome (to the Congregation for the Propaga-

---

[14] For the first, see the report in the *New York Times* (November 27, 1858) p. 2, repeating a story from the Genoese *Corriere Mercantile*. The opposite view can be found in the *New York Tablet* (November 20, 1858) p. 3, carrying an article from the Turin *Armonia*.

[15] See August Bernhard Hasler, *Wie der Papst unfehlbar wurde: Macht und Ohnmacht eines Dogmas* (Frankfurt am Main, 1981), pp. 251–52.

[16] John Henry Newman, "On Consulting the Faithful in Matters of Doctrine," *Rambler* (July 1859), pp. 198–230, edited and republished by John Coulson (London, 1961).

tion of the Faith). At the same time Brown also admonished George Talbot, an English prelate functioning in Rome as an unofficial agent of the English hierarchy, to make sure that the case was brought directly to the pope's attention, charging Newman with "positive heresy." Talbot, an extraordinarily active gossip of would-be importance who later ended his days in a mental institution, did as he was bidden. Because of his denunciation, Newman was effectively put on ice and denied the role he might have played in the church of his choice. Only two decades later, at the time of his rehabilitation and the award of the cardinal's hat, did he learn of the foundation for those many years of unexplained suspicion and mistrust.[17]

These examples of denunciation, however, only presaged a much more virulent struggle for control of thought and utterance within the Roman Church. From the last decade of the nineteenth century until the First World War there raged throughout the Catholic Church a war over so-called Modernism.[18] Led by a small number of scholars, intellectuals, and concerned thinkers, the Modernist Movement was an effort on the part of deeply committed members of the Roman Church to integrate into its thought, teachings, and belief system the most profound and persuasive results of contemporary science, history, and theory. The institutional leadership of the church, however, could only see this enterprise as an attempt to change the most basic tenets of Christian belief and history while at the same time undermining the authority of the ecclesiastical hierarchy and thus its ability to govern Christianity. Whatever the Modernist program may or may not have been, it is clear that the anti-Modernist agenda was quite simply the survival of hierarchical power and control. As the controversy intensified, so did the methods used to achieve victory. Excommunications (e.g., of Loisy in 1908 and of George Tyrrell in 1907), official encyclicals condemning a variety of fabricated doctrinal positions, suspensions, and disciplinary actions: all these were arrows in the institution's quiver. Many such actions resulted from denunciations made to Rome, often directly to Cardinal Merry del Val, the secretary of state, or to Pius X, pope since 1903.

[17] In regard to the *Rambler* article, see my *Witness to the Faith: Cardinal Newman on the Teaching Authority of the Church* (Shannon, 1971), pp. 86–93. For Newman's red hat, see my "Newman: The Roman View," in *Newman and the Modernists,* ed. Mary Jo Weaver (Washington, D.C., 1985), pp. 161–82, and now also in my *"Odd Fellows" in the Politics of Religion: Modernism, National Socialism, and German Judaism* (Berlin, 1995), pp. 93–109, esp. 94–95.

[18] Among the ocean of studies dedicated to this interlude, see esp. Lester R. Kurtz, *The Politics of Heresy: The Modernist Crisis in Roman Catholicism* (Berkeley and Los Angeles, 1986); and more recently Marvin O'Connell, *Critics on Trial: An Introduction to the Catholic Modernist Crisis* (Lanham, Md., 1994). For the larger setting, see my "Modernism and 'Modernism': Christianity as Product of Its Culture," *Journal for the Study of Religion* 1, no. 2 (1988): 97–111, now in my *"Odd Fellows" in the Politics of Religion,* pp. 110–27.

Most instructive is the case of Tyrrell, certainly one of the leading intellectual lights of the movement. As early as 1900, long before he became a powerful cardinal, Merry del Val was receiving intimate reports on Tyrrell and others.
The excommunication of 1907 was only the culmination of a long campaign
to silence this particular thinker. Not content with that, after Tyrrell's death two
years later (1909) Cardinal Merry del Val used his influence to deny Tyrrell a
church burial. Henri Bremond braved the order and provided a graveside service in an Anglican cemetery, and within a week Merry del Val had suspended
Bremond from universal church service. And Maude Petre, Tyrrell's last and
most faithful disciple, was forbidden access to the sacraments in her diocese
of Southwark; for thirty years, until her death in 1942, this suspension was
upheld in England. The local bishop, Peter Amigo, later admitted that he had
imposed this sentence on secret orders from Rome after Petre's biography of
Tyrrell (1912) had been denounced.[19]

Even more astounding was the case of the seminary at Wonersh. Francis
Bourne, archbishop of Westminster, fervently desired the cardinalate, and
Merry del Val kept reassuring him that it was just around the corner. As late as
1908 prospects for his red hat appeared strong. By the next year, however,
Bourne's hopes had evaporated. How had this come to be? The major problem,
of course, was that Merry del Val was suddenly no longer well disposed to
Bourne, and rumors began to fly. Who the precise agents were is now impossible to tell, but it is clear that term papers from students at the Wonersh seminary were sent by zealous guardians of the truth directly to Merry del Val along
with suggestions that Archbishop Bourne was "soft" on Modernism. Various
actors denied participation, but the damage had already been done. As with all
denunciations, it soon made little difference whether the charges were true or
not: "His Eminence [Cardinal Merry del Val] has listened and his listening
brings trouble. The worst of listening is that it is not cured by a denial. It is a
bad habit."[20]

Further afield, the ax of denunciation also struck at the Catholic University
of America. Henry Poels (1868–1948), a Dutch Old Testament scholar teaching there, had refused to swear an oath that he would accept and teach all
decisions of the Pontifical Biblical Commission at a time when the rector,
Denis O'Connell, was trying to present a clean orthodox front at the university
in the wake of Modernism's condemnation in 1907. O'Connell promptly re-
layed Poels's refusal to Merry del Val, without, of course, telling Poels about

[19] For the details see my "Merry del Val and Tyrrell: A Modernist Struggle," *Down-
side Review* 102 (1984): 133–56, now in my *"Odd Fellows" in the Politics of Religion,*
pp. 55–76, esp. pp. 68–73.
[20] Lease, "Merry del Val and Tyrrell," pp. 73–76. The quote is from Bishop Cahill
(Portsmouth), p. 75.

it. The secretary of state reacted without hesitation: it is impossible, he opined, that anyone should be allowed to occupy a chair of scripture without teaching and holding all that is taught and held by the Holy See. Poels's sincerity was simply not enough. Under direct order from Rome, the university's trustees met with Poels in November 1909 and demanded his oath. Like Abelard before him, Poels declined to swear to an oath formulated by someone else and demanded that he be allowed to craft the language of any oath he would perform. This was, naturally enough, denied him, and he was dismissed, in conformity with the wishes of Rome as provided by Merry del Val. Just as in the earlier case of Tyrrell, the cardinal had been able to silence a voice that disturbed his anti-Modernist tack without having to be directly involved—another hallmark of denunciation at work.[21]

These were "terrifying" times and the victims felt the scourge no matter how far they were from its source.[22] The fear on all sides had great justification. There was not only the possibility that the all-powerful cardinal and secretary of state might happen, by chance or design, upon something as innocuous as a student's term paper, sending a promising career up in smoke, but in addition there was, it turned out, a systematic organization in place to make sure that such denunciations were forthcoming. In 1909, with the support of the highest figures in Rome's institutional hierarchy (including Merry del Val), Umberto Benigni (1862–1934), a staunch conservative prelate living in Rome, founded the "Sodalitium Pianum," also called the "Sapinière." Establishing a network of like-minded Catholic periodicals and journals, together with a sophisticated and encoded system of internal correspondence, Benigni sought to encourage denunciations in order to preserve the church's control over its members' thought and expression. The German army, upon its invasion and occupation of Belgium in 1914–15, discovered a cache of documents detailing the history and operations of this effective secret organization.[23] Formulating their goals and actions in the language of war, Benigni and his associates saw themselves as legitimated by a struggle to preserve authority, save the church from internal

[21] The particulars can be traced in the correspondence between Merry del Val and Cardinal Gibbons, then the archbishop of Baltimore; for more details see my "Merry del Val and the American Church," in *"Odd Fellows" in the Politics of Religion,* pp. 77–92, esp. pp. 91 and 253. Poels's career as an Old Testament scholar was effectively ended by this episode, but upon return to his native Holland he was able to develop a fruitful second career in the social apostolate.

[22] Emile Poulat's trenchant term; see his *Integrisme et catholicisme integral: Un reseau secret international antimoderniste: La "Sapinière" (1909–1921)* (Paris, 1969), p. 7.

[23] See Kurtz, pp. 161–65. The documents themselves have since been edited and published in magisterial fashion by Poulat (*Intégrisme et catholicisme intégral*). See also Poulat's later study, *Catholicisme, démocratie et socialisme: Le mouvement catholique et Mgr. Benigni de la naissance du socialisme à la victoire du fascisme* (Paris, 1977).

betrayal, and oppose the revolution of modernity. The group decried feminism and the separation of church and state, while promoting the spirit and fervor of the Counter-Reformation.[24] For such causes no tool could be denied. Operating in strict secrecy, including the concealment of its very existence, this small but tight-knit band enjoyed the approval and, indeed, encouragement of the Vatican itself. According to one of its harshest critics, espionage was its main weapon, which it used to "discredit faithful Catholics" everywhere. Benigni viewed denunciation as a natural product of the Catholic movement and defended it to the end.[25] Indeed, one critic, reporting in 1921 on the papers discovered by the Germans, saw denunciation as the chief work of the Sapiniere. His account of the individuals, institutions, and publications denounced by this organization covers two and one-half pages.[26] Cardinals (e.g., Van Rossum, Mercier, Amette, Piffl), professors, leaders of suspect religious orders, entire faculties (e.g., all the Dominicans at the University of Fribourg), journalists, editors, research institutes, and publications: you name it and the Sapiniere was against it. The group even speculated in 1913 on the outcome of the next papal conclave (as it turned out, it was just a year away), listing those it thought "dangerous" to its work and those it thought favorable. Merry del Val was listed as "La Peur."[27]

But all good things come to an end. Criticism grew against the high-handed and destructive operation of the Sodality. The successor to Pius X, Benedict XV, sought to restrict the group's operations, and in 1921 it was at last formally disbanded. The damage, however, had been extensive: careers shattered, spirits broken, service replaced by fear. As Kurtz observes, Benigni's operations had "created disruptions in the lives and careers of countless Catholics, introduced chaos into a number of institutions, and precipitated a strong undercurrent of suspicion, mistrust, and insecurity throughout the church, almost paralyzing scholarly inquiry within it."[28]

One example that stands for many is the case of the great French Dominican and exegete, R. P. Lagrange (1855–1938), whose career was brought to an early end by denunciations—some dating as early as 1898, but culminating in

---

[24] Poulat, *Intégrisme et catholicisme intégral,* pp. 119–23. See, too, Maurice Pernot, *La politique de Pie X (1906–1910)* (Paris, 1910), esp. chap. 15, "La *Correspondance de Rome* et la France," pp. 254–97.

[25] For the first, Kurtz, p. 164. For the second, Poulat, *Integrisme et catholicisme integral,* p. 69.

[26] The "anonymous memo" by Fernand Mourret (1854–1938), a Sulpician priest and seminary professor (church history), is to be found in Poulat, *Intégrisme et catholicisme intégral,* pp. 548–63; the list of people and organizations denounced by Benigni and his colleagues is on pp. 551–54.

[27] Ibid., pp. 328–31.

[28] Kurtz (n. 18 above), p. 164.

the attacks on the Dominican Biblical Institute in Jerusalem and on Lagrange's own work on the Hebrew Scriptures, in particular his commentary on Genesis (never to be published). By 1907 he was forbidden to publish any of his scholarship in this field, and in order to work at all Lagrange abandoned entirely his work on the Hebrew Scriptures and dedicated himself to a new field—the New Testament. And by 1909 the Vatican had founded its own Pontifical Institute of Biblical Studies as a counterweight to the Dominican school in Jerusalem. Lagrange endured another quarter of a century unable to contribute fully to the fields of study he knew and loved so well.[29] As late as the 1950s the effects of this suppression continued to work their magic. Seminarians at the French School in Rome were warned against Loisy and especially de Lubac, while work at the Dominican Biblical Institute in Jerusalem was still performed under a cloud.[30]

In this connection I find it difficult not to offer a personal experience of the power of denunciation in a religious context. The year 1969 found me returning from doctoral studies at the University of Munich to a position at Loyola University (now Loyola-Marymount University) in Los Angeles. Within a year of my arrival the anachronistic department of theology had been replaced with a Department of Religious Studies featuring a major in which students might concentrate their work. Enrollments grew and the curriculum expanded. As one might imagine, however, sentiments were not positive on all sides. Some members of the Jesuit community attached to the university were not pleased with the demise of the theology department; as one disgruntled professor put it: "What we need is not only more Catholic theology, but [also] more Jesuit theology!" Some students, enthused over their exposure to contemporary biblical criticism, talked eagerly about their course work at home. As a result, some parents become alarmed and communicated their concerns to selected trustees of the university, who then alerted the Jesuit leaders on campus. Of course, no one spoke to me. The silent circle, so necessary for denunciation to work, was complete.

Only later was it revealed that some of the Jesuit leaders had recruited Jesuit novices, teaching in a downtown Los Angeles high school, to appear on campus in mufti and to infiltrate my classroom, where I was lecturing on early Christian history. Their task was simple: to ask leading questions, carefully formulated in advance, and then report back to their superiors. The topic that created the most disturbance, as I recall, was the issue of the Assumption of

[29] See Lagrange's memoirs as *Pere Lagrange: Personal Reflections and Memoirs* (New York, 1985), pp. 62–63 (denounced), 129–31 (suspicion, prohibition), 155–65 (his "terrible year").

[30] See the arresting account by Emile Morin in his *Confession d'un prêtre du xxe siècle* (Paris, 1991).

Mary. Queried about its development in early Christian thought, I replied that the earliest traces of this belief were considerably later than the first century and likely had arisen in connection with the emerging doctrine of Jesus' divinity. That response, however, did not satisfy my interlocutors. Did I believe in the Assumption? The question was repeated again and again. My retort was that it was none of the students' business what I believed in, but if they wished to work with me after class on the relevant Greek and Syriac texts that detailed the development of that particular doctrine, I would be happy to do so. As it turned out, of course, none of my interrogators was interested in that level of scholarship.

Further controversies arose between me and one of the Jesuit historians on campus, who not only espoused a firm commitment to the notion of papal infallibility also believed that it had long been held and acted upon. In a number of conversations I adduced in opposition to his position the fifteenth-century episode of conciliarism, and in particular the case of Pius II, who had been such a fierce enemy of papal infallibility until elected pope but who then quickly espoused a doctrine more suitable to his own newly acquired powers. This faculty member, as it turned out, promptly denounced me to his Jesuit community colleagues as a "heretic," confirming once and for all what they already knew through the testimony of the shills placed in my classroom earlier.

In 1971 I was awarded a National Endowment for the Humanities grant for study in Germany: the time was ripe for action. While I was away on research leave, the Jesuit community brought pressure to bear on the dean, and my dismissal was accomplished in my absence. My terminal year in 1972–73 was a tension-filled period of hearings, charges, and countercharges with the reasons for my dismissal never fully disclosed. Only years later did former colleagues admit to the informants placed in my classroom and to the claims of my "heretical" teaching bandied about in the Jesuit community. Once again, a religious community had rid itself of a potentially disruptive influence by exercising the time-honored tactic of denunciation.[31]

Denunciation as exercised within a religious community and belief system is an especially potent agent of destruction. As these examples illustrate, it suits particularly well the conviction that one possesses the truth and that all weapons against its denial are justified. Indeed, heretics—those who would

---

[31] The relevant committee reports, campus newspaper articles, and correspondences are all available in my personal files. "Like Nicodemus in the night," to cite the late Senator Sam Ervin, various faculty came privately to assure me of their support and their recognition of the trumped-up nature of the charges against me. Of course, they continued, in the light of such denunciations they were quite powerless to do anything publically. This illustrates another effect of denunciation: the paralysis that infects observers and witnesses.

deny one's possession of the truth—not only endanger those who control the institutional nurturing of that truth but also are themselves outside it. Denouncing such cases to the proper authorities is seen as a genuine duty, one that ensures survival and, ultimately, growth. In such instances denunciation serves political goals elevated to the level of salvific actions. And in the name of salvation there is nothing that can be left undone.

Signals from Below: Soviet Letters of Denunciation of the 1930s*

Sheila Fitzpatrick
University of Chicago

> DENUNCIATION (*donos*). A weapon of war of reactionary forces of the bourgeoisie and Black Hundreds against the revolutionary movement—information [given] to the Tsarist or other reactionary government about revolutionary acts that were secretly being prepared. [Examples] *Acting on a denunciation from a traitor, Tsarist gendarmes broke up an underground Bolshevik organization. Fascists threw a group of Komsomols into prison on the basis of a provocateur's denunciation.*
> SIGNAL (*signal*). 2. A warning about something undesirable that may happen, a putting on guard (*predosterezhenie*). [Example] *The Bolshevik Party demands sensitivity to the signals coming from below by way of self-criticism.*[1]

Denunciation—the voluntary reporting of wrongdoing by other citizens to the authorities—is a highly ambiguous practice. In some contexts, a denunciation may be read as an exemplary act of civic virtue motivated by altruistic concern for the public good. More often, however, denunciations are construed as acts of betrayal motivated by venality or malice. Language reflects these ambiguities and complexities. Two different terms for the practice may exist simultaneously, one neutral or positive and the other pejorative (French *délation* versus *dénonciation;* Russian *signal* versus *donos*). Euphemisms abound, like the contemporary American term *whistle-blowing*. The related and almost universally despised practice of informing—that is, regular denunciation that is paid or otherwise rewarded—has generated whole hosts of colloquial pejoratives.

How to distinguish "good" denunciation from "bad" has exercised many

---

* I am grateful to the National Council for Soviet and East European Research (NCSEER) for supporting the research in Russian archives on which this article is based. An earlier version of the article was submitted to NCSEER in 1994 as part of the Final Report on the Denunciations project. I would also like to thank all those who made helpful comments on the article as it went through various revisions, particularly Jonathan Bone, David Fitzpatrick, Catriona Kelly, and Andrew Verner. Thanks also to V. V. Shishkin (Novosibirsk) and S. A. Krasil'nikov (Novosibirsk) for supplying materials.

[1] D. N. Ushakov, ed., *Tolkovyi slovar' russkogo iazyka,* 4 vols. (Moscow, 1935–40).

This essay originally appeared in *The Journal of Modern History* 68 (December 1996).

86   *Fitzpatrick*

writers. Contemplating the moral status of practices of public accusation (delation) in ancient Rome, an early twentieth-century edition of the *Encyclopaedia
Britannica* concluded that the key distinction was between interested and
disinterested accusation: "When exercised from patriotic and disinterested
motives, [the] . . . effects [of delation] were beneficial; but the moment the
principle of reward was introduced, this was no longer the case."[2] Diderot's
encyclopedia suggested a more complex division based on intention: "One is
inclined to think that the delator is a corrupt man, the accuser an angry man,
and the denouncer an indignant man," while noting that "these three person-
ages are equally odious in the eyes of the people."[3]

Denunciation has attracted less attention from twentieth-century thinkers
than it did from those of the eighteenth century. When it has been discussed in
English-speaking countries, it has usually been with reference to the Nazi and
Stalinist regimes and in the context of totalitarianism. Yet denunciation is
a phenomenon of everyday life that exists in every society, albeit with great
variation in type, visibility (the degree to which the practice is recognized and
problematized), and incidence. The Soviet Union of the 1930s, with its multiplicity of types of denunciation, strong visibility, and high incidence, provides
a rich but by no means unique case study.

There were well-established traditions of denunciation in Russia long before
the Bolsheviks took power in 1917.[4] The Bolsheviks and other Russian revolutionaries despised these traditions and associated them with the corruption of
the old regime, as their counterparts in the French Revolution had done before
them. Yet at the same time it quickly became clear to the Bolsheviks, just as it
had to the Jacobins, that revolutionary denunciation was both necessary and
virtuous. It was necessary to encourage citizens to denounce enemies, spies,
and plots because of the danger of counterrevolution. Within the revolutionary
party, moreover, denunciation of backsliders and hypocrites was the duty of
every member, a guarantee of the continued purity and transparency on which
the revolution depended. Unlike the Jacobins, the Bolsheviks did not philoso-
phize about the principle of denunciation.[5] But they instinctively adopted the
practice, just as every other sect of revolutionary or religious enthusiasts has
done over the ages. There can be no secrets in the community of saints.

[2] *Encyclopaedia Britannica,* 11th ed., s.v. "delator."
[3] *Encyclopédie ou Dictionnaire raisonné des sciences, des arts et des métiers, par
une Société de Gens de Lettres mis en ordre et publié par M. Diderot,* vol. 10 (Lausanne/
Berne, 1779).
[4] On denunciation in the Muscovite and Petrine periods, see A. M. Kleimola, "The
Duty to Denounce in Muscovite Russia," *Slavic Review,* vol. 31, no. 4 (December 1972);
Richard Hellie, "The Origins of Denunciation in Muscovy," *Russian History* (in press);
Evgenii Anisimov, "Donos," *Rodina,* no. 7 (1990).
[5] See Colin Lucas, "The Theory and Practice of Denunciation in the French Revolution," in this volume.

With time came routinization. The Bolshevik Party's concern for purity was institutionalized in the periodic party "cleansings" or purges (*chistki*) of the 1920s and 1930s in which each member had to give a public account of himself and respond to questions, criticisms, and accusations. The practice of denunciation of Communist by Communist was embedded in this ritual, though it also existed independently of it.

As for popular denunciation, the type actively encouraged by the regime was citizens' denunciation of wrongdoing by officials. This was conceived as a kind of popular monitoring of bureaucracy that was also a form of democratic political participation. One institutional product was the workers' and peasants' inspectorate that was much on Lenin's mind in his last years. Another was the recruitment of worker and peasant correspondents for newspapers (*rabkory* and *sel'kory*)—volunteer amateur stringers whose job was to serve as "the eyes and ears of Soviet power," reporting local abuses of power by Soviet officials as well as keeping watch on the activities of class enemies like kulaks and priests. A third product was the institution of "self-criticism" sessions in factories and enterprises to stimulate the airing of workers' grievances and the denunciation of wrongdoing and incompetence on the part of managers and specialists.[6]

Denunciation as a social practice was greatly encouraged by the regime's decision in the late 1920s to expropriate, deport, and otherwise punish whole categories of class enemies, notably kulaks (prosperous peasants) and Nepmen (the private entrepreneurs whose existence had been tolerated under the New Economic Policy [NEP] of the 1920s). "Bourgeois" (i.e., non-Communist) specialists and "former people" (members of the old privileged classes) also came under fire at this time. Class enemies, who were prone to conceal their identities, had to be "unmasked," and denunciation was an important part of this process. A few years later, denunciation acquired its official hero and martyr in Pavlik Morozov, a Young Pioneer (or so the story had it) murdered by relatives after denouncing his own father for trying to cheat the Soviet government by hoarding grain. For more than fifty years, until his monuments were (literally) toppled by resentful citizens in the Gorbachev era, Pavlik remained an exemplar of the virtuous Soviet child who put public interests above private and family loyalties.[7]

The Great Purges of 1937–38 gave further impetus to popular denunciation, as citizens were exhorted to watch out for spies and saboteurs and to unmask

---

[6] In Bolshevik jargon, "self-criticism" originally meant the self-criticism of the collective. But the meaning it acquired in practice was public criticism of bosses by the rank and file and the bosses' acceptance of such criticism (q.v. Ushakov's definition of *Signal*).

[7] On the cult of Pavlik Morozov, see Robert Conquest, *Harvest of Sorrow* (New York, 1986), pp. 293–96; and my *Stalin's Peasants: Resistance and Survival in the Russian Village after Collectivization* (New York, 1994), pp. 254–56.

hidden "enemies of the people"—a term applied primarily to disgraced Communists who had formerly held responsible administrative positions. Soon the tide of denunciation rose so high that party leaders became disturbed by its disastrous impact on government efficiency and industrial output and started to inveigh against "false [*lozhnye*] denunciations," meaning accusations that were hysterical and unfounded or that served the denouncer's private interests rather than the public good. It should be noted, however, that citizens' denunciations constituted only one of a number of sources of what was known in Soviet parlance as "compromising information."[8] The Soviet secret police was a large organization, and in addition to exploiting its network of regular informers (*sekretnye sotrudniki*) it also collected a great deal of the material used against "enemies of the people" through interrogation of prisoners and members of the free population.

Contrary to the stereotype of denunciation in a police state, Soviet denunciations were not addressed exclusively or even mainly to the secret police (NKVD).[9] Communist denunciations of other Communists were usually sent to some organ of the Communist Party.[10] Other denunciations were sent to the government and to individual government agencies such as Rabkrin, the People's Commissariat of Workers' and Peasants' Inspection.[11] Some people sent their denunciations directly to Stalin, Molotov, or another Politburo member, or to the first party secretary in their area, who was often the object of a regional "cult of personality" similar to Stalin's. Citizens also sent denunciations directly to the procuracy (Public Prosecutor's office) and the NKVD.

Newspapers received many denunciations, especially those of the whistle-blowing and "abuse of power" types. A few such letters from readers were

---

[8] In contrast to Gellately's findings on Nazi Germany, freely offered denunciations seem not to have been the typical starting point for a Soviet secret police investigation. A Russian scholar working with materials from the KGB archives in the Urals reports that most denunciations in investigatory files are statements obtained by the police in the process of investigation, and only a few are voluntary "signals" from members of the public: S. M. Popova, "Sistema donositel'stva v 30-e gody (K probleme sozdaniia bazy dannykh na materialakh Urala)," *Klio,* no. 1 (1991), pp. 71–72. (Thanks to Hiroaki Kuromiya for alerting me to this article.)

[9] From 1934 to the war NKVD was the name of the secret police. In the early 1930s it was called the OGPU, and before that the GPU. In the 1940s, the agency was divided into the MVD and the MGB. In the last decades of the Soviet period, the name of the reunified institution was the KGB.

[10] The Central Committee, the Central Control Commission (Commission of Party Control) and its regional branches, regional party committees, the political administrations of the Red Army and other quasi-militarized sectors, and so forth.

[11] Here *government* means the all-Union and republican Sovnarkoms (Councils of People's Commissars) and the executive committees of the all-Union and republican parliaments, called TsIK and VTsIK (Russia) before being renamed Supreme Soviets in the late 1930s.

published, usually boiled down to a paragraph each under the heading "Signals from the Grassroots" (*Signaly s mest*) or "Signals from Below" (*Signaly snizu*). But the main point of writing a letter to the editor in the Soviet Union (not only during the Stalin period but continuing right up to the late 1980s) was not to get the letter published but to provoke an official investigation. All Soviet newspapers maintained large departments for dealing with readers' letters. Selection and editing of letters for publication was only a minor function of these departments. Their main function was that of ombudsmen, forwarding complaints and denunciations to the appropriate agencies (government, party, procuracy, NKVD, and so on) and following up to see that those agencies conducted proper investigations.[12] Thus, there was really no substantive difference between sending a denunciation to a newspaper and sending it to the NKVD or some other official agency. In fact, many denunciations were sent to newspapers and to the relevant government and party bodies, even though each letter cost the sender twenty kopecks in postage.

There has been almost no scholarly analysis of the phenomenon of Soviet denunciation,[13] though a number of actual denunciations from the archives have appeared in Russian publications in the past few years. The lack of scholarly discussion is undoubtedly related to the fact that historians have only recently gained access to denunciations in Soviet archives. Along with other categories of citizens' letters to the authorities, denunciations were usually filed in the "secret" sections of the archives that were not previously available to scholars, particularly Westerners.[14]

The database for this article consists of two hundred denunciations located in twelve archives of different types (central and regional, party and state, city, newspaper, and so forth).[15] There is no way of making a truly representative

[12] A major central newspaper like *Pravda* might also conduct its own investigation, sending out a journalist to research the situation and write up the results as an exposé article, but this was much less common than the forwarding procedure.

[13] The subject is tackled peripherally in two studies that deal primarily with petitions: Merle Fainsod, *Smolensk under Soviet Rule* (Cambridge, Mass., 1958), chap. 7; and Margareta Mommsen, *Hilf Mir, Mein Recht zu Finden: Russische Bittschriften von Iwan dem Schrecklichen bis Gorbatschow* (Frankfurt, 1987).

[14] Common headings for the archival files containing denunciations, along with other citizens' letters, are *Pis'ma trudiashchikhsia, Zhaloby i zaiavleniia trudiashchikhsia, Pis'ma v redaktsiiu,* and *Pis'ma na imia* [*predsedatelia Sovnarkoma, sekretaria obkoma,* and so on]. In party archives, denunciations of Communists were sometimes separately filed under the heading "Compromising information on . . ." (*Komprometiruiushchie dannye na . . .*).

[15] The denunciations in the database were mainly collected in research trips to Russia in 1993–94. Their archival provenance is as follows: Gosudarstvennyi arkhiv Novosibirskoi oblasti (hereafter cited as GANO), total of eight denunciations, f. 47 (Novosibirsk kraiispolkom, secret sector) and f. 288 (Rabkrin/Control Commission, Novosibirsk oblast); Gosudarstvennyi arkhiv Rossiiskoi Federatsii (hereafter cited as GARF; for-

sample of denunciations, since the letters that survive constitute only a randomly preserved part of a much larger original corpus. My selection represents the diversity of types of denunciation that I encountered in various archives. Denunciations from the KGB archive, to which I was refused access, constitute the major lacuna in my database. This does not mean that my sample lacks all denunciations sent to the NKVD (the KGB's precursor), since under the bureaucratic handling procedures in force during the Stalin period, denunciations were filed in the archives of the institution with which the denouncee was affiliated, not the institution to which the denunciation was originally addressed.[16] But the KGB archive does contain denunciations filed in the NKVD's dossiers on persons under investigation (*sledstvennye dela*), as well as denunciations of NKVD personnel, and consequently both types are absent from my sources.

---

merly TsGAOR SSSR), total of twenty-nine denunciations from f. 1235 (VTsIK Secretariat), f. 3316 (TsIK Secretariat), and f. 5446, op. 81a (Sovnarkom SSSR: Vyshinskii's Secretariat) and op. 82 (Sovnarkom SSSR: Molotov's Sovnarkom Secretariat); Gosudarstvennyi arkhiv Sverdlovskoi oblasti (hereafter cited as GASO), total of one denunciation from f. 88 (Sverdlovsk oblispolkom); Latvijas valsts arhiva social-politisko dokumenta nodala (hereafter cited as LVA SPDN, former Latvian Party Archive, located in Riga, Latvia), total of two denunciations from f. 101 (Central Committee of the Latvian Communist Party); Partiinyi arkhiv Novosibirskoi oblasti (hereafter cited as PANO), total of fourteen denunciations from f. 3 (Novosibirsk kraikom); Rossiiskii gosudarstvennyi arkhiv ekonomiki (hereafter cited as RGAE, formerly TsGANKh SSSR), total of sixty-four denunciations from f. 396, op. 10 and 11 (letters to the newspaper *Krest'ianskaia gazeta,* 1938–39) and f. 7486 (Secretariat of Narkomzem SSSR); Rossiiskii tsentr khraneniia i izucheniia dokumentov noveishei istorii (hereafter cited as RTsKhIDNI, formerly the Central Party Archive, TsPA IM-L), total of twenty-six denunciations from f. 17, op. 85 (Central Committee: Sekretnyi otdel), op. 114 (Central Committee: Sekretariat-Orgbiuro), and op. 125 (Central Committee: Upravlenie propagandy i agitatsii), f. 475 (Glavsevmorputi—thanks to John McCannon for alerting me to this rich source of denunciations), and f. 613 (Central Control Commission); Smolensk Archive (located in the United States, U.S. National Archives), total of seventeen denunciations from WKP 190, 355, 362, 386, and 415 (Western oblast party committee); Tsentral'nyi gosudarstvennyi arkhiv goroda Moskvy (hereafter cited as TsGAOR g. Moskvy), total of three denunciations from f. 1474 (Rabkrin: complaints bureau); Tsentral'nyi gosudarstvennyi arkhiv goroda Sankt-Peterburga (hereafter cited as TsGA S-P), total of three denunciations from f. 1024 (Rabkrin/Control Commission, Leningrad guberniia) and f. 1027 (Rabkrin/Control Commission, Leningrad oblast); Tsentral'nyi gosudarstvennyi arkhiv istoriko-politicheskoi dokumentatsii Sankt-Peterburga (hereafter cited as TsGA IPD, formerly the Leningrad Party Archive, LPA), total of thirty denunciations from f. 24, op. 2g and 2v (Leningrad obkom: special sector); and Tsentral'nyi munitsipial'nyi arkhiv Moskvy (hereafter cited as TsMAM), total of three denunciations from f. 3109 (thanks to Viktoriia Tiazhel'nikova and her team for making available these denunciations from their database on *lishentsy*).

[16] See Kozlov, "Denunciation and Its Functions in Soviet Governance," in this issue, p. 887.

For the purposes of this article, a denunciation is defined as a written communication to the authorities, voluntarily offered, that provides damaging information about another person.[17] There was no standard form by which
authors identified their letters as denunciations, though the word "Statement"
(*Zaiavlenie*) or "Complaint" (*Zhaloba*) was sometimes written at the head of
the letter. I classified a letter as a denunciation by its content. The denunciations in my database span the period 1929–45, and the great majority (191 out
of 200) date from the 1930s.

The first three sections of this article deal with three major genres of denunciation: those concerning loyalty, social class, and "abuse of power." The subject of the fourth section is denunciations written by family members or dealing with moral offenses. The fifth section discusses the manipulative uses of
denunciation, with particular reference to professional feuds and rivalries and
"apartment" denunciations. The sixth section deals with anonymous denunciations and the general issue of secrecy, and the seventh section with the outcomes of denunciations. In the conclusion, I address more general questions
about the meanings and functions of denunciation in Stalin's Russia.

LOYALTY DENUNCIATIONS

This is the paradigmatic form of Communist-against-Communist denunciation. The most frequent specific accusation in these letters was that a Communist was hiding something disreputable in his past, usually support for Trotsky
or friendship with Trotskyites. Other allegations ran the gamut from "anti-
Soviet conversation" to terrorism and counterrevolutionary conspiracy. "Compromising facts" commonly cited include past membership in non-Communist
political parties, supporting the White armies during the Civil War, participat-
ing in uprisings against Soviet power, membership in opposition factions in
the party (Trotskyite, Zinovievite, Rightist), and contacts of any kind with Oppositionists, foreigners, or émigré relatives.

It was the duty of Communists to make known to the party any compromis-

---

[17] This follows the definition of denunciation (*donos*) given in a standard Soviet dictionary, namely, a secret communication to a representative of the regime or a superior
about somebody's illegal activity (S. I. Ozhegov, *Slovar' russkogo iazyka* [Moscow,
1964]). I have substituted "damaging information" for "illegal activity" because the
latter is too narrow to cover the range of proscribed, hence denunciable, behaviors. (It
was not illegal, e.g., to have been a supporter of Trotsky in the 1920s, yet many Communists were denounced for this in the 1930s.) Note that my definition covers only letters
written by citizens on their own initiative and in a private capacity. It excludes the
following types of written documents: reports (*doneseniia*) by regular police informers
or by officials writing in the line of duty, and denunciatory statements (*pokazaniia*)
solicited from citizens and prisoners by the NKVD in the course of interrogation or otherwise.

ing information about other Communists that came to their attention. Some writers of loyalty denunciations used the formulaic preamble "I consider it my party duty to inform you." But many dispensed with any introductory phrase or used the more ambiguous "I consider it necessary to inform you." Many such denunciations were evidently written out of fear of the consequences of *not* writing, especially during the Great Purges, when the volume of loyalty denunciations increased markedly.

Some loyalty denunciations appear to have been written in a spirit of public service, though such subjective evaluations of decontextualized texts are obviously fallible. For example, the Leningrad Communist writer Vera Ketlinskaia conveyed a kind of civic spirit, albeit on the hysterical side, in her letter to Leningrad party secretary Andrei Zhdanov about enemies in the Communist leadership of Komsomol'sk, a new town in the Soviet Far East from which she had just returned in the fall of 1937.[18] In more measured terms, a group of young South Osetian Komsomols working on the construction of the Moscow Metro wrote a collective letter addressed to Stalin, Kaganovich, Molotov, and Kalinin warning them of the degeneration of the party leadership in South Osetia as a result of Mensheviks and "opportunists" worming their way in.[19]

Other denunciations had a sound of genuine outrage. One indignant citizen, probably a young engineer, wrote to Nikolai Ezhov[20] in 1936 asking him to "pay attention to some outrageous facts" about the director of the "Red Flag" factory in Leningrad who made fun of young Communist engineers, mocked the factory party committee, helped people who had been arrested as terrorists by the NKVD, and on top of that was of alien social origin—the son of a rich merchant under the old regime.[21]

As might be expected, malice made itself felt in many denunciations, though no doubt the more skillful writers were able to conceal it. Perhaps more disconcerting than everyday malice was the spirit of the Young Avenger that imbued some denunciations from adolescent vigilantes. A fourteen-year-old village Komsomol member, for example, wrote to Stalin in 1937 in a tone of excited self-congratulation and blood lust about the local Trotskyites that remained to be arrested in his district, not to mention the bandits in the forest. This boy, eager to make his mark in the Pavlik Morozov mode, boasted that he had already "bagged" one kolkhoz chairman.[22]

During the Great Purges, as in several earlier periods of Russian history,

[18] TsGA IPD, f. 24, op. 2v, d. 2222, ll. 202–8.

[19] GARF, f. 5446, op. 82, d. 42, l. 103.

[20] The same Ezhov who headed the NKVD during the Great Purges. This denunciation, however, was sent to him (by name) at his earlier post in the Commission of Party Control.

[21] TsGA IPD, f. 24, op. 2v, d. 1570, ll. 216, 219.

[22] The verb *posadit'* whose colloquial meaning is to cause to be imprisoned, fortunately has no English analogue. Ibid., f. 24, op. 2v, d. 2226, ll. 78–79.

failure to denounce could have very serious consequences, particularly for a Communist. The archival files for 1937–38 contain many denunciations from Communists that were surely written from fear, or at least to be on the safe side, rather than out of any real sense of duty, outrage, or even malice. One such denunciation was sent to Gamarnik, head of the Red Army's political administration, in 1935.[23] Its subject was an anti-Soviet conversation at a drinking party the previous summer. In the presence of the writer (and "a lot of other comrades"), "comrade Smirnov, having had a bit to drink, made a speech in defense of Zinoviev and especially Trotsky." He said that "if Lenin were alive, Trotsky, Zinoviev, Bukharin, and the others would be in the Politburo and would have worked for the good of the party, and that in general the wheel of history would probably have turned in another direction." He also called Trotsky "exceptionally talented," second only to Lenin in the party. The comments were sufficiently rash that at least one listener was likely to pass them on—which meant that the others present would be in trouble for keeping silent. The writer's basically self-defensive motivation and lack of enthusiasm for his task was palpable: "I cannot, as a party member, fail to report this, despite the fact that it was at an evening party [*vecherinka*] and despite the fact that Smirnov was half drunk." The letter ended on a fine note of bathos: since Smirnov was reportedly "a professor of dialectics," the writer concluded, he "should not make such remarks even when drunk."

The Great Purges stimulated many denunciations about conspiracies and sinister signs and connections whose full import (the authors write) had only just become clear. In Siberia, a semiliterate woman farmworker wrote to the regional party committee in 1937 to say that reading "all those articles by comrade Zhdanov and Vyshinskii"[24] had made her wonder about the loyalty of a party organizer who had worked at her state farm in 1933: his mother-in-law, who came from Latvia, used the prerevolutionary salutation "sir" (*gospodin*), and the man himself had inherited sixty dollars from a Latvian relative.[25]

Early in 1937, a local prosecutor wrote in, apropos of the recent suicide of the Leningrad oblast prosecutor, Palgov, to say that he had just thought of something sinister: Palgov had a friend called Nechanov, also a prosecutor, whose wife had once denounced or threatened to denounce her husband as a Trotskyite. Were Palgov and Nechanov involved in some sort of plot together? Might this not explain both Palgov's suicide and Nechanov's strangely rapid promotion?[26]

An engineer wrote a loyalty denunciation about an official named Uralov

[23] Ibid., f. 24, op. 2v, d. 1518, l. 94.

[24] Andrei Zhdanov was the party leader who took over in Leningrad after Kirov's assassination. Andrei Vyshinskii was the state prosecutor in the famous show trials of former opposition leaders held in Moscow in 1936, 1937, and 1938.

[25] PANO, f. 3, op. 11, d. 41, l. 97.

[26] TsGA IPD, f. 24, op. 2v, d. 2478, ll. 25–26.

who was in charge of purchasing aircraft and determining their routes. Uralov always made the wrong decisions, and the writer had many conflicts with him. "At the time it seemed to me that Uralov was simply ignorant, uninformed, not a real engineer but just an incompetent," the engineer wrote to the Political Administration of the Northern Sea Routes in November 1937. "But after my investigation of the Tiumen' air route I analyzed a number of facts and came to the conclusion that *Uralov is an enemy, a wrecker*."[27]

Such illumination was sometimes conveyed in exalted tones. "I accuse Popov'ian, a party member since 1918, of being an enemy of the people, a Trotskyite," wrote M. P. Gribanova, a Communist, to her local party committee in October 1937. Gribanova had worked with Popov'ian when he was chief physician in a hospital on the island of Spitzbergen. She remembered that he and his wife had a very suspicious meeting behind closed doors with a Norwegian who came to the hospital at eight o'clock in the morning. "The conversation was conducted rather quietly, in English and sometimes in German. Before [the Norwegian] left, Popov'ian gave him a package and added something in German, but I don't know what it was."[28]

Sometimes there was a note of urgency, almost desperation, about the fact that an obvious enemy had so far escaped detection. "I don't understand why up to the present time S. P. Vaniushin still enjoys honor and respect. . . . Who is protecting him?" asked one baffled denouncer in May 1938.[29] "I have already written eight times to various places, but for some reason Vaniushin still survives unscathed." Given the facts cited in the letter, notably Vaniushin's close contacts with prominent Communist leaders who had been shot as enemies of the people, it was indeed surprising that Vaniushin remained at liberty. Such people were not only in great danger themselves but also constituted an involuntary danger to all around them. This was perhaps why the author, probably a colleague of Vaniushin's, was so anxious for Vaniushin to be arrested and removed from his environment.

Similar concerns are evident in one of the most striking denunciations I have encountered, a letter sent to the editor of *Pravda* (Lev Mekhlis) by a Komsomol student of a Leningrad technical institute in 1936.[30] The student was in "torment," he wrote, because N. V. Kitaev, another student at his institute, had just been reinstated in the party despite having supported Zinoviev in the party debates of 1925–26 and, worse, having been a coworker and perhaps even friend of one of the Leningrad oppositionists executed for complicity in Kirov's murder. "How can a parasite WHO ALWAYS SOBS WHEN HE HEARS LENIN'S

[27] RTsKhIDNI, f. 475, op. 1, d. 10, ll. 356–57.
[28] Ibid., l. 2.
[29] RTsKhIDNI, f. 475, op. 1, d. 16, ll. 180–82.
[30] TsGA IPD, f. 24, op. 2b, d. 1628, ll. 79–82.

NAME AND GROANS WHEN HE HEARS STALIN'S (those are not just words, comrade Mekhlis, but the appalling truth), how can such a person be allowed to remain within the walls of the institute; how can we, comrade Mekhlis, shelter such a snake in our bosom?" Since he became "so agitated" about Kitaev's continued presence, the author wrote, Mekhlis might suspect that he had some personal grievance against Kitaev. "No, comrade Mekhlis, it's much worse— for four years, until February 1935, we venerated him as a 'real party man,' politically highly developed, an activist, someone who always spoke up at every meeting and assembly, who could quote Lenin and Stalin and in our [the Komsomol members'] eyes was the INCARNATION OF PARTY CONSCIENCE, ethics, and PARTY SPIRIT." It was painful to recall that the Komsomol students of the institute had defended Kitaev a few years ago when the institute tried to expel him for academic failure. But now this previous admiration had turned to hatred.

Since Kirov's murder, [Kitaev] arouses an animal fear in me, an organic disgust. Just as I previously venerated him and respected him, now I fear him and expect him to do something terribly evil, some irreparable harm to the whole country. If you could have seen the unfeigned joy we all felt . . . when we learned of his expulsion [later revoked] from the institute after the execution of Zinoviev and Kamenev. . . . It is impossible and criminal to allow him to finish his studies at the institute, because, comrade Mekhlis, even THE CAMPS OF THE NKVD WILL NOT REFORM HIM. . . . I am terribly sorry now that he was not sitting next to his heroes Zinoviev and Kamenev [in the court that ordered their execution].

CLASS DENUNCIATIONS

An individual's social class (or the social class ascribed to him) was a key attribute in the Soviet Union in the 1920s and 1930s.[31] According to Bolshevik/ Marxist thinking, certain classes were ipso facto enemies of the revolution, and their members had to be stigmatized and marginalized by various discriminatory measures (deprivation of voting rights, restricted access to higher education, ineligibility for party and Komsomol membership, and so on). The main objects of stigmatization were members of the urban bourgeoisie (both the old prerevolutionary and the new "NEP" bourgeoisie), the old nobility, kulaks, and the clergy. Such people were categorized as "social aliens" (*sotsial'no-chuzhye, chuzhdye elementy*), much as Jews, Gypsies, and other "asocials" were categorized as *Gemeinschaftsfremde* in Nazi Germany.

To avoid stigma, many people with "bad" class backgrounds tried to conceal them. This in turn made it imperative for Communists and other friends of the

[31] On this theme, see my article "Ascribing Class: The Construction of Social Identity in Soviet Russia," *Journal of Modern History* 65 (December 1993): 745–70.

revolution to uncover the identities that had been hidden. An important category of denunciations consists of the unmasking of class enemies. Class was an equally popular subject with urban and rural writers. Interestingly enough, among urban writers non-Communists seem to have been more likely to write class denunciations than Communists were. Their letters often hinted that party and government leaders were too lenient on questions of class.

A good proportion of class denunciations simply stated that someone who was a member of the party or held a responsible position was of alien class origin and ought to be expelled from the party and dismissed from his job. For example, a person identifying himself as nonparty wrote to the Leningrad party committee in 1935 to say that there were many class enemies (whom he named) in the local soviet: two daughters of a rich kulak who had been arrested and died in prison were working in the education department, the daughter of a former landowner was employed as court secretary, and there were kulaks in the agriculture department and "no fewer than three kulaks" in the State Bank.[32]

A more passionate denunciation came from nine "old party members, civil war veterans," who wrote to Molotov in 1934 about class enemies in responsible positions in the Crimean party organization: four merchants' sons; two priest's sons, including one who was a former tsarist officer; three mullah's sons, one of them rector of the local Communist University; and so on. Everybody knew about this but kept quiet. The authors were afraid to sign their letter for fear of retaliation. But if Molotov did not respond to their letter, they wrote, "then we will appeal to comrade Stalin, and if comrade Stalin does not take measures, then one must say straight out that our regime is not socialist but KULAK."[33]

A Siberian miner wrote to the regional party secretary to denounce the chairman of the local trade union, whom he had just heard was "the son of a big merchant," married to a kulak's daughter, who had gotten into the party by changing his name and concealing his real identity. "This bastard should be driven out of the trade union," the miner wrote. "If you don't take measures, I will write directly to the Central Committee of the party."[34]

The implied threats in these last two denunciations were atypical but by no means unique. A small but distinct subgroup of denouncers seemed to enjoy the sensation of bullying the important man to whom they addressed their letters and/or hinting that he, and perhaps the regime as a whole, shared the sins of the individual being denounced.

The underlying theme of many class denunciations was resentment that

[32] TsGA IPD, f. 24, op. 2v, d. 1518, ll. 164–66.
[33] GARF, f. 5446, op. 82, d. 27, l. 172.
[34] PANO, f. 3, op. 9, d. 801, l. 209.

"they" (the formerly privileged and powerful, who had retained at least part of their power under the new regime) "still treat us as they used to in the old days." When the Siberian Waterways Administration was going through a routine purge in 1930, several workers with memories of the old days wrote to the purge commission to denounce "bourgeois specialists," holdovers from the equivalent prerevolutionary bureaucracy.[35] These were people who had been responsible for having sailors flogged and workers arrested before the revolution, the letters stated. They had served Kolchak's (anti-Bolshevik) administration willingly in 1918; they were protectors of counterrevolutionaries. "This citizen Gavril Meshkov is cunning," one worker wrote about the specialist who had headed the Waterways Administration under the tsar. "I know his tricks since 1905 as well as I know my own five fingers." According to the writer, Meshkov pretended to be loyal to Soviet power, but in fact his record showed that he would work for any regime—tsarist, Kolchak's, or Soviet.[36]

Women workers at the Leningrad Knitting Plant wrote to a newspaper in 1931 to denounce the manager of their plant, a former entrepreneur (they claimed), whose associates were of the same bourgeois ilk. This "former petty boss" (*byvshii khoziaichik*) treated the workers like any capitalist, "making them have hysterics, and he answers just like a little capitalist, 'If you don't like it you can leave, I will hire others in your place.'"[37]

In a similar vein, a group of peasants denouncing their kolkhoz chairman in 1938 recalled that his father, a labor contractor, had always exploited and cheated poor peasants: "That's how Romanenkov's father carried on the whole time up to the revolution, and made people's lives miserable and beat them like a Fascist contractor; the old people in the district know that, but the rural soviet [leaders] themselves, being young, don't know it."[38]

Class discrimination was deeply embedded in Soviet law as well as custom until it was abolished (at least in theory) by the new Soviet Constitution of 1936; and many class denunciations had the aim of invoking a specific legal or administrative sanction against the person denounced.[39] For example, a trade unionist wrote to the Central Electoral Commission in 1929 arguing that a woman living in his neighborhood should be deprived of the vote because she was not an unskilled laborer, as she claimed, but a former nun who made a

---

[35] This kind of purge (*chistka*) was a review of white-collar personnel in government agencies whose purpose was to weed out (i.e., to dismiss, not to arrest) social and political undesirables.

[36] GANO, f. 288, op. 2, d. 902, ll. 4–5, 6.

[37] TsGA S-P, f. 1027, op. 2, d. 860o, l. 52.

[38] RGAE, f. 396, op. 10, d. 128, ll. 66–69.

[39] For denunciations of persons deprived of voting rights, see Golfo Alexopoulos, "Rights and Passage: Marking Outcasts and Making Citizens in Soviet Russia, 1926–1936" (Ph.D. diss., University of Chicago, 1996), chap. 2.

good living trading in icons and crosses.[40] Another denunciation was sent to the Commission on Passportization in 1933 with the aim of preventing the issue of passports to persons the author claimed were class aliens.[41]

When Communists wrote denunciations on class grounds, the purpose was usually to unmask another party member who was concealing an "alien" class background. In one such letter (1935), an old Communist (of Civil War vintage) wrote to the regional party committee to denounce a Communist woman called Khomlianskaia, currently residing in Novosibirsk. According to the writer's information, Khomlianskaia claimed to have joined the party organization in his district in 1922. That was impossible, he said, because he knew her to be the sister of a rich wool and leather merchant who had fought against the Reds in the Civil War and subsequently had been exiled. Evidently, therefore, she had obtained her party card fraudulently and had lied about her social origin. Moreover, the writer added, she was probably still in touch with her capitalist brother, in whose home she had been reared and educated, for "according to my information Khomlianskaia's brother is also in Novosibirsk at the present time and trades in cigarettes in a kiosk opposite the Soviet Hotel."[42]

Vigilance about class enemies was particularly strong in the late 1920s and early 1930s, the time of collectivization, dekulakization, expropriation of urban Nepmen, and mass arrests of priests. Any Communist worth his salt was going to be watching local "kulaks" like a hawk, as did the Komsomol from Kuntsevo who wrote to the district security police (OGPU) in 1933:

Pay attention to the citizens living in Usovo village, Stepan Vasil'evich Vatusov and his wife Nadezhda Senafant'evna, since according to my observations of them they . . . are like kulaks working *by stealth;* up to 1930–31 they had their own separate farm with about five hectares of land which they worked by exploiting the *bedniak* population. The land has now been transferred to the kolkhoz, but [the Vatusovs] are making money on their well-appointed house, which has all kinds of extensions, by renting it out to vacationers. . . . In all probability they have gold because when they come from Moscow they bring all kinds of packages whose wrapping could only be from Torgsin.[43]

Some "class" denunciations have the look of preemptive strikes by people whose own origins made them vulnerable to attack. For example, in 1937 a statistician denounced the party secretary of his district, a man he had apparently known from childhood, saying that he was the son of a local scribe who had himself worked as a scribe (a damaging sign of willingness to serve the

[40] TsMAM, f. 3109, op. 2, d. 2140.

[41] TsGAOR g. Moskvy, f. 1474, op. 7, d. 79, ll. 86–87.

[42] PANO, f. 3, op. 9, d. 801, l. 10.

[43] GASO, f. 88, op. 2, d. 62, ll. 125–26. In the early 1930s, state Torgsin stores sold scarce goods for hard currency, gold, and silver only (no rubles).

old regime, despite the lowly status of the job) and had also rented out part of his house as a commercial teahouse. The writer added that this same man had been spreading slander about *his* social origins.[44]

Despite the 1936 Constitution, old class stigmas and suspicions were not forgotten even in the late 1930s. Reading in 1938 of the appointment of V. S. Tiukov as deputy chairman of the State Bank, an alert resident of the village of Maksimovka in Voronezh oblast realized that a class enemy might have penetrated the highest ranks of government. He wrote to Molotov to warn him that this could be Valentin Tiukov (or perhaps his brother Vitalii), the son of a big local landowner, Stepan Tiukov, who had suddenly vanished from the district with his entire family around 1925.[45] As late as December 1940 a Communist wrote in to complain that one Mikhailov, recently admitted to candidate membership of the party, was ineligible for party membership on class grounds[46] "since his parents were former owners of furnished rooms and commercial bathhouses in the city of Tambov."[47]

"ABUSE OF POWER" DENUNCIATIONS

"Abuse of power" (*zloupotreblenie vlast'iu*) is one of the most interesting categories of Stalinist denunciation.[48] These letters in fact straddle the boundary between denunciation (where the emphasis is on wrongdoing by another person) and complaint (where the emphasis is on injury to the writer). In the Soviet period, as before the revolution, most writers of "abuse" denunciations were peasants, though one sometimes encounters urban denunciations of a similar type against small-town bosses, factory directors, and so on.[49] Kolkhoz chairmen were by far the most popular target of peasants' accusations. These denunciations are quintessential "weapons of the weak," containing many references to the writers' powerlessness and poverty and invoking natural justice rather than formal law.

Unlike the peasant petitions from the 1905 period analyzed by Andrew Verner, Soviet "abuse" letters rarely came from the whole village commu-

[44] TsGA IPD, f. 24, op. 2g, d. 15, ll. 3–8.

[45] GARF, f. 5446, op. 82, d. 65, l. 53.

[46] In fact, the party had dropped formal class criteria in the selection of members a few years earlier.

[47] RTsKhIDNI, f. 475, op. 1, d. 28, l. 395.

[48] In the *Krest'ianskaia gazeta* archive for 1938–39 (RGAE, f. 396, op. 10 and 11), such denunciations are collected in files headed "Wrecking and Abuses in the Collective Farms" (*Vreditel'stvo i zloupotrebleniia v kolkhozakh*) or variants thereof.

[49] For example, PANO, f. 3, op. 11, d. 41, ll. 31–36; TsGA IPD, f. 24, op. 2g, d. 48, ll. 22–25.

nity, though it was not uncommon for more than one kolkhoznik to sign (but not more than five or six).[50] But it was equally rare for an "abuse" letter to be written as if it represented only the opinion of the individual writer. "All the kolkhozniks are indignant," is a standard phrase. Often an individual author will name other kolkhozniks who have denounced the same offender to the authorities,[51] or list the names of kolkhozniks who will back up his version of events,[52] or even enclose a copy of the minutes of a kolkhoz meeting censuring the offender.[53]

The "abuse" letter of the 1930s had a Soviet as well as a prerevolutionary antecedent—namely, the reports sent to newspapers by rural correspondents (*sel'kory*) in the 1920s.[54] By the late 1930s, however, that movement had withered. Only a small minority of peasant writers to the newspaper *Krest'ianskaia gazeta* in 1938 called themselves *sel'kory* or had the *sel'kor*'s typical self-identification with Soviet power and the Communist Party, though a larger number had borrowed something of the style of the *sel'kor* reports published in newspapers over the years, using Soviet terms like *unmask* and *wrecker,* and occasionally providing titles for their letters (e.g., "Who is plundering kolkhoz assets?"). Most writers of "abuse" denunciations in the late 1930s were just ordinary peasants with grievances against the kolkhoz leaders. The purpose of writing the denunciation was to get the chairman or brigade leader dismissed from his job (or, for those of a more vengeful character, arrested).

Despite the *sel'kor* antecedent, rural "abuse" denunciations were sent not only to newspapers. Peasants sent exactly the same kind of letter—sometimes literally copies of their letters to the newspapers—to district and regional prosecutors, regional party and soviet leaders, land departments, and the NKVD.[55]

Unlike the "loyalty" and "class" denunciations discussed earlier, the typical "abuse" denunciation does not focus on a single or central attribute or action. Instead, it is a grab bag of all the crimes, shortfalls, mistakes, defects, and black marks that can plausibly be attributed to the denouncee, particularly those that are likely to weigh heavily with higher authorities. At the top of the list in my sample is "stealing" from kolkhozniks. This is not ordinary theft (usually) but, rather, the kind of misappropriation of kolkhoz funds that was

[50] See Andrew M. Verner, "Discursive Strategies in the 1905 Revolution: Peasant Petitions from Vladimir Province," *Russian Review* 54, no. 1 (1995): 65–90.

[51] RGAE f. 396, op. 10, d. 161, l. 289.

[52] Ibid., d. 128, ll. 276–78.

[53] Ibid., d. 142, ll. 493, 496–97.

[54] See above, p. 833. For a detailed study of *sel'kory,* see Steven R. Coe, "Peasants, the State, and the Languages of NEP: The Rural Correspondents Movement in the Soviet Union, 1924–1928" (Ph.D. diss., University of Michigan, 1993).

[55] Reference to such copies may be found in many letters to *Krest'ianskaia gazeta,* e.g., RGAE, f. 396, op. 10, d. 128, ll. 158–59; d. 142, ll. 84–87, 173–77, 493, 496–97; d. 161, ll. 289, 317–18.

easily done by kolkhoz chairmen and accountants: cheating kolkhozniks on labor-day payments, confiscating their animals, imposing illegal fines and a variety of other forms of extortion, treating the kolkhoz horses as personal property, drawing money out of the kolkhoz bank account for personal use, and so on.

One such denunciation described how kolkhoz leaders refused to give a deserving kolkhoznik twenty-four kilos of flour, extorting his fur coat in payment: "These kulak scum take grain themselves, they sell sixteen kilos [on the market] for fifty rubles a *pud,* while honest toilers go hungry. Comrades, where is your vigilance? Twenty years of Soviet power and this kind of abomination and terrorizing of the dark masses continues."[56]

Next on the list of offenses cited in rural "abuse" denunciations was "suppression of criticism," a catchphrase that covered a range of arbitrary and tyrannical practices on the part of the chairman. "Kolkhoz chairman F. A. Zadorozhnyi does not allow kolkhozniks to talk at the meeting, if somebody tries to say something he Zadorozhnyi says why are you trying to disrupt the meeting you are not our man; because of that kolkhozniks don't go to meetings, they say why should we go if Zadorozhnyi won't let us speak and stifles criticism and self-criticism."[57]

Writers of such denunciations often complained that the chairman in question was a district appointee who had been forced on the kolkhozniks against their will. One letter to *Krest'ianskaia gazeta* described how the kolkhozniks of "Freedom" kolkhoz had tried to dismiss the chairman at a general meeting but were prevented by the head of the district land department. When they asked why they could not choose their own officers, "he said straight out that's impossible and wouldn't let the kolkhozniks speak." (Whatever the ultimate outcome of this complaint, it was forwarded to the district party secretary with a strong recommendation from *Krest'ianskaia gazeta* that the land department should respect "kolkhoz democracy" and remove the offending chairman.)[58]

Glaring economic disasters such as unmet procurement quotas, potatoes left to rot in the field, or the flight of hungry kolkhozniks from the kolkhoz were frequently listed in denunciations among the sins of kolkhoz chairmen. No less frequent were indignant reports of the chairmen's and brigade leaders' offenses against the peasants' dignity: treating kolkhozniks with contempt (*izdevatel'-stvo*); insulting, beating, and cursing them ("He curses all the kolkhozniks in foul language; he can't find words bad enough to call the kolkhozniks").[59]

---

[56] Ibid., f. 396, op. 10, d. 128, ll. 158–59.
[57] Ibid., d. 86, ll. 71–73.
[58] Ibid., d. 65, ll. 238–40.
[59] Ibid., d. 161, ll. 84–87.

Favoring relatives in the allocation of jobs and tasks, use of kolkhoz horses, and selection of candidates to go on study courses to the district center was another standard accusation in "abuse" letters. Drunkenness was often on the list of offenses, particularly in connection with "drinking up" kolkhoz assets (as in "the chairman took two pigs to market but stayed in town for three days and drank up all the money").

Just as peasants quickly learned to use the term *kulak* to discredit kolkhoz chairmen with higher authorities, so also they were quick to pick up the preferred rhetorical terms of indictment of the Great Purges period: "enemy of the people," "terrorist," "Trotskyite."

The position in our kolkhoz is pitiful. Comrades, answer us please where we can find justice. We often read the papers and see in them what great evil has been done in our Soviet Union by enemies of the people of the rightist-Trotskyite bloc, how widely it has spread, how they wrecked agriculture, how many horses perished and pedigreed cattle.... We as kolkhozniks people still unenlightened cannot get justice, for example in our kolkhoz there is a very large amount of stealing of kolkhoz property [details follow on thefts by brigade leaders].... How many times we have told our local authorities about this, both the kolkhoz board and also the chairman of the rural soviet, Savoni, who has now been exposed as an enemy of the people and the police chief Arkhipov who has also been taken away by organs of the NKVD ... but there were no results.[60]

The peasants understood the mechanism of smearing by association and used it often when district leaders—who could always be more or less accurately represented as the patrons of lower-level bosses like rural soviet and kolkhoz chairmen—were arrested as "enemies" during the Great Purges. For example: "Many times I as a *sel'kor* have sent signals to Chistiakov, chairman of the rural soviet, and the Bol'shesol'skii district [leaders] about wrecking by the kolkhoz chairman and stableman, but they were deaf to these signals. Now the district soviet chairman Bugeev has been sent to prison as a wrecker [and it is] time to get all the other wreckers."[61]

Peasants who denounced their kolkhoz chairmen or other local officeholders wanted them to be punished—"given what they deserve." They asked higher authorities to "help us purge the kolkhoz of these rascals," "help us to rid ourselves once and for all of these criminals," "deliver us from these enemies of the people who have gotten into the kolkhoz."[62] Some letters explicitly asked that the offender be dismissed from his post or prosecuted.[63] One writer, who

---

[60] Ibid., d. 65, ll. 212–14.
[61] Ibid., d. 161, ll. 29–32; see also ibid., d. 142, ll. 173–77.
[62] Ibid., f. 396, op. 10, d. 26, ll. 137–39 and 158–59; d. 87, ll. 125–26 and 281–84; d. 161, ll. 203–4; TsGA IPD, f. 24, op. 2b, d. 1570, l. 49.
[63] RGAE, f. 396, op. 10, d. 142, ll. 141–42; d. 161, ll. 84–87.

had already sent material on her kolkhoz chairman to the local NKVD, was particularly forthright about the importance of arresting him. What the authorities needed to do, she wrote, was to "interview kolkhozniks on site, expose Bakaliaev as an enemy of the people, remove him from his job, prosecute him, and take him away from the kolkhoz."[64]

FAMILY AND MORALS DENUNCIATIONS

The intense publicity given to Pavlik Morozov's denunciation might suggest that denunciation of one family member by another was commonplace in Stalin's Russia. But the archives of the 1930s (in contrast to those of the late Imperial period studied by Jeffrey Burds, as well as those of later Soviet times) offer little support for this hypothesis.[65] To be sure, there are individual cases of denunciation within the family. But in general this genre of denunciation is conspicuous by its absence. Thus, the story to be told in this section is essentially that of the dog that failed to bark.

The archives of the 1930s do contain a large number of "family" letters that are not denunciations. There are many letters from parents asking that their children be given medical help, be admitted to technical schools and universities, or be placed in orphanages (on the grounds that the parents lacked the means to support them). There are letters from wives asking that their absent husbands be traced and required to pay child support, and there are "confessional" letters (*ispovedi*) in which women write to a distant authority figure, usually a regional party leader, describing their misery at their husband's unfaithfulness or desertion. From the late 1930s, the archives contain an enormous number of appeals and inquiries from wives whose husbands have been arrested during the Great Purges, together with similar letters from the husbands, parents, and children of victims. Such letters almost invariably assert the innocence of the arrested relative and plead for his or her release.[66]

In the last type of letter we can perhaps find a clue to the rarity of denunciatory letters about family members. Reading these letters, it is difficult not to feel that, contrary to Hannah Arendt's "atomization" thesis,[67] family bonds in Russia were strengthened, not weakened, by Soviet terror.[68] But there were

---

[64] Ibid., d. 161, ll. 84–87.

[65] See Jeffrey Burds, "Culture of Denunciation," in this issue.

[66] See my "Supplicants and Citizens: Public Letter-Writing in Soviet Russia in the 1930s," *Slavic Review* 55, no. 1 (Spring 1996): 78–105.

[67] Hannah Arendt, *The Origins of Totalitarianism,* new ed. (New York, 1973).

[68] In interviewing refugees from the Soviet Union after the war, the Harvard Project found that respondents from all social levels were more likely to say that "under Soviet conditions the family drew closer together" than the reverse. This response was particularly common from members of families in which a close relative had been arrested by

also practical reasons not to denounce a close family member during the Great Purges, as well as in the earlier rural terror associated with dekulakization. If one family member was dekulakized or branded an "enemy of the people," the whole family suffered. When kulaks were deported in the early 1930s, their families were deported with them. In the late 1930s, special camps were established in the gulag for "wives of traitors to the motherland."

Of course, there are exceptions to all rules. In 1927, the wife of an assistant prosecutor in the Ukraine wrote to Stalin complaining about the abuse she had been suffering at her husband's hands since she had denounced him as an Oppositionist involved in preparing for an armed uprising(!).[69] In 1938, an angry ex-husband, denied custody of his young daughter by the court in the divorce settlement, wrote to the office of President Kalinin to denounce his former wife for debauchery and for the fact that her lover had been arrested as an enemy of the people.[70]

Ex-spouses, of course, fall into a special category. Many people have grievances against former husbands and wives, and denunciation was one way to settle the score. This thought evidently occurred to someone in the Soviet propaganda machine. In mid-1937, just after the secret courts-martial of Marshal Tukhachevskii, General Iakir, and other leaders of the Soviet Army, *Pravda* announced that it had received a letter from the former wife of Iakir in which she "renounces and curses [*proklinaet*] her former husband as a traitor and betrayer of the motherland."[71] Like the Pavlik Morozov story, this had the look of an example for others to emulate. But a year later the newspaper changed its tune and deplored "false" (i.e., malicious) denunciations from angry ex-spouses.[72]

As far as Pavlik Morozov's example is concerned, there certainly was a type of adolescent Young Avenger who wrote denunciations freely and recklessly in the hope of becoming a hero. But even would-be Pavliks did not usually write about their own fathers and mothers. The denunciations of this type that

---

the secret police. Alex Inkeles and Raymond A. Bauer, *The Soviet Citizen: Daily Life in a Totalitarian Society* (1959; New York, 1968), pp. 211–13.

[69] RTsKhIDNI, f. 17, op. 85, d. 492, l. 37.

[70] GARF, f. 3316, op. 29, d. 312, ll. 12–13.

[71] *Pravda* (June 18, 1937), p. 6. This announcement was made in the "Chronicle" section. *Pravda* did not publish the text of the letter.

[72] The example cited in *Pravda* (June 8, 1938), p. 6, was a "false denunciation" from a former wife and her brother alleging that the husband had sold his passport to foreigners on a trip abroad. Although *Pravda*'s intervention suggests that denunciations from ex-spouses were common, this is not confirmed by my reading of the archives of the 1930s (though, judging by the Latvian party archives of the postwar period [see n. 78 below], it certainly became common a decade later). It is possible, of course, that some ex-spouses were disguising their identity or writing anonymous denunciations.

I have encountered target people in the surrounding community—neighbors, teachers, schoolmates.[73]

While spontaneous written denunciations of parents by their children seem to have been rare, it was not uncommon during the Great Purges for the school-age children of arrested "enemies of the people" to be forced to repudiate them orally in public at school or Komsomol meetings. Occasionally, as in the Iakir case, such repudiations appeared in print. But such practices evidently aroused popular revulsion, and in the spring of 1938, despite the official endorsement of the Pavlik Morozov cult, a regional newspaper, *Krasnaia Tatariia,* protested strongly against them. The occasion was the publication in a smaller local newspaper of a letter in which a young man accused his father, an agricultural laborer, of being an "enemy of the people" because he had stolen feed from the state farm where he worked. "The whole tone of the letter is obviously phoney," *Krasnaia Tatariia* commented, clearly hinting that the district news-paper had fabricated the letter or forced the author to write it. "This letter did not meet with the reader's approval. It only morally crushed the unfortunate father. What kind of joke is this, that a man's own son would publicly [*vsenar-odno*] call his father an enemy of the people and repudiate him."[74]

Occasional denunciations of in-laws are to be found in the archives, though in most cases there is an obvious self-protective motive. One Communist de-nounced his father-in-law as a kulak in 1930, when the older man fled the village and took refuge in the writer's city apartment. He did this unwillingly, and he lived to regret it (as he wrote indignantly seven years later) when in 1937 his "kulak ties" (i.e., his relationship with his father-in-law) led to his expulsion from the party.[75]

Letters from wives about child support, as well as "confessional" letters from abandoned wives, sometimes had an element of denunciation, but this was not their predominant flavor. With rare exceptions, such letters did not ask that the delinquent husband be punished. The letters about child support were focused on collecting the money,[76] while the "confessional" letters asked for moral support, understanding, and the opportunity for a personal meeting with

[73] See TsGA IPD, f. 24, op. 2v, d. 2226, ll. 78–79; GARF, f. 5446, op. 81a, d. 335, l. 29, and op. 82, d. 94, l. 19. For a typical Young Avenger denunciation, see above, p. 838.
[74] *Krasnaia Tatariia* (Kazan') (April 5, 1938), p. 2.
[75] PANO, f. 3, op. 11, d. 542, ll. 240–41. See also the quasi-denunciation of a father-in-law, recently arrested by the NKVD, from one of Molotov's stenographers in GARF, f. 5446, op. 82, d. 56, l. 22.
[76] One exception was the 1934 letter from a deceived and abandoned wife of a Com-munist, who, while noting that he had paid her nothing for support of their child, seemed more interested in getting him punished or at least damaging his reputation than in the financial aspect. TsGA IPD, f. 24, op. 2g, d. 769, l. 78.

the addressee. No doubt women did not frame these letters as denunciations in the 1930s because the regime was still relatively uninterested in punishing people for moral delinquency. It is true that the antiabortion law of 1936 introduced short prison terms for nonpayment of child support and raised the price of divorce, but "no fault" divorce remained.[77] When a much stricter divorce law was introduced after the war, requiring demonstration of fault, the letters written by abandoned wives quickly acquired the character of denunciations.[78]

Questions of sexual morality were not major concerns in Soviet society in the 1930s, judging by their infrequent appearance in denunciations. After 1936, when it became a criminal offense punishable by imprisonment to perform an abortion or to force a woman to have one,[79] a few abortion denunciations appeared: for example, a 1938 denunciation of a kolkhoz chairman in Kursk included the allegation that he had forced his wife to have an abortion, from which she had died.[80]

Although male homosexuality was outlawed in 1934, I have encountered no denunciations for this or any other "deviant" sexual act. The only sexual offense that seems to have interested writers of denunciations was female promiscuity. Allegations that women administrators, or the wives of administrators, had lovers and rewarded them with favors and advancement were not uncommon. These letters follow the familiar "Catherine the Great" trope, in which a woman's power is juxtaposed with her unbridled sexual appetites and both are condemned as perversions of nature. "All this gossip about my past is meant to discredit me as a leader," wrote a woman party official in a complaint about denunciations that falsely accused her of having affairs with male colleagues.[81] One anonymous denunciation, written in block capitals by "an employee of the *raikom* [district party committee]" in 1935, dispensed with any talk of lovers and focused on a woman's undue sexual influence on her husband, who headed the district party committee in which she worked: "Zolina is Kasimov's second wife and therefore all the *raikom* staffers are in Zolina's hands, and if she doesn't like someone, then under the influence of a sweet minute in bed she only has to say [something] to Kasimov and the next day Zolina's

[77] Decree of June 27, 1936, "On the prohibition of abortions, . . . the strengthening of criminal penalties for nonpayment of alimony, and on certain changes in the legislation on divorce" (*Izvestiia* [June 28, 1936]).

[78] There are many such denunciations in the Latvian Central Committee files for the late 1940s and early 1950s: see LVA SPDN, f. 101, op. 12, d. 290; op. 13, d. 387; op. 15, d. 597, and so on.

[79] See n. 73 above. Women who had abortions were not liable to any penalty but "public contempt" (*obshchestvennoe poritsanie*) and fines for repeat offenders. I have not come across any denunciations of women for having abortions.

[80] RGAE, f. 396, op. 10, d. 87, l. 207.

[81] TsGA IPD, f. 24, op. 2v, d. 1514, ll. 28–30.

request will be carried out and the staffers have to suffer. . . . It is necessary to mount a campaign against sexual debauchery [*razvrat*] in the organizations and dismiss Zolina from the *raikom*."[82]

Women rarely denounced men for sexual harrassment (to use an anachronistic term). In the *Krest'ianskaia gazeta* archive, for example, there are very few denunciations of local officials by peasant women alleging that the men had forced the women to have sex with them, although we know from other sources that this was by no means an unusual phenomenon.[83] One of the rare exceptions, a letter by a peasant woman named Suslova from Krasnodar, gave a vivid description of her attempted rape by a local official, Pavlenko:

On March 2, 1938, [Pavlenko] came to Dakhovskaia stanitsa, drank himself stupid at eight in the evening came to the apartment of Elena Suslova and said: "Come to the soviet the NKVD summons you." The woman was frightened and asks why. He answers you won't come back from there, and on the way he says everything is in my hands I can save you Suslova. She began to implore him he throws himself on her and begins to do unspeakable things. Suslova began defending herself and begging him Pavlenko says if you are stubborn it will be worse we'll throw you in prison. . . . Despite Pavlenko's threats Suslova still managed to run away home. He caught her and pulled at her, trying to rape her. Suslova continued to cry out and defend herself. Pavlenko seeing that he is losing takes hold of Suslova and tries to throw her in the well but because he was drunk he slipped and lost the chance. And Suslova ran into the house all beaten up after that she lay in bed all bruised, with swollen arms. But Pavlenko wasn't punished. . . . I Suslova beg the editors of *Krest'ianskaia gazeta* to help me bring this criminal to justice.[84]

MANIPULATIVE USES

The Soviet state was very responsive to denunciations. This responsiveness meant that it was always vulnerable to manipulation by denunciation writers with personal agendas. Regional officials were well aware that peasants were using mutual denunciation as a tool to pursue village feuds.[85] In one case the newspaper *Krest'ianskaia gazeta* uncovered an elaborate confidence trick exploiting the convention of "abuse of power" denunciation. Two Belorussian con men joined a kolkhoz in Krasnodar and set out to discredit the kolkhoz chairman. Their method was to encourage the kolkhozniks first to criticize the chairman at kolkhoz meetings and then to use these data to write plausible and

---

[82] Ibid., d. 1518, l. 62.

[83] See, e.g., the statements (*pokazaniia*) that the NKVD collected from five kolkhoz women in the course of a broader investigation of a kolkhoz chairman: Smolensk Archive, WKP 355: 48.

[84] RGAE, f. 396, op. 10, d. 66, l. 180. I have retained some of the grammatical and syntactical peculiarities of the original.

[85] See Fitzpatrick, *Stalin's Peasants* (n. 7 above), pp. 259–61.

circumstantial "abuse" denunciations. The aim was to force the chairman out of office, have their own man appointed, and get control of kolkhoz assets.[86]

A different kind of manipulative use of denunciations occurred in the cultural and scientific professions, which were often characterized by intense factional fighting as well as by close client-patron relations between leading members of the professions and political leaders. The use of denunciations as a weapon in the factional struggles of Soviet architects has been well illustrated from archival materials by Hugh Hudson.[87] The files of Viacheslav Molotov (chairman of Sovnarkom and member of the Politburo) contain many denunciations sent to him by "clients" who sought his support against their professional rivals. For example, the wife of a biologist denounced a powerful Communist in the same profession as "a vulgarian who pulls the wool over people's eyes, a pitiful scientific pigmy, a plagiarist and compiler" who had conducted a five-year persecution of her husband.[88] In the humanities, academician Derzhavin denounced academician Deborin in similar terms;[89] and the Communist historian I. I. Mints begged Molotov to save him from the consequences of a false denunciation alleging that he was a friend of the disgraced literary journalist Leopol'd Averbakh.[90]

A young Communist mathematician at Moscow State University was the author of a denunciation of the physicist Petr Kapitsa that, despite its postwar date, echoed the militant spirit of the Cultural Revolution of the early 1930s. Kapitsa, regarded with suspicion by many Communist and "nativist" colleagues on account of his Cambridge sojourn in the early 1930s, was accused of expressing antisoviet views, leading a Western-oriented clique that monopolized funds and appointments in physics, and behaving contemptuously toward Soviet physicists outside the clique—especially those who were Communists and Soviet patriots, of lower-class origin, and less cosmopolitan than Kapitsa and his friends. It is a measure of Kapitsa's standing with the top party leadership that, despite the fact that these accusations were perfectly credible, the denunciation was dismissed by a high official as nothing more than a product of professional feuding and rivalry.[91]

[86] RGAE, f. 396, op. 10, d. 67, l. 219. For a similar case, see TsGA IPD, f. 24, op. 2v, d. 1534, ll. 105, 109.
[87] See Hugh D. Hudson, Jr., "Terror in Soviet Architecture: The Murder of Mikhail Okhitovich," *Slavic Review* 51, no. 3 (Fall 1992): 455, 462–63.
[88] GARF, f. 5446, op. 82, d. 51, l. 144.
[89] TsGA IPD, f. 24, op. 2v, d. 2220, ll. 103–5. This letter, although sent to Molotov, was forwarded to Zhdanov at the Leningrad party committee.
[90] GARF, f. 5446, op. 82, d. 53, l. 130.
[91] RTsKhIDNI, f. 17, op. 125, d. 361, ll. 19–31, 37–49 (Central Committee department of agitation and propaganda). The official who commented was Sergei Kaftanov of the Committee for Affairs of Higher Education. These documents come from 1945–46. Presumably, similar denunciations would have been found in the agitprop depart-

Theaters, particularly the Bolshoi Theater in Moscow and the Kirov Theater in Leningrad, were notorious for the volume of mutual denunciations they generated. "Anonymous letters on the ballet company of the Kirov Theater are coming in almost every day to various institutions," stated a memo from a Leningrad official to Zhdanov in 1940.[92] The agitprop files in Moscow contain many letters from leading actors, actresses, and opera singers denouncing the theater directors who had insulted them and failed to give them appropriate roles.[93]

"Apartment" denunciations provide a particularly good example of the manipulative uses of denunciation. In the former Soviet Union, even now, the term "apartment denunciation" is instantly comprehensible. The context it evokes is that of the acute urban overcrowding that lasted for decades—in its most severe form from the beginning of the 1930s to the 1960s. During this time, apartments formerly occupied by a single family became "communal," with one family per room; the kitchen and bathroom were shared by all the inhabitants. An "apartment" denunciation is the denunciation of neighbor by neighbor, often motivated by the desire to increase living space.

In 1933, I. A. Leont'ev, a resident of 19, Bolshoi Spasobolvanskii Lane, Moscow, wrote a denunciation about his neighbors.[94] Although his house was small, eighteen families lived in it. Most apartment denunciations focused on one person or family, but Leont'ev preferred the scattershot approach and gave all the damaging information he had on everybody. E. M. Dmitrieva, who had owned the house before it was municipalized and remained one of its residents, had been disenfranchised as a bourgeoise. Several other residents, relatives of Dmitrieva, were in the same "alien" class category. E. I. Tregubova was a formerly disenfranchised woman who had taken over the chairmanship of the housing council, the better to protect her own dubious relatives, also residents of the house. V. N. Suslin, an office worker, probably came from a priest's family. Z. E. Ekshtein, unemployed, "probably trades in something (you should check)." V. G. Shenshev, a government employee, "has bourgeois inclinations, especially his wife"—and so the list went on. Leont'ev addressed his letter to the Commission on Passportization, which was currently (March 1933) issuing internal passports and urban registration permits to residents of the capital and at the same time purging the city's population of "social aliens."

In another case, two Communists, husband and wife, each wrote a denunciation of a man named Volodarskii, also a Communist, who had lived in

---

ment's archives for the 1930s, but they are not available in RTsKhIDNI and may have perished during the war.

[92] TsGA IPD, f. 24, op. 2g, d. 226, l. 1.

[93] RTsKhIDNI, f. 17, op. 125, d. 216, ll. 33–35 and 51–54 (letters of 1941 and 1943).

[94] TsGAOR g. Moskvy, f. 1474, op. 7, d. 79, ll. 86–87.

their apartment and still had legal claim to a room.[95] When these denunciations were shown to Volodarskii, he said they were the result of a complicated quarrel about living space.[96] According to his story, the wife wanted his room for her sister and had suggested an exchange, which he refused, causing bad feelings. Then he had gotten a new job in another place and moved out, leaving the spouses in effective possession of his room—to which, however, he retained title. Now he was trying to organize an exchange that would bring a new permanent resident into the apartment—hence, Volodarskii implied, the denunciations.

An eloquent testimony to the power of apartment quarrels came in an appeal sent in 1939 to Andrei Vyshinskii, deputy chairman of Sovnarkom and former state prosecutor. The writer was a Moscow teacher whose husband was serving an eight-year sentence for counterrevolutionary agitation.[97] The family (the parents and two sons) had lived for nineteen years in one comparatively large room—forty-two square meters—in a communal apartment in Moscow. "For all these years our room has been the apple of discord for all residents of our apartment," the teacher wrote. Neighbors sent an endless stream of denunciations to various local authorities. As a result, the family was disenfranchised; then the adults were refused passports; and finally the husband was arrested as a counterrevolutionary, leaving the rest of the family to fight eviction orders. When Vyshinskii called for a report on this case, the prosecutor's office conceded that denunciations by hostile neighbors lay at the root of the family's troubles. But the neighbors were hostile, the prosecutor explained, because the family was anti-Soviet.[98]

SECRECY

It is hard to form an accurate assessment of the proportion of denunciations that were anonymous, but it appears surprisingly small. According to the registry of incoming letters kept by the secretariat of the Leningrad party committee in the mid-1930s, fewer than one letter in a thousand was anonymous.[99] This is much lower than the proportion in *Krest'ianskaia gazeta*'s files for 1938, which is around 20 percent.[100] We should take account of the fact that a cer-

---

[95] RTsKhIDNI, f. 475, op. 1, d. 9, ll. 82, 83. The wife denounced him for being a Trotskyite, the husband for his dissolute lifestyle.

[96] RTsKhIDNI, f. 475, op. 1, d. 9, ll. 87–88.

[97] GARF, f. 5446, op. 81a, d. 94, l. 209.

[98] Ibid., l. 207.

[99] TsGA IPD, f. 24, op. 2g, d. 13, ll. 3, 12–14; d. 46, ll. 31–77. The "letters" category includes appeals, complaints, and other types of letters from citizens, not just denunciations.

[100] Eighteen out of a sample of ninety-four denunciations from RGAE, f. 396, op. 10, were anonymous (count by Golfo Alexopoulos). A quick survey of the *Krest'ian-*

tain proportion of signed letters were signed with false names—that is, they were in fact *anonimki*.[101] But even so, anonymous denunciations remain the exception.

The main reason for signing a denunciation was that it added verisimilitude. "We ask you to regard this not as an *anonimka* but as reality," wrote one anonymous collective.[102] Writers of anonymous denunciations frequently addressed the possibility that their letters, as *anonimki,* would not be taken seriously, although on the basis of the available archival materials it is not clear that this was actually the case. Zhdanov's office in Leningrad, for example, seems to have handled anonymous communications in much the same way as signed letters.[103]

Some writers were coy about their anonymity, like the man who wrote to Moscow city authorities about a financial scam in 1933: "I am obliged to write anonymously for the following reason—I am no coward, but this is my second letter to the OGPU for 1933, and after the first letter they ground me to powder although I had done a big service for the Republic—so I am fed up with being insulted and I decided not to give my name but if you guess it I will just congratulate you."[104] Anonymous denouncers often promised to reveal their names as soon as they saw that action was being taken on their denunciations.[105] As "Unknown for the Time Being" wrote chattily to Kalinin in 1937 after informing him of a terrorist plot against Mikoian, "*Ekh*, Mikhail Ivanovich! Check this out, and when this group figures in the press I will make my appearance and unmask [them]."[106]

While most anonymous writers presumably wished to avoid the attention of the NKVD, some seemed positively to court it. "So long *until further work with you,* and [then] I will give you my name and everything," wrote one anonymous author of a denunciation, a man who claimed to have served as an informer before, not to mention having helped Kirov trap the Whites in Astrakhan and having a revolutionary pedigree that "went back to 1888 [*sic*]."[107] This writer seems to have been hoping for an invitation to work as an informer

skaia gazeta files for the late 1920s (ibid., f. 396, op. 6 and 7) suggests that, for unknown reasons, anonymous letters were more frequent then than a decade later.

[101] For example, the 1939 denunciation signed "A. Mitrofanov" in GARF, f. 5446, op. 81a, d. 154, l. 2. As an accompanying memo indicates, an NKVD investigation found that Mitrofanov was not the author of the letter, who remained unknown. See also TsGA IPD, f. 24, op. 2v, d. 1534, ll. 105–9, for a letter signed in the name of one kolkhoznik but actually written by two others without his knowledge.

[102] GARF, f. 5446, op. 82, d. 27, l. 172. See also ibid., f. 1235, op. 141, d. 2070, l. 4.

[103] TsGA IPD, f. 24, op. 2v, d. 1518 (1935 file of anonymous letters to the first secretary of the Leningrad party committee).

[104] TsMAM, f. 3109, op. 2, d. 2140.

[105] GARF, f. 5446, op. 82, d. 27, l. 172.

[106] Ibid., f. 1235, op. 141, d. 2070, l. 4.

[107] TsGA IPD, f. 24, op. 2v, d. 945, l. 3 (my emphasis).

(*sekretnyi sotrudnik*) for the NKVD. The NKVD did in fact recruit informers from the writers of anonymous denunciations. In one such case the writer was a high school student, whose subsequent reports as an informer—and presumably his original denunciation as well—turned out to be worthless fantasies, much to the NKVD's chagrin.[108]

Despite the fact that most writers of denunciations signed their names, secrecy remained a major concern. Some denunciations were marked "Secret" or "Top Secret" by the senders. Many writers stated that they feared retaliation, particularly when their bosses were the objects of denunciation.[109] Peasants denouncing kolkhoz chairmen and other rural officials were particularly anxious on this score (and, as we shall see, their fears were quite justified). Although usually signed, their letters abound with anxious warnings: Don't let the district know our names because they will tell the kolkhoz bosses and "they will drive us out of the kolkhoz." Don't write directly to me "because the Doronins will get it." "Please don't make my name known, otherwise I will be in trouble."[110]

OUTCOMES

In March 1936, the Starodub district branch of the NKVD received a denunciation of the head of the local prison, Georgii Molotkov, an NKVD officer and party member since 1918.[111] Its author had encountered Molotkov on vacation and reported that in casual conversation Molotkov had slandered various named NKVD personnel, calling them "fascists" unworthy of their positions. Molotkov had also mentioned that he had a girlfriend in Moscow, Katia, who worked as a cook for a foreign consulate, and he had said that through her he had met the consul and his wife.[112]

This denunciation set in motion a complicated process. First, the Starodub party organization decided that Molotkov was a suspicious character and suspended his party membership. Since an exchange of party cards (i.e., a membership purge) was currently in process, this was done simply by failing to issue a new card. Then, because Molotkov no longer had a party card, he was fired from his NKVD job. Nobody told Molotkov the reason for this. He concluded correctly that he had been the victim of a denunciation but made

[108] This example is given in a 1939 memo to Vyshinskii on the case of V. M. Grekov: GARF, f. 5446, op. 81a, d. 94, l. 19.
[109] For such a statement in an anonymous denunciation of a factory director, signed "Production worker," see TsGA IPD, f. 24, op. 2v, d. 1518, l. 8.
[110] RGAE, f. 396, op. 10, d. 128, ll. 66–69, 158–59, and 262. See also ibid., d. 65, ll. 212–14; d. 86, ll. 71–73; d. 87, ll. 281–84; d. 142, ll. 40–41; d. 161, l. 289.
[111] Or Sergei Molotkov. The documents give two versions of his first name, though agreeing on his patronymic, Grigor'evich.
[112] Smolensk Archive, WKP 355: 10–11.

the wrong guess about who had written it. He thought the author was his boss, Strigo, head of the Starodub NKVD, and surmised that its content had something to do with a case of wrongful imprisonment that was currently under investigation. So he sent off his own counterdenunciation to Ezhov in Moscow, blaming Strigo for this and other similar occurrences.

The central office of the NKVD then ran a check on Molotkov and found he had a number of blots on his record, including expressions of dissatisfaction with life in the Soviet Union and "praising the way of life abroad" in the presence of nonparty people. But it was Katia and her foreign employers that evidently bothered the investigators most: "We attach very serious significance to the materials received on Molotkov's links with one foreign consulate in Moscow." The outcome was a decision that Molotkov should no longer be employed in the NKVD.

It is rare to find so detailed a record of the outcome of a denunciation as this one. Often there is no information at all in the archival file about what action, if any, was taken in response to a denunciation. In other cases, the information consists only of a marginal note indicating the initial bureaucratic processing: "File [*Arkhiv,* i.e., no action]"; "Send to the NKVD"; "Send to the prosecutor"; or "Ask the *raikom* for information."

The *Krest'ianskaia gazeta* archive is one of the best sources of information on outcomes because of the assiduity with which the newspaper followed up on denunciations and complaints.[113] In July 1935, the paper published a summary of outcomes on 746 letters recently forwarded to various institutions for investigation and action: 103 persons who were the targets of "abuse" denunciations had been dismissed, prosecuted, or otherwise punished, and in 110 cases the accusations had been found to be groundless.[114] This implies that out of every seven denunciations sent to *Krest'ianskaia gazeta* in mid-1935, one was successful (i.e., resulted in punishment for the person denounced), one was unsuccessful, and the other five fizzled without any particular result.

This ratio may not hold for all denunciations, since "abuse" denunciations from peasants seem to have had an abnormally high chance of backfiring on their authors. Nevertheless, the three types of outcome are universal. Successful outcomes usually involved dismissal from jobs, expulsion from the party, arrest, criminal charges, or a combination of the four. For example, a Siberian engineer denounced by two workers in separate letters in 1930 failed to get past the state purge commission and thus presumably lost his job.[115] The head of a department of the Central Committee who was denounced for softness on

---

[113] For a more detailed discussion of outcomes to denunciations and complaints to *Krest'ianskaia gazeta,* see my "Readers' Letters to *Krest'ianskaia gazeta,* 1938," *Russian History* (in press).

[114] *Krest'ianskaia gazeta* (July 10 and 22, 1935).

[115] GANO, f. 288, op. 2, d. 902, ll. 4–5, 6.

Trotskyism in 1937 was immediately dismissed from his position.[116] A kolkhoz chairman was dismissed from his job, expelled from the party, and arrested by the NKVD following his denunciation by kolkhozniks for abuse of power.[117] Criminal charges were brought against a band of hooligans terrorizing a kolkhoz as a result of a kolkhoznik's denunciation, and an audit of kolkhoz books was ordered after a denunciation of the accountant.[118] A multitarget anonymous denunciation of 1935 against class enemies in a district soviet was spectacularly successful: at least four people lost their jobs after an immediate NKVD investigation.[119]

The most straightforward type of unsuccessful denunciation produced an investigation that concluded that the charges were groundless. For example, an anonymous denunciation purporting to be from a worker at the Putilov plant denounced a construction foreman as "a former contractor and exploiter" in 1934. The factory's party organizer, to whom the accusation was forwarded in 1934, said it was without foundation, and the case was dropped.[120] A woman worker's denunciation of the director of a nursery for neglect and mistreatment of the children in her care was investigated in 1935 and found to be ill founded, although the investigator admitted that the director's manner was stern and abrupt; no charges were brought.[121] Suslova's accusation of attempted rape was also dismissed by the local prosecutor, though in this case it is not clear that any real investigation took place: the key finding reported by the prosecutor to *Krest'ianskaia gazeta* was that "Suslova herself is the wife of an enemy arrested by organs of the NKVD"—and thus her complaint had no standing.[122]

Charges against kolkhoz chairmen in peasants' letters to *Krest'ianskaia gazeta* were often dismissed after investigation by the local authorities to which the newspaper had forwarded them. This was particularly likely to happen if a district rather than a regional prosecutor handled the investigation, lending credence to the allegation frequently made by peasant writers that district and rural officials were all part of the same mutual-protection network.

Peasants' denunciations of local officials sometimes backfired, leading to the punishment of the author, not the object of the denunciation. In a number of cases in the *Krest'ianskaia gazeta* archive, for example, a local authority's report on a denunciation not only dismissed the allegations but also stated that

[116] RTsKhIDNI, f. 17, op. 114, d. 822, l. 62.

[117] RGAE, f. 396, op. 10, d. 161, l. 53. For other cases of dismissal and arrest, see ibid., d. 161, ll. 84–87 and 203–4, and d. 142, ll. 162–66 and 173–77.

[118] Ibid., d. 121, ll. 52–55, and d. 142, ll. 493 and 496–97.

[119] TsGA IPD, f. 24, op. 2v, d. 1518, ll. 164–66. Note that in this case the investigation was so prompt and the endorsement of the anonymous denunciation so complete that one is inclined to suspect a put-up job.

[120] Ibid., f. 24, op. 2v, d. 727, l. 325.

[121] Ibid., d. 1534, ll. 166, 168–70.

[122] RGAE, f. 396, op. 10, d. 66, l. 180.

the writer was a known troublemaker or a "socially alien element." Sometimes *Krest'ianskaia gazeta* was informed that, as a result of the investigation, its correspondent was facing prosecution on criminal charges or had been arrested by the NKVD.[123]

In the case of peasants who had written "abuse" denunciations, the criminal charges often involved stealing, slaughtering animals without permission, and similar economic offenses. But there was a specific criminal charge that could be brought for wrongful denunciation: slander. A Leningrader who denounced his Communist neighbors as "kulaks" and "Zinovievites" had an earlier conviction on his record for slander of these same neighbors, probably with similar allegations.[124] A kolkhoznik was imprisoned, evidently on a conviction for slander, after his denunciation of a kolkhoz chairman was judged "clearly slanderous" and motivated by a desire for revenge after losing his job as head of the kolkhoz animal farm.[125]

Occasionally even a successful denunciation backfired. In one such case, a kolkhoznik's allegations of abuse by a kolkhoz chairman were found to be basically correct and the chairman was dismissed. But "during the investigation of the letter it was established that the author of the letter, Mednikov, is a habitual thief with several convictions, including one in 1933 for robbing a freight train. He does no work at all in the kolkhoz. In 1937 Mednikov was taken away by the NKVD as a socially harmful element."[126] In another case, local authorities reported that, as a result of their investigation of a denunciation, "kolkhoz chairman Manenkov has been dismissed from his job, and criminal charges have been brought against a number of people, *among them being the author of the letter* . . . [who] is under arrest for antisoviet activities, obstruction of work in the kolkhoz, drunkenness, hooliganism, slander of honest workers, and so on."[127]

Prolonged investigations of a denunciation in which an initial outcome was reversed are occasionally recorded in the archives. A denunciation of a factory manager sent to the Leningrad purge commission in 1931 was investigated with great thoroughness: extra witnesses were sought out and interviewed, the background of the accusers was examined, and a lengthy statement was taken from the accused. At first it seemed that the denunciation had hit its mark, for the commission ruled that he should be dismissed from his job and not allowed to hold a senior position for three years. But this decision was reversed on appeal, and he evidently kept his job.[128]

A more dramatic version of the same pattern occurred after *Krest'ianskaia*

[123] For example, ibid., d. 64, l. 165.
[124] TsGA IPD, f. 24, op. 2v, d. 1516, ll. 88, 90.
[125] RGAE, f. 396, op. 10, d. 68, l. 78.
[126] Ibid., d. 143, l. 211.
[127] Ibid., l. 325 (my emphasis).
[128] TsGA S-P, f. 1027, op. 2, d. 860o, l. 52.

gazeta forwarded a denunciation of a kolkhoz chairman to the district prosecutor in October 1937. The prosecutor had the chairman arrested and began criminal proceedings against him. But then the chairman was released and returned to his old job; no reason is given, but presumably patrons in the district leadership intervened. Evidently he knew who had denounced him, because the denouncer (a kolkhoznik named Pavlenko) was immediately arrested. "There he sits in Ust'-Labinskaia jail," Pavlenko's wife wrote pathetically to *Krest'ianskaia gazeta* in November, "and the other kolkhozniks say look what happens when you write to the paper and expose wrongdoing; you get sent where you don't deserve."[129]

CONCLUSION

We can think about the function of denunciation in several ways. One is to ask what a regime gets out of receiving denunciations from citizens. Another is to ask what citizens get out of writing denunciations. These approaches are complementary, not mutually exclusive. Each highlights a different set of functions that denunciation may serve.

In postwar Sovietological scholarship, the regime perspective was almost always privileged. Denunciation was treated as a form of totalitarian control—in Fainsod's words, "one of the important techniques developed by the regime to use the Soviet citizenry to spy on one another and to report on the abuses of local officialdom, to take the measure of popular grievances and to move, where necessary, toward their amelioration."[130] Implicit in this approach was the assumption that denunciation was innately associated with totalitarianism, being a product of the climate of vigilance and mutual suspicion engendered by totalitarian regimes and a response to their insistence on ideological orthodoxy, conformity, and the exclusion of "alien elements" from the community.

The regime-centered approach highlights the surveillance functions of denunciation. While the totalitarianism model is the traditional scholarly reference point, and literary works inspired by the model like George Orwell's *1984* provide its classic representation, there are other theoretical contexts in which these functions can be placed—for example, as Robert Gellately shows in his article in this collection, Foucault's concept of the Panopticon.[131] In the

---

[129] RGAE, f. 396, op. 10, d. 68, ll. 77–78. After receiving Pavlenko's wife's letter, *Krest'ianskaia gazeta* sent a journalist to investigate, but he ended up agreeing with the district party committee's decision that Pavlenko's denunciation was malicious and the chairman essentially innocent.

[130] Fainsod (n. 13 above), p. 378.

[131] See Robert Gellately, "Denunciations in Twentieth-Century Germany," pp. 937–41.

Soviet context, Pavlik Morozov's denunciation—at least in its Soviet-mythical form—is a fine exemplar of the surveillance function in action.[132] Communist-on-Communist "loyalty" denunciations[133] also fit well into a surveillance schema. The same could be said of the broader category of "busybody" denunciations from ordinary citizens.[134]

The surveillance function of denunciation has to do with the disciplining of citizens—the exertion of state or collective power to enforce conformity to certain socially accepted norms. The primary motivation associated with performing the surveillance function is duty, expressed either as "my duty as a Communist" or "my duty as a Soviet citizen."

The second way of thinking about the function of denunciation is to take the citizen's perspective and ask what the individual citizen could achieve by denouncing another citizen. This citizen-centered approach highlights the manipulative functions of denunciation.[135] In a "manipulative" denunciation, the motivation is to provoke a state response from which the denouncer would derive some specific benefit or satisfaction. The benefit might be the disgrace of a professional rival or competitor in village politics, the eviction of a neighbor from a crowded communal apartment, the punishment of a former spouse, or the settling of scores with a personal enemy. Or the denouncer might have the less tangible aim of satisfying that envious desire to "cut down the tall poppies" that flourished under the guise of egalitarianism in Soviet society.

The manipulative function of denunciation has to do with "working the system"—how citizens protect and advance their individual interests within a given society.[136] In the Soviet case, "manipulative" denunciations should be considered part of a complex of informal mechanisms of citizen agency, including client-patron relations and "pull" (*blat*), that were the sociocultural equivalent of the Stalinist "second economy" or black market.

In the Soviet Union and elsewhere, denunciation may also serve functions of justice. In all societies, there are citizens who use public accusation as a means of correcting injustice or protecting the interests of the community. They may be American "whistle-blowers," seeking to disclose wrongdoing in

---

[132] For a deconstruction of the myth, see Iurii Druzhnikov, *Voznesenie Pavlika Morozova* (London, 1988).

[133] See above, pp. 840–47.

[134] Kozlov ("Denunciation," in this issue), discusses these under the heading of "'Disinterested' Denunciations."

[135] See above, pp. 853–856. Kozlov uses the label "'interested' denunciations" for this category.

[136] For an ingenious, if paradoxical, theory linking manipulative denunciations with totalitarianism, see Jan T. Gross, "A Note on the Nature of Soviet Totalitarianism," *Soviet Studies* 34 (July 1982): 3 (discussed above, "Introduction to the Practices of Denunciation in Modern European History, p. 757).

corporations and government departments,[137] or Frenchmen exercising "the competence of justice," in the words of the sociologist Luc Boltanski, by writing letters to *Le monde* exposing scandals or seeking rectification of injustices done to them.[138]

The justice functions are characteristic of what may be called "subaltern" denunciations—those made by ordinary people against people with power. Denunciations of this type are "weapons of the weak," in James C. Scott's phrase.[139] Into this category fell Soviet "whistle-blowing" denunciations, in which subordinates in a factory or government office exposed wrongdoing or institutional cover-ups by superiors, and the "abuse of power" denunciations that peasants wrote against local officials who mistreated them.[140]

In Soviet practice, the justice function of denunciation can often be understood quite literally, since a denunciation involving criminal behavior often served as the initiation of a lawsuit after the receiving institution had forwarded it to the public prosecutor. Indeed, many Soviet citizens sent denunciations of this type directly to the prosecutor. It is easy to see why they did this, since the chances of success in a legal action initiated by the prosecutor were undoubtedly greater than one initiated in a lower court by a private plaintiff. This raises the intriguing question of whether prosecutorial legal systems in general tend to encourage citizen denunciation.

Denunciations are never written in a vacuum. First, and most important, they are letters to authority, and authority in any given context has its own codes, conventions, preferences, and spheres of action. People write the kinds of denunciations they think are likely to be heard and acted upon by authority. One thing this means in practice is that they denounce offenses that authority condemns and punishes. Writing to the public prosecutor to denounce a crime is the most obvious example of this, but it is by no means the only one.

In Stalin's time, Soviet citizens denounced "class aliens" because alien social origin (though not, strictly speaking, a crime) was punishable by disenfranchisement and other penalties. They denounced "kulaks" because kulaks were liable to expropriation and deportation, as well as disenfranchisement. They did not often denounce people for being Jews (as they would have done in Nazi Germany) because the Soviet regime in the 1930s did not marginalize Jews

[137] On whistle-blowing, see Alan F. Westin, ed., *Whistle Blowing! Loyalty and Dissent in the Corporation* (New York, 1981).

[138] See Luc Boltanski, *L'amour et la justice comme compétences: Trois essais de sociologie de l'action* (Paris, 1990), pt. 3; and his article, with Yann Darré, and Marie-Ange Schiltz, "La dénonciation," *Actes de la recherche en sciences sociales*, vol. 51 (1984), on which it is based.

[139] James C. Scott, *Weapons of the Weak: Everyday Forms of Peasant Resistance* (New Haven, Conn., 1985).

[140] See above, pp. 845–49; and Kozlov.

and condemned anti-Semitism. They did not often denounce people for sexual misbehavior, either because the authorities were perceived to be uninterested or because it was not a dominant preoccupation in the society.

During the Great Purges, when Soviet authorities were calling for denunciations of many kinds, citizens responded generously, often using the party's nomenclature of "Trotskyites," "enemies of the people," "wreckers," and "spies." Yet it would be wrong to think of denunciation as something a regime can turn on and off at will, or order up with any precision. As we have seen, real-life Pavlik Morozovs seemed usually to denounce someone other than their parents, and this may have reflected their awareness that most people, even Communists, found familial denunciation reprehensible. Ex-spouses generally found it more prudent to refrain from following the denunciatory example of General Iakir's ex-wife, despite *Pravda*'s encouragement.

Denunciation is always a matter of individual choice, whatever incentives regimes may offer and whatever personal advantages may be gained. The word *denunciation* (*donos*) was already pejorative in Russian in the 1930s, implying that many or most people condemned the practice.[141] If most people thought it was bad to write denunciations, why did so many people do it?

In the first place, not everybody wrote denunciations, and only a minority of people wrote denunciations often. Among those who wrote often, the historian comes to recognize some familiar types: paranoids, who felt they were being persecuted; people consumed by anger and malice, who wanted to hurt someone; graphomaniacs (perhaps a peculiarly Russian type),[142] who wrote for the love of writing and being read; and compulsive busybodies, who were always interested in other people's affairs and misdeeds.

In the second place, many writers of accusatory letters undoubtedly saw the practice as something other than denunciation. It is a familiar human trait to classify acts differently depending on who performs them. (If I write a denunciation, I am a public-spirited citizen; if my enemy writes one, he is a contemptible informer.) Many of those who wrote "abuse of power" letters must have located them mentally in a category other than denunciation.[143] This was all the easier since Soviet citizens were in the habit of writing all sorts of letters to the authorities (complaints, petitions, appeals, and so on) that were not denunciations and to which no odium was attached.[144]

Finally, a major reason for writing denunciations, even if one deplored the

---

[141] This is noted implicitly in Usakov's 1935 definition (n. 1 above) and explicitly in Ozhegov (n. 17 above).

[142] See Svetlana Boym, *Common Places: Mythologies of Everyday Life in Russia* (Cambridge, Mass., 1994), chap. 3.

[143] See Kozlov ("Denunciation," in this issue), pp. 876–77.

[144] On the range of citizens' letters, see Fitzpatrick, "Supplicants and Citizens" (n. 66 above).

practice in principle, was that Soviet citizens had so few options for action. Law functioned poorly, the bureaucracy worse. There were few mediating institutions to deal with government on the individual's behalf, and those that existed, like the trade unions, were weak. In Stalinist society, some people were well connected and could pull strings to remedy injustices and mistakes or bypass bureaucratic roadblocks. But for the great majority who were not powerful or well connected, denunciation was one of the few available forms of agency, a way that the little man (as well as the malicious one) could hope to impose himself on his environment.

Denunciation and Its Functions in Soviet Governance: A Study of Denunciations and Their Bureaucratic Handling from Soviet Police Archives, 1944–1953*

Vladimir A. Kozlov
State Archive of the Russian Federation

According to Vladimir Dahl, author of the *Interpretive Dictionary of the Living Great-Russian Language* published in the second half of the nineteenth century, a denunciation is "not a petition or complaint on one's own behalf, but the revelation of the illegal acts of another."[1] In the nineteenth century the word "denunciation" did not convey a clear pejorative meaning. Alexander Pushkin considered "Kochubei's denunciation of the evil hetman to Tsar Peter" a completely positive act (the reference is to the treason of the Ukrainian hetman Mazeppa during a war between the Swedes and the Russians in the early eighteenth century). Most probably it was only in the Soviet period, especially after the wave of bloody political denunciations in the thirties, that the word "denunciation" took on a negative, even repugnant, connotation. S. I. Ozhegov, compiler of the *Dictionary of the Russian Language,* noted this development along with his definition: "a secret revelation to government representatives of some kind of illegal activity."[2]

The negative connotation of the word "denunciation" in the modern Russian language not only reflects essential shifts in the traditional culture of Russian society but also sets up psychological obstacles to understanding the actual social phenomenon signified by the word. The fact is that archaic survivals within the political culture of the USSR—the almost complete absence of a tradition of legal resolution of conflicts between political institutions and the individual, between the rulers and the ruled; the extremely limited legal rights of the population to organize autonomously; the anxiety generated in the individual by the feeling of a direct psychological connection to the central power—made denunciation more than anything else an essential element in Russia's traditional system of bureaucratic governance and only secondarily a moral problem, understood within the context of conceptions of good and evil.

While the denunciation of a person close to one—of a relative, a neighbor,

---

* Translated by Christopher Burton, Matthew Lenoe, and Steven Richmond.

[1] V. Dahl, *Tolkovyi slovar' v chetyrekh tomakh: Tolkovyi slovar' zhivogo velikorusskogo iazyka,* vol. 1, *A–Z* (Moscow, 1989).

[2] S. I. Ozhegov, *Slovar' russkogo iazyka,* 3d ed. (Moscow, 1953), p. 149.

This essay originally appeared in *The Journal of Modern History* 68 (December 1996).

or a coworker—was always considered an act deserving of moral censure (thus "everyday ethics" did mark out and protect the boundaries of the autonomous personality against the state), matters stood otherwise when it came to denunciations of the malfeasance of "the bosses"—local officials and bureaucrats. Making such a move often demanded courage and a readiness to suffer "for the people." It is simply impossible to imagine how the central government could have maintained any control over its local agents without many such acts, carried out every day, year in and year out. For long periods of time bureaucrats scattered throughout the vast spaces of Russia were able to act independently and arbitrarily, following the dictates of their own self-interest rather than pursuing the greater good of the state. Within the complex of interrelations among the populace, the bureaucracy, and the central power (and in this instance it is not important who the central power was, whether the monarch, the party chiefs, or even the Central Committee of the Communist Party), the institution of the denunciation functioned as a communicative back channel in the cumbersome, ineffective, but nonetheless stable governing apparatus. Denunciation was an important element of the culture of governance for many centuries.

The denunciation, along with petitions of complaint to the "big bosses" over the heads of the bureaucrats and officials who oppressed and abused the people, substituted for courts and other institutions of civil society. It gave the population a final hope that justice would be done, preserved for the central power an aura of infallibility and righteousness, and redirected the population's dissatisfaction into the channel of "local criticism." For these reasons, I would argue that the evolution of the institution of denunciation in Russia must be viewed within the framework of overall research into the history of Russian government, as a specific case of paternalistic statism in an "underdeveloped" country.

To verify this hypothesis, I turned to the documents of one of the most important organizations of Stalinist Russia—the USSR People's Commissariat of Internal Affairs, or NKVD (from 1946 renamed as the USSR Ministry of Internal Affairs, or MVD).[3] The NKVD/MVD archive is stored in the State Archive of the Russian Federation (GARF), which combines the former state

---

[3] Translators' note: The change of name from NKVD to MVD in 1946 was part of a general shift in nomenclature from People's Commissariats to Ministries. But the NKVD also suffered other organizational changes during the war and postwar periods. From 1943 to 1953, the political security administration (Glavnoe Upravlenie Gosudarstvennoi Besopasnosti) was separated from Internal Affairs as a distinct People's Commissariat-Ministry of State Security, the NKGB/MGB. Other police functions, including issuing passports and administering the labor camp system (gulag), remained with NKVD/MVD.

archives of the Soviet Union (TsGAOR SSSR) and the pre-1991 Russian Republic (TsGA RSFSR). Some archival materials are no longer classified, and the classifications of "secret," "top secret," and "special file" will be lifted for others in the near future.[4]

My research covers the years 1944–53. I chose the first date for purely practical reasons: in 1961, NKVD/MVD materials for the years 1944–60 were handed over to TsGAOR for storage. Analogous documents for the second half of the 1930s and the early 1940s are stored in other archives and are less easily available. The reason for my selection of 1953 as the last year of my research period is self-evident: it is the year of Stalin's death.

I studied denunciations filed among the materials of the Secretariat of the All-Union NKVD/MVD, above all those filed under certain standard headings: correspondence over the signature of the People's Commissar himself (Beria and later Kruglov) or that of the commissar's deputy (Kruglov, Zaveniagin, and others).[5] A large number of denunciations have been preserved with this correspondence (as either originals or duplicates). Likewise, the paper trail for these denunciations has been saved. This includes copies of notes appended when the denunciation was forwarded for "verification and administrative action" to party committees, the executive organs of the Soviet state, local NKVD organizations, the counterespionage organ SMERSH, or the People's Commissariats or state ministries, as well as the replies of these organizations and institutions regarding the results of their investigations.

I should note right away that in my opinion the denunciations sent to the NKVD from 1944 to 1953 differ little from denunciations of earlier or later periods in terms of the motivations for composition, the denouncers' psychology, or the rhetoric they employed (which usually either was borrowed from official propaganda or used the traditional Russian schema of the "Good Tsar," protector of the people, versus his evil servants). This latter case illustrates the

---

[4] In cooperation with the U.S. Center for the Study of Russia and the Soviet Union, GARF has published catalogs of the so-called Special Files (*Osobye papki*) of Stalin and Molotov (consisting of letters and reports sent from the NKVD/MVD personally to Stalin and Molotov). See Gosudarstvennaia Arkhivnaia Sluzhba Rossiiskoi Federatsii, Gosudarstvennyi Arkhiv Rossiiskoi Federatsii, *Arkhiv noveishei istorii Rossii,* vol. 1, *"Osobaia papka" I. V. Stalina: Iz materialov Sekretariata NKVD-MVD SSSR 1944–1953 gg. Katalog dokumentov,* ed. V. A. Kozlov and S. V. Mironenko (Moscow, 1994), vol. 2, *"Osobaia papka" V. M. Molotova: Iz materialov Sekretariata NKVD-MVD SSSR 1944–1956 gg. Katalog dokumentov,* ed. V. A. Kozlov and S. V. Mironenko (Moscow, 1994). Volumes on the "Special Files" of Khrushchev, Beria, and Malenkov are in preparation.

[5] The "All-Union NKVD" was the ministry of internal affairs for the Soviet Union as a whole. Subordinated to it were republican NKVDs (Ukraine, Georgia, etc.). (Translators' note.)

stability and persistence of denunciation as a back channel in the system of bureaucratic governance of Russia and the USSR.

Of course, the 1944–53 denunciations are colored by the period (by war and postwar difficulties, various political campaigns, etc.). But the unique character of the denunciatory letters sent to the NKVD/MVD lies not only in their addressees, their style, their themes, and their dates of composition but also in their targets. These were higher officers of the NKVD (e.g., the Deputy Commissar of Internal Affairs for the Estonian Soviet Socialist Republic, the Commissar of Internal Affairs for the Dagestan Autonomous Soviet Socialist Republic, the commander of the NKVD Rear Area Security troops for the Second Belorussian Front), agents of city or district (*raion*) NKVD branches, NKVD plenipotentiaries stationed at labor camps and "special hospitals," NKVD military branch officers, agents at educational institutions and secret scientific research institutes under NKVD jurisdiction, prison wardens (e.g., the warden of the notorious Taganka jail in Moscow), and so on.

When the author of a denunciation addressed him- or herself to the NKVD on a matter not under its jurisdiction (i.e., not concerning the malfeasance of NKVD operatives)—and some trusting and honest people really did consider the NKVD a font of higher justice—the letter was immediately forwarded to another office with the notations, "to proper jurisdiction" and "for verification and administrative action." "Incorrectly addressed" denunciations (i.e., those not dealing with NKVD officers) of local officials' activities were forwarded to regional (*oblast'*) Communist Party committees, enterprise managers, the appropriate People's Commissariats, state and party officials, the Central Committee's Department of Cadres, officials in the public prosecutor's office (e.g., the prosecutor general of the USSR, Gorshenin), the leadership of the housekeeping department of the Economic Administration of Sovnarkom, the Council of People's Commissars (Sovnarkom's office manager [*upravliaiushchii delami*], Ia. P. Chadaev), and so on.

Sometimes the NKVD received denunciations of the entire governing apparatus of some agricultural district (e.g., a denunciation written by one Khoron'ko, a kolkhoznik, from Turukhansk *raion*); in such cases NKVD officers were among the denounced. In a denunciation of defects in the renovation of the Moscow movie theater Uran, sent to Beria, there was not a word about any NKVD connection—but the denunciation's author served in the local anti-aircraft defense system, which was under NKVD jurisdiction. In another complaint against a military doctor, a former secret informant of the NKVD complained of the disclosure of his assumed name.[6]

The People's Commissar and his deputies naturally showed an interest in all

---

[6] Gosudarstvennyi arkhiv Rossiiskoi Federatsii (GARF), f. 9401, op. 1, d. 4934, ll. 270–74.

such cases, and they did not simply forward the denunciations to other jurisdictions without retaining records of them. Whoever the target of the denunciation was, a paper trail was nearly always preserved in the archives of the NKVD, since the leadership wished to be informed of the results of investigations into forwarded denunciations. Another current of paperwork flowed in the opposite direction: the Central Committee, the ministries, and other departments forwarded "incorrectly addressed" denunciations of NKVD operatives to the NKVD.

There are very few instances of political denunciation among those I have studied. This is due to the fact that, after the division of the NKVD into two independent People's Commissariats, political denunciations were investigated (and stored) by the People's Commissariat of State Security of the USSR (NKGB), which had the functions of a secret political police. The NKVD principally retained regular police functions, such as battling crime, managing places of incarceration, utilizing and controlling forced labor, organizing the passport system, and so on. In addition, some of the denunciations that served as the basis for juridical or extrajuridical repression ultimately ended up in the files of courts and investigative agencies, which were stored in other archives.

Most denunciations in the NKVD/MVD archive are devoted to the ordinary themes of Russian denunciation: abuse of power; bureaucratic neglect of duties or financial misdemeanors; and so-called moral breakdown, ranging from alcoholism to marital infidelity, corruption, bribe taking, and theft of state funds. In this sense they have a routine, "timeless" character, and they give us an opportunity to look into the ordinary, traditional forms of denunciatory activity in Russia and the USSR. They differ somewhat from the hysterical denunciations made during the "Great Terror" in the 1930s, but the differences lie more in their numbers than in their motivations, techniques of composition, and rhetoric. At the same time it is obvious that precisely this persistent tradition of denunciation, existing at all times as an instrument of back channel communication in the Russian administrative system and as a part of the political culture of the people, could in certain situations be dry kindling for a bonfire of massive political repression. The leader's exhortation and the eagerness of subordinates and deputies to get their bosses' jobs no matter what the cost were enough to get the machinery of denunciation working at full speed. This machinery always had an opportunity to use experienced, clever "cadres" and a numerous "reserve army" of "amateurs," and it enjoyed great legitimacy in the eyes of the people, who hungered for order and for the punishment of the bureaucrats who constantly abused and insulted them.

For these reasons, this article deals less with denunciations in and of themselves than with the whole complex of problems connected with their social and administrative functioning, from the complicated NKVD procedures for the processing of denunciations to the methods and results of investigations and administrative action. The structure of this article in fact mirrors the social history of the denunciation, addressing in turn the types of authors, their motivations for writing, the peculiarities of their style and rhetoric, the means of registering their complaints, the procedural controls and investigative routines, the bureaucracy's self-defense mechanisms, the efficacy of denunciation, and the subsequent fates of both denouncers and denounced.

Clearly, it is impossible to present the results of such a broad investigation in a single article. I shall focus on only a few of the more important points, attempting to formulate a series of working hypotheses without making any claim to comprehensive research coverage or to totalizing conclusions. Nor have I set myself the task of presenting a complete classification of denunciations and denouncers: there are too many facets to the subject. One could do an entire study of the characteristics of lower-level denunciation of managers or of coworkers within the bureaucracy, or of the distinction between rural/provincial denunciations and those written by city residents. For the latter the local government was too abstract and distant an entity to justify a general denunciation of corruption within the entire urban apparatus. Such broad denunciations were more typical of rural localities or small towns where bureaucrats' activities and personal relationships were constantly in public view, where administrative connections had a deeply personalized character, and where the circle of collective accountability among bureaucrats (*krugovaia poruka chinovnikov*) was more developed. Another entirely separate topic might be the comparison of anonymous denunciations, written over pseudonyms or made-up names, with those whose authors did not hide their identity.

This article touches on all of these questions, but I have chosen to base my typology on the identity of the denouncer and on his or her motivation—in particular, on the presence or absence of motives of personal gain in his or her turning "to those above."

"Disinterested" Denunciations

Among the documents of the NKVD one very often finds denunciations written without any obvious personal motives and imbued with an abstract striving toward justice, a desire to expose "the enemies of the party and the people." In such denunciations the author did not achieve anything for himself—at least not directly.

One denunciation from the Zaporozh'e district reads:

> Prosecutor Ostrokon' of the Mikhailovskii district is a criminal. He destroys Red Army families, misappropriates kolkhoz produce, undermines the kolkhoz finances, and is rude to those who register complaints. Such plaintiffs get bad treatment. Often the prosecutor refuses to receive a plaintiff who has traveled many kilometers. During working hours he goes about his personal business. It is time to investigate this person!

He is repeating the year 1933. This fellow has traveled down the wrong path. Although he cheers, "Long Live Soviet Power!" he quails before Soviet power. There are many signs of trouble here, and the people are concerned.
> Red Army soldier K. Sokolov
> Just let us finish the war and we'll clean things up!
> December 2, 1944[7]

Such attempts to unmask others are often so angry and convoluted that they seem nonsensical. They were authored by people who sincerely believed in the fairness of the central government and in the possibility of restoring justice. Often such a complaint was simply a cry from the soul of a person from the lower levels of society, directed to the higher arbiter and not referring to any real facts. The role of the selfless defender of justice was also filled often by members of the local intelligentsia, and in taking it on, they condemned themselves to long and fierce battles with corrupt bureaucrats.

Some "disinterested" denunciations were directed against specific individuals (immediate supervisors and coworkers). One example is the official report of the deputy chief of police of the Estonian Soviet Socialist Republic, Golubkov, to a deputy commissar of the Estonian NKVD, Kiselev:

> I consider it essential to inform you of the following:
> On Saturday, 8 August of this year I had a discussion with the Director of the NKVD Police Command, Comrade Logusov. In the discussion he told me that one of the Deputy Commissars of the NKVD, Comrade Kal'vo, is a nationalist and has a very bad attitude toward Russians.[8] According to Comrade Logusov, Comrade Kal'vo once asked him during conversation (they always speak in Estonian) if he were concealing something from him (Kal'vo), since it seemed to him that Logusov was not passing on to him necessary information.
> On receiving Logusov's answer that he (Logusov) was concealing nothing from him (comrade Kal'vo), comrade Kal'vo then said to Logusov: "All right, don't worry. When we go to Estonia, we'll show them our teeth."
> This "We'll show them our teeth," Logusov explained to me, "refers to Russians."[9]

The above "report" demonstrates, or in any case allows us to assume, the existence of a specific personality type especially inclined to write denunciations. It is characteristic that the main source of compromising information in the "report"—Logusov—did not write the denunciation. This dirty job was taken on by another person, who himself had no incriminating information on Kal'vo.

The author of the denunciation of Kal'vo does not put forward any personal requests: this is a classic example of the selfless "announcement of the illegal actions of another person." Devoid of any special rhetorical strategies, it con-

---

[7] Ibid., d. 2184, l. 1413.
[8] There were two deputy commissars, Kal'vo and Kiselev (translator's note).
[9] GARF, f. 9401, op. 1, d. 4935, l. 273.

tains only information touching upon a single fact known to the denouncer. The only thing of which the author can be suspected is a concealed careerism, and the documents we have reviewed neither refute nor confirm this suspicion. However, there is a much more important point here. The report quoted above was swiftly used in a complicated judicial intrigue. Logusov's oral communication went into the written report of Lieutenant Colonel Golubkov, which in turn became an extremely important part of the denunciation that followed—presented this time not as a "report" (*raport*) but as "reference materials [*spravki*] on Deputy Commissar of Internal Affairs of the Estonian Soviet Socialist Republic, Police Colonel A. Ia. Kal'vo," signed by Deputy Commissar Kiselev. This document is a typical denunciation, but its author is obviously attempting to make the details it includes more believable by labeling it "reference materials," like an ordinary bureaucratic document.

Mislabeling of this kind—denunciations headed "reference materials" (*spravki*), "memoranda" (*dokladnye zapiski*), or even "collegial notes" (*tovarishcheskie pis'ma*)—are encountered quite often. It is relatively easy to distinguish such documents from those that were genuine official correspondence. For example, *spravki* were usually written in response to some official request or were attached to some other document as additional information. When a *spravka* was written without reference to other documentation, on the sole initiative of its author, then something else was obviously being hidden under this label. A "memorandum" (*dokladnaia zapiska*) was usually the result of a full-scale bureaucratic investigation and was prepared in order to resolve some sort of specific problem. In short, an attempt by a denouncer to expose an official on his own personal initiative cannot be regarded as a real *spravka* or *dokladnaia zapiska,* much less a real "collegial note." The only bureaucratic genre that could plausibly give the denunciation a decorous title was the "report" (*raport*). Indeed, this term is often synonymous with "denunciation." Like the denunciation, the "report" often begins with the formulaic phrase "I consider it essential to inform you of the following."

To return to the *spravka* about Kal'vo: in using this term for his denunciation Kiselev was attempting to follow the canons of composition for such a document. In trying to prove the devotion of Kal'vo to the ideas of Estonian nationalism, he was creating the impression of objective research into Kal'vo's life. The author of the *spravka* quoted "several verbal denunciations about the 'strange' attitude and manner of conduct Kal'vo maintained toward colleagues of Russian nationality." "They [Kal'vo's Russian colleagues] report," he wrote, "that Kal'vo carries out any requests made by Estonian colleagues and refuses all those made by Russians. Recently he has begun to surround himself with Estonian police workers who are under investigation by the counterintelligence department SMERSH."[10]

[10] Ibid., l. 272 ob.

In his *spravka,* Colonel Kiselev utilized Lieutenant Colonel Golubkov's written "report" as the only real evidence of Kal'vo's guilt. The *spravka* initiated a whole series of political accusations and graphically demonstrates how denunciation could serve not only as an effective instrument of official intrigue but also as an important means of forcing government bureaucrats to adhere to state policies. In this case the attack on Kal'vo fizzled out; in the upper margin of the *spravka* there was noted the bureaucratic resolution typical of such cases: "To be filed." The central authorities probably did not consider the accusation serious enough. However, the resolution of this particular case does not change my overall interpretation of the social function of such communications to the upper-level "bosses."

An officer of the NKVD was always threatened with denunciation, and this constant fear guaranteed his political and bureaucratic loyalty. In fact, most Soviet bureaucrats lived under the weight of this illusion of constant oversight (*kontrol'*) over their political reliability and behavior. (I speak of an "illusion" because it was not the oversight that was constant but, rather, the fear generated by the potential for continuous oversight, the unrelenting sense of looming danger.) The fear of the "stool-pigeon" (*stukach*) so characteristic of Soviet life was founded not on a myth of mass denunciation but on the perpetual risk of being "misunderstood" and becoming the victim of a routine "disinterested" denunciation.

While the denunciation of colleagues and immediate supervisors leads one to suspect concealed bureaucratic intrigue and secret personal motives, the "disinterested" denunciations of local authorities' malfeasance appear to be the offspring of a peculiar denunciatory "graphomania." Some such denunciations may have been born of the play of demented imagination and paranoia. The deputy director of the Moscow district NKVD office, one Polukarov, described in this way the author of more than three hundred denunciations, addressed to every imaginable (and unimaginable) destination: "He systematically wrote letters of a troublemaking and slanderous character . . . to central and regional organizations, both Party and Soviet,"[11] adding that "as a rule, investigation did not confirm the allegations made in the letters."[12] In contrast, the author of another denunciation, Ivanov, complained that "I have also given you information in the past. While I have never been charged with deceiving you, I have suffered unpleasantness at the hands of several individuals."[13] Ivanov represented an unusual type, the professional fighter for justice (*borets za spravedlivost'*)—though it is true that he did strongly resemble a traditional "troublemaker" (*sklochnik*). It was not coincidental that while serving with troops of the Moscow antiaircraft defense force (MPVO) he was deputy chair-

[11] Ibid., d. 4933, ll. 119 ob. –20.
[12] Ibid., l. 120.
[13] Ibid., d. 4934, l. 273.

man of the People's Court and a member of the cafeteria "control commission": in short, he was constantly watching the people around him and "educating" them. Ivanov carried a reputation with him from one workplace to the next. Coworkers feared him and told potential victims of Ivanov's "vigilance": "He is a very dangerous man; when he was serving in the battalion, he informed on us."[14] Word that someone was capable of "disinterested" denunciation of coworkers or acquaintances spread widely, surrounding the denouncer with a wall of estrangement and fear. (Ivanov complained about this to Beria, incidentally.) "Writers" afflicted with the mania of suspecting and exposing others were not loved even within the NKVD system, especially if their "artistic compositions" were directed against coworkers. They "got the squeeze," "got nailed," or were denied promotion.[15]

Another fighter against malfeasance and disorders, Kovalev, a prisoner at the NKVD labor camp in Noril'sk, was, judging by the texts of his denunciations, as sincere and disinterested as Ivanov. He was in the habit of numbering his statements at the top, and his persistence may be judged by a document I came across bearing the number 318. Naturally, this flood of complaints aroused the ire of the camp's administrators, who accused Kovalev of making "provocative declarations." (These same administrators had originally proposed Kovalev for early release from camp; it was only later that his accusations began to escalate.) The Deputy Commissar of the All-Union NKVD was relatively tolerant of this behavior, but he also instructed the administrators to give the truth seeker "a really serious warning" about "the inappropriateness of submitting one statement after another, to a total of over three hundred," and to rebuke him on that account.[16]

Such denunciations frightened those in the vicinity precisely because they were written, as it were, "from love of the art," and so it was not possible to use standard defenses against them—discrediting the denouncer or exposing his personal interest in the matter. Nonetheless, most of the authors of the denunciations I studied did not suffer from this kind of denunciation mania. I have encountered many "pure" denunciations—"pure," that is, from the point of view of the authors' motives—that were written by completely normal people who despaired of getting justice on the local scene.

(When I had nearly finished this paper, I was surprised to discover that I had been unconsciously using a certain "code" to reflect the difference between "interested" and "disinterested" denunciations. The authors of "interested" denunciations I unhesitatingly called "informers" [*donoshchiki*], using a word that has clear pejorative connotations in contemporary Russian. But to refer to

[14] Ibid., d. 4934, l. 277.
[15] See, e.g., ibid., d. 4930, ll. 363–68.
[16] Ibid., d. 4933, l. 57.

those who did not have obviously self-serving motives, who did not engage in slander but fought for justice however they understood it, I used the term "denouncer" [*donositel'*], which has a more neutral meaning and simply signifies a type of activity without attaching a negative attitude to that activity.)

As a rule, the authors of "disinterested" denunciations give the impression of being fearless and ready to fight stoically for justice. Yet some of them appear to be driven by forces beyond normal dedication or even denunciation mania; we might think of such individuals as being afflicted by a particularly severe and incurable sort of "denunciation virus," whose symptoms include the use of highly politicized rhetoric and a set of images and metaphors standard for Soviet political culture.

"Disinterested" denunciations based not on concrete facts but on a general moral indictment of "the bosses'" corruption were often anonymous or had in place of a signature a pseudonym or label—such as "One of your own" (*Svoi*), "Partisan," "Red Army soldier," "Party member," and so forth—designed to present the author to the higher authorities as "one of their own." A pseudonym might also be used to forestall the unfortunate psychological impression created by anonymity: the absence of a signature would automatically provoke doubt about the "pure motives" of the denouncer, leading to suspicions that he was personally interested in the results of his denunciation.

Local authorities often criticized "disinterested" denunciations as an "anti-Soviet activity" growing out of an alternative political culture that transgressed the limits of permissible Communist rhetoric. In denunciations of this kind, criticism and exposure of "unjust state servitors"[17] went beyond the conventional dichotomy between a "good" central authority and "bad" local bureaucrats and turned into criticism of the political system itself. During Khrushchev's time this type of denunciation evolved into a specific form of "anti-Soviet propaganda": anonymous letters, addressed to the highest Soviet leaders, criticizing the regime. Copies of these letters were mailed to many people and usually dealt with problems in the country at large rather than focusing on any particular district.

I offer as an example one of the these "proclamation denunciations," which was written in 1944:

I want to scream!
When I look around at what is happening, I cannot keep silent. Once upon a time there was the autocracy of the tsar. Things were clear: there were the lord and his workers. One had rights and the other responsibilities. But in the so-called socialist republic where there is supposed to be socialist rule of law [*zakonnost'*], the purity of which

---

[17] The Russian phrase (*nepravednykh gosudarevykh slug*) is archaic, recalling the language of traditional Russian petitions to the tsar (translators' note).

is supposed to be maintained by the Soviet government, something unbelievable is going on.

This government, the only one of its kind in the world, was born with great difficulty: so much priceless workers' blood was spilled, so many strong young lives were given up with total faith in the shining future. Happy are they who died in that faith, the faith in a shining future for their oppressed, forgotten, but nonetheless beautiful motherland. They did not live to see the scandalous injustice of today.

For three long years, the Soviet land has been drinking human blood, even as it still soaked in the blood of previous wars. For three long years the Soviet people has carried on its back the heavy burden of war. The weight presses upon people, crushing them into the earth. And this burden has been distributed very unevenly. For some the war is immeasurable physical suffering and spiritual torture; for others it is not so much war as pleasure. Beside those who have emaciated faces, who are wracked by scurvy, who are barefoot and unclothed, you see others who are sated, who have more than they need, who are dressed smartly, lack nothing, and live in spacious apartments which are light, warm, dry, and well furnished. What is the war to them? . . . [*sic*] And right next to them . . . [*sic*] naked degradation. People huddle together in dugouts, crushed in until no more can fit. It's humid; the air is unbearably heavy. The so-called healthy are here and also the sick. Dressed in rags, people die from hunger although there is food, die in cold, damp shelters although there is firewood. Nobody helps them. And this is inside Soviet territory, thousands of kilometers from the front. Where is this sad corner? It is the Turukhansk district of the Krasnoiarsk region . . . [*sic*] The town of Turukhansk— a regional center with a district Party Committee, a Party Executive Committee, a Prosecutor's office, a People's Court, and so on and so forth, where there sit (and I do mean sit—on their behinds) leaders who do not care for the condition of the district, but only for their personal well-being. They don't care that people are dying of hunger, are dying in the dugouts; it doesn't matter to them that hundreds, indeed thousands of tons of foodstuffs are rotting. . . .

Money does not make it easier to buy things. And there's no money anyway. There is only one exit: death by starvation. We've got the right to "employment" (as forced labor!) and the right to eternal rest. The greatest number of deaths occur in transport contingents (Volga Germans and Greeks). But among the regional authorities the opinion about these people is, "It's all the same if they croak." And so people die. . . .

Can one protest? Say a word, and you'll disappear! Lawless arbitrariness . . . [*sic*] It can be compared only with serfdom. That was a hundred years ago. . . . Wartime is used to cover up all kinds of incompetence, indifference, and even crime, like a "fig leaf." And this is happening thousands of miles from the front. If only this leaf were torn away as it should be, that would be a lesson to others!

I just don't have the time or energy to describe all the dirt. No energy, when I see the uselessness of it all. For I am not cheering "Hurrah!" but shouting "Danger!" And that, only as long as I still have my voice. And for that I could lose my voice, too. What I lose once, I won't have to lose again, but the best I can hope to get is prison. You new gentry bastards! It's hard to acquire new habits, forget old ones. . . . [*sic*]

These are all trifles. But when will trifles be treated as great, important matters, and the great matters as trifles? Surely great matters boil down to trifles.

"A Partisan."[18]

---

[18] GARF, f. 9401, op. 1, d. 2184, ll. 836–39.

The author of this denunciation makes no personal requests or demands. Against the background of a typical denunciation of the local authorities and the usual wartime charges that "the rats in the rear" are "provisioning themselves" (*samosnabzhenie*—the Stalinist equivalent of "corruption"), the author trumpets much louder political motifs: the bureaucratic degeneration of the socialist system ("You new gentry bastards!"), the leaders' betrayal of their avowed principles, and an indictment of the government for demagogy and deception.

"INTERESTED" DENUNCIATIONS

"Interested" denunciations are those written to protect the personal interests of their authors. They occupy an intermediary position between the ordinary petition and the denunciation in the narrow sense of the word, as it was understood by Vladimir Dahl. It is not surprising that documents like these are addressed against immediate supervisors, coworkers, and neighbors. One almost never finds in them an abstract desire to achieve justice.

I know of one curious case in which a denunciation that was apparently a "disinterested" exposure of local corruption and "counterrevolutionary statements" among NKVD agents turned out upon investigation to be an "interested" document. Sakhnenko, the regional fire inspector of the Buriat-Mongolian Autonomous Soviet Socialist Republic (the fire command was a part of the NKVD system) accused some collective farm directors of engaging in sabotage during the 1943 harvest. He also accused some local NKVD officials (names were not provided) of Buriat nationality "of rubbing their hands in satisfaction at the prospect of Japan's arrival, saying that when the Japanese come, we Buriats will show you Russians."[19]

The higher leadership of the NKVD naturally became interested in this denunciation, but an investigation proved it to be totally false. It turned out that Sakhnenko wanted only to be transferred back from Buriat-Mongolia to Ukraine. According to the author's own naive confession, the denunciation was written "as a supplement to my official request to be sent on a mission to Ukraine," with the sole "aim of making an 'argument' for a positive decision"—that is, it was an attempt to impress his superiors with his vigilance and perspicacity.[20] The only thing the author achieved with his denunciation was a transfer to another district within the same Buriat-Mongol Republic he disliked so much.

The "interested" denunciation was sometimes used as a means of self-

[19] Ibid., d. 2141, l. 1441.
[20] Ibid., l. 1440.

defense. People who learned that they were about to be accused of abuses and indicted took to writing denunciations against their persecutors, hoping to carry off a preemptive strike that would make them appear to be victims of "suppression of criticism." In materials related to the investigation of such cases there appeared supplements of the following type: "I must also note that the authors of this statement, Ermakov and Sharapov, were themselves involved in embezzlement of government property and are violators of labor discipline, for which they were removed from their responsibilities by the director of Enterprise Group No. 100. Materials related to their case have been handed over to the proper organs for indictment."[21]

A typical example of such a denunciation is the accusation of one Fediainov, a former employee in the prosecutor's office, against the chief military prosecutor, Afanasiev. In August 1941 Fediainov was caught in a surrounded pocket and lived for two years in German-occupied territory. By the standards of that time this was in itself a serious transgression. Nor was Fediainov able to produce any proof that he had taken part in the resistance against the Germans. In short, he had been "sitting things out" behind the German lines. After an investigation, Fediainov was expelled from the party and thus automatically lost the right to work in the prosecutor's office.

In the opinion of officials at the Communist Party's Central Control Commission (TsKK pri TsK VKP), Fediainov had written a denunciation against his longtime acquaintance, the chief military prosecutor, "only because he himself was in a bad position, as he had lived in occupied territory, and Comrade Afanasiev, as the chief military prosecutor, was obligated (for there was nothing else he could do) to hold off on the decision whether to restore Fediainov to his former job as a military prosecutor until a clarification of the question about his party standing."[22]

Fediainov had chosen not to wait for that decision, but instead had answered with a strike against Afanasiev, charging that he had ties with an "enemy of the people," former Chief Military Prosecutor Rogovskii, who had been arrested six years earlier. Afanasiev was fortunate. The Control Commission concluded: "Everything that Fediainov writes about Afanasiev has been collected or thought up by him only now, six to seven years after the fact."[23]

One motive for an "interested" denunciation could be the desire to take secret revenge on someone who had offended the writer. One example of this was an anonymous denunciation against the commander of the First Detached Division of the NKVD Special Service troops, Engineer-Major Iadroshnikov. Iadroshnikov had had longtime relations with a former commander of the divi-

[21] Ibid., d. 4935, l. 60.
[22] Ibid., d. 4930, ll. 542–43.
[23] Ibid., d. 4930, l. 538.

sion, Colonel Khrychikov. Khrychikov used a tried-and-true tactic: he created a commission composed of people loyal to him that was to collect compromising material against his deputy and "drown" him. Even this commission, which the Leningrad District (*okrug*) NKVD counterespionage department (SMERSH) concluded had "tendentious origins," was not able to find any evidence of corruption on Iadroshnikov's part. A repeat attempt to use the same tendentiously selected commission against Iadroshnikov was undertaken, in the opinion of a newly created commission of inquiry, "with clearly slanderous intent by persons [whom] Engineer-Major Iadroshnikov had 'offended.'"[24]

A special type of "interested" denunciation is the "petition denunciation." The authors of such documents are clearly pursuing personal goals as they struggle against some sort of injustice done to them, but the pathos of appealing to central authorities goes beyond the limits of a single episode (e.g., "Help a family that was robbed get back their stolen goods") and reaches the level of generalization ("No one is fighting against crime in our region; the people's complaints are ignored"). In this manner a petition on the writer's own behalf is given a higher status—one of a denunciation or complaint that is "not for oneself" but "a declaration of the unlawful acts of another." This is meant not only to make a personal petition more convincing but also to wash away any taint of suspicion that the author had self-interested motives in turning to the highest authorities.

Once a personal request was turned into a denunciation, it was cast as part of a fight for higher justice in the name of the "common good," of "the people," of "the state." Authors of such declarations to the authorities tended to be more educated and consciously or unconsciously exploited Russian statist traditions in order to achieve their personal goals. Not only did they place their request within the symbolic system of the dominant political culture but also they used the most effective rhetorical tactics for that system.

For example, Captain N. A. Beliaev wrote to the deputy commissar of the NKVD, Kruglov, "This is why, Comrade Kruglov, I am turning to you concerning this small matter and asking you to demand from the authorities of the city of Serpukhov that effective measures be taken to protect the families of soldiers, especially at such a difficult time. One understood the situation when it was the fascists who pillaged and burned, but something must be done now about the Russian bandits. Send help from Moscow to Serpukhov and protect our families and workers. This situation is a major political issue in Serpukhov."[25] Having opened with a request for the return of his family's stolen property (for they had lost everything), Beliaev veiled his main motive behind a concern for the common good, presenting his own problem as one brush stroke

---

[24] Ibid., d. 4936, ll. 60–64.
[25] Ibid., d. 4933, l. 123.

in the terrifying total picture of a city submerged in a crime wave. This folding of a personal problem into a "big political question" through constant references to the heavy lot borne by the families of military servicemen defending the fatherland was a typical rhetorical approach. It was not coincidental that this passage of the petition denunciation was underlined in blue pencil by an upper-level NKVD official.

Beliaev's request was the product of high-quality creative work by an experienced petitioner. Ordinary petitioners would often, without giving it any deep thought, simply reinforce their very specific petition with more general accusations against the people they were complaining about.[26] Thus they composed supplementary accusations, often of a political nature, in transparent attempts to fortify their personal requests with "higher" motives, to present their petitions as "selfless," to obscure their private motives with concern for the general welfare. The existence of various methods for making ordinary petitions mimic denunciations both demonstrates the latter form's higher status and confirms the proposition that denunciations had a special social function in postrevolutionary Russian society.

THE RHETORIC OF DENUNCIATIONS

In almost any denunciation one can find a kind of compulsory minimum of ideological beliefs and moral judgments. The widespread logic was: Soviet power is the best and most just in the world, so how can it bear the illegal and amoral actions of its bureaucrats? Or: A war is on, millions of people are dying at the front, and these traitors who have dug in at the rear are committing offenses against the wives and children of the fighting troops. Or: The authorities are disgracing the title of Communist. Sometimes denunciations against the malfeasance of local authorities concluded with symbolic threats (e.g., "Just let us finish the war and we'll clean things up").[27]

As noted above, such pronouncements—intended to signify that the author of the denunciation was "one of ours," to key into the ideological codes that would open the door to mutual understanding with the higher authorities— often concealed quite different motives. Some authors used standard ideological "frames" sincerely, almost subconsciously; others quite cynically exploited the Communist regime's favorite themes. All strove to establish their right of petition to the higher authorities by presenting positive facts about themselves; often this presentation resembled that used in "the lives of the saints."

The motif of "a few words about myself" (*nemnogo o sebe*) was one of the most popular rhetorical ploys. When the author of one denunciation wrote that

[26] See, e.g., ibid., d. 4934, ll. 291–92.
[27] Ibid., f. 9401, op. 1, d. 2184, l. 1413.

he was a participant in the October Revolution, a Red Guard in 1917, twice wounded, with permanent war injuries, and so on, he was actually trying to "activate" in the consciousness of the reader a whole system of symbols that reflected the basic ideological and political preferences of the government—in this case including the revolutionary past, the author's worker origins and social status, and Soviet patriotism.

The use of applicable ideological codes was supposed to set up a special, almost intimate connection between the informer or denouncer and the regime and to indicate that the author was deserving of special trust. An ably (professionally?) written denunciation invariably utilized at least one of the rhetorical strategies described above. In the majority of the denunciations I examined, however, the authors also strove not to overuse political rhetoric. Only in a few, relatively rare cases did the denunciators deviate from the principle of the "quick prayer"—that minimal expression of moral and political sentiments that was almost as routine as saying grace before meals in a religious family, which would be enough to activate in the mind of the bureaucrat the system for "recognizing one's own." In the unusual cases where more than a "quick prayer" was offered, the denunciation came to resemble a front-page article from *Pravda,* with a quotation from the latest "great" speech of Comrade Stalin serving as the central support for the argument (e.g., "People must be evaluated and judged according to the results of their activities, according to their abilities").[28] The abuses detailed in the denunciation would then be presented to the reader as contravening the Great Chief's Great Precepts; that is, they would be turned into a political crime.

In addition, some "writers" clearly misused references to their "revolutionary services." As a result, the effective approach of "a few words about myself" turned into its opposite: "a lot of words about myself." And this was bound to provoke a negative reaction from the bureaucrats who were required to read and verify the long confessions and autobiographies.

The techniques employed in the writing of denunciations depended primarily upon the nature of the author's motives—disinterested pursuit of the truth or personal gain—as well as upon his or her level of education. In spite of superficial similarities, such as the use of rumors or fabrications, there were also fundamental differences.

The phraseology of "disinterested" denunciations against local authorities was directly determined by the educational level of the denouncer. Semiliterate people usually just detailed concrete facts, making no claim to generalization. As a rule they did not employ the devices of political demagogy. "Disinterested" denunciations of this type were founded on a deep conviction that it was possible to convey the "real truth" and get justice "up there" (*naverkhu*).

[28] Ibid., d. 4934, l. 400.

These authors not only lacked the ability (because of their educational defi-
ciencies) to provide proof of things that were self-evident to them but, to all
appearances, also lacked the desire to do so. They simply appropriated the
traditional Russian myth (which could still be applied in a Soviet context)
about "the good tsar" and his "bad servants" who deprived the people of truth
and justice. In such a system of social concepts, the central authority was supposed to act as an agent "of the people"; it was through this authority that the
people were supposed to achieve justice. Without a doubt, the morality of this
authority was accepted as a kind of given. In the traditional view, the higher
authorities had but one problem: that the immoral and self-serving bureaucrats
who represented authority in the regions were not telling them "the whole
truth." And since this was so, there was no need for further verbal "stimulation"
of the "chiefs" (*vozhdi*): once they knew the truth, they themselves would
restore justice.

The naive traditional faith in the limitless fairness of the highest authorities
normally accompanied another traditional motif: "The lord [*barin*] will come,
and then the lord will sort it out [*nas rassudit*]." Authors of many denunciations
wrote insistently to Stalin or Beria: "I beg you to come here yourself." Many
denunciations repeated this request in various forms and contexts, but one can
always discern the paternalistic traditions of the authoritarian Russian state and
the last hope of the "oppressed and debased" for the personal intervention of
the leader who was almost as powerful as the Lord God himself.

It was not only in such petitions to higher authority that traditional consciousness found its expression. Archaic rhetoric, including the expression of
values condemned at least officially by Communist ideology, such as anti-
Semitism, was generally characteristic of many types of denunciation. It was
as if traditional consciousness slipped up here, introducing forbidden motifs.
Yet at the same time there was an essential difference between the truly archaic
everyday anti-Semitism of the uneducated, with their complaints that Jews
dominated trade, and the appeals of educated and semieducated denouncers
who called upon Beria to save "Georgian sports" from Jewish sabotage.[29] This
latter denunciation was written a few years before the beginning of the anti-
Semitic political campaign officially dubbed "the battle against cosmopolitanism." The author of the denunciation apparently was attempting to make use
not only of the official system of political symbols but also of the chauvinistic
prejudices deeply rooted (and carefully concealed) in the consciousness of the
regime leaders. And quite probably (as the text of the denunciation allows us
to suppose) the author knew that these prejudices existed.

Denunciations were often rigged with a system of supplementary arguments
that were supposed to strengthen their emotional and logical power. "Social

[29] Ibid., d. 4932, ll. 420–23.

origins as a factory owner," kulak, Nepman, landowner, and so on were often cited as incriminating circumstances.[30] In the political culture of Stalinist Russia, belonging to one of these categories was in itself no small sin. And again, some of the authors sincerely believed that simply belonging to such social categories was practically a crime, while others obviously were using the class preferences of the authorities to further their personal interests.

In many cases "disinterested" accusations were clearly written by people who were mentally ill or (as one bureaucrat who had to check out denunciations observed) were inclined to interpret facts incorrectly, giving them a wider meaning than necessary. In other words, "disinterested" informers of this type saw "enemies of the people" everywhere, and their brains built up logical frameworks of "betrayal" from completely innocuous facts.

Such pathological cases would not merit even passing mention in this report except for the fact that I have discovered an analogous logic in "self-serving" denunciations written by completely normal people. For example, the only more or less real fact mentioned in a denunciation against the chairman of the All-Union Arts Committee, Khrapchenko, was the nationality of his wife's relatives (German). Everything else was conjecture and innuendo. On these grounds Khrapchenko was portrayed as the next thing to a German spy, since he had the opportunity to meet with Stalin and might then tell what he heard to his German relatives (who, by the way, lived in another town).[31]

Most slanderous denunciations, in fact, were constructed according to this ingenuous schema. For instance, the denunciation written by one Dombrovskii against the director of a Moscow institution of higher education was based on the following real fact: he had recently dismissed eight persons from the institute. On this basis the denouncer concluded that the director was "poisoning and smashing cadres [meaning here "personnel" or "human resources"]." Investigation revealed that some of the workers had been fired before the tenure of the present director and that others had simply been transferred to new posts upon their graduation from the institution. Only one relevant case was found: "The management of the Institute intends to relieve Comrade Chernaia . . . from her post for neglect of her clerical duties."[32]

Other accusations made use of a similar method. In actuality Dombrovskii's slander of the director was constructed like a myth: it contained one real fact and a completely fantastical interpretation. Some "disinterested" denunciations following this pattern were written by people who were clearly mentally ill—but the difference between their letters and Dombrovskii's slander is obvi-

[30] A Nepman was a private trader or entrepreneur during the New Economic Policy period in the 1920s, when economic controls were relaxed (translators' note).

[31] GARF, f. 9401, op. 1, d. 4930, l. 372.

[32] Ibid., l. 388.

ous. What was for them a genuine "model of the world" was for Dombrovskii a consciously applied stratagem, a pretense.

A comparison of the rhetorical devices and techniques of "disinterested" and "interested" denunciations suggests that we are dealing with two completely different cultural systems: one that is traditional, sincere, and naive and another that is its cynical imitation. On the one hand, we have the genuine sacralization of leaders; on the other, hypocritical paeans to them. On the one side there is an almost mystical belief in the traditional paternalism of the higher authorities; on the other, a sanctimonious appeal to that paternalism that relies on the "concern for the common good" sanctioned by official ideology. A sincere faith in socialism as heaven on earth, which for many replaced religious faith, contrasts starkly with the calculating use of the symbols and substance of that faith for personal gain.

In truth the legitimacy of the Communist regime rested on a system of traditional Russian values only lightly swathed in the clothing of socialist ideology. This legitimacy was destroyed not by Gorbachev or the democratic movement but by an egotistical individualism that had begun to develop at the core of Stalinist society, which understood the value of socialist demagogy and was able to use it for its own goals. This individualism touched not only "the people" but also the party elite itself.

Those who destroyed the traditional system of values and concepts, among them the authors of many "interested" denunciations, seem unappealing as historical actors. However, the "knights of the era of primitive capitalist accumulation"—representatives of the young and greedy bourgeois class—looked equally unappealing, especially in comparison with the "noble lords" of the waning feudal era.

Fortunately, cynicism was not the only refuge for people torn out of their traditional culture. Oppositional defiance and the beginnings of a new ideology of protest existed in embryo within the shell of the traditional "disinterested" denunciation. It is enough to recall, for example, the letter from "A Partisan," quoted above, with its criticism of the system as opposed to the system's own devious servants, in order to understand that base compromise and hypocritical egotism were not the only products of the decomposition of the old value system. From it also sprouted sincere and noble protest.

PROCEDURE FOR PROCESSING DENUNCIATIONS

When the denunciation was completed, a multiplicity of bureaucratic procedures still lay ahead. First of all, the writer wanted his letter to have an audience. For "professional" writers of denunciations, the usual method was to send the denunciation simultaneously to several addressees at once, just to be sure. A typical heading in such cases might read roughly as follows:

To the People's Commissar of Internal Affairs, Marshal of the Soviet Union, Comrade
  Beria
Copy: Central Committee of the Communist Party
Copy: General Prosecutor of the USSR

Regrettably, the files contain no information about any interaction between
the various authorities that received copies of one and the same denunciation.
But it seems that it was purely the contents of the denunciation—more precisely, the institutional affiliation of the officials against whom it was written,
or the ministry whose activity it discussed—that determined where it would
be investigated. Under these circumstances, it was not important exactly who
received the original and who the copy.

All denunciations received by the NKVD/MVD were processed by its Secretariat, which handled "correspondence between the People's Commissar and
his deputies and all institutions and organizations in the USSR, as well as correspondence arising out of all statements and letters from citizens [*zaiavleniia
i pis'ma trudiashchikhsia*] that came in to the NKVD." If the denunciation
was sent to the NKVD from another institution or organization, then the First
Department of the Secretariat dealt with it. The majority of denunciations I
have studied bore the registration stamp of the Second Department, which was
in charge of "letters from citizens."[33] Both departments kept track of which
documents were sent to what office and monitored the fulfillment of the orders
issued by the People's Commissar (later, Minister) of Internal Affairs and his
deputies.

There were many ways of investigating information received through denunciations. Important cases were assigned to the so-called Special Inspectorates
of the NKVD in the various Soviet republics and in the regional (*krai* and
oblast') NKVD offices set up in 1941 after the division of the agency into the
NKVD and the NKGB. Until that time Special Plenipotentiary agents of the
republican and regional branches of the NKVD had fulfilled analogous functions. There also existed a Special Inspectorate within the central NKVD command. An NKVD circular of May 15, 1941, delegated to the Special Inspectorate the fulfillment of special assignments: investigations into matters related to
crimes perpetrated by NKVD personnel; the checking of statements, complaints, and reports of crimes committed by NKVD personnel on or off duty;
and so on. From these investigative materials the Special Inspectorate prepared
reports for the NKVD leadership and also proposed measures to be taken in
response to the denunciation.

As a rule the Special Inspectorate handled only cases with good "judicial
prospects"—those that were covered by the Disciplinary Rules (*distsiplinarnii*

---

[33] Literally, "toilers" (*trudiashchiesia*) (translators' note).

ustav) or NKVD internal regulations. The majority of the denunciations I have studied belong to the other category: those without good judicial prospects. Denunciations that did have good judicial prospects most likely ended up in the prosecution files for cases against NKVD officers.

Sometimes the Special Inspectorate would decide to close an investigation and would send this decision for ratification to the leadership of the all-Union and republican NKVDs and the heads of regional NKVD branches. In such cases, the denunciation sent to the Special Inspectorate for investigation was returned to the Secretariat and then, after a final report to superior agencies, was filed away.

It is clear that the majority of denunciations preserved in the Secretariat's files were of a routine character, with the exception of some exceptional bureaucratic situations when, after the Special Inspectorate's report, Beria personally decided to close the investigation in spite of the seriousness of the alleged crime (there were such instances).

A denunciation that arrived in the normal way in the NKVD/MVD was immediately sent "for checking" (*na kontrol'*) with a special card labeled "Document check" (*kontrol' po zaiavleniiu*) attached. The card gave the name of the writer of the letter and his address, identified the addressee, provided a short summary of the letter's contents and a word-for-word transcript of any decisions taken by the People's Commissar or his deputies, and noted whether the document had been forwarded to other bureaucratic agencies.

Sometimes the higher officers of the Secretariat (at the instance of the People's Commissar or on their own initiative) would summon the writer of the denunciation for a personal interview. In this case the bureaucratic machine cranked out yet another document, as a supplement to the denunciation—a report on the results of the interview, written by the interviewer.

After the denunciation was registered with the Secretariat, its movement from office to office was a matter of bureaucratic routine. It is interesting that the bureaucrats in their pragmatic cynicism quickly crossed out all of the ideological rhetoric with which the denouncers had so painstakingly decorated their compositions. The People's Commissar or one of his deputies usually underlined with pen or pencil only the concrete facts: that which it would be possible to verify; that for which someone could be fired or arrested. (This does not mean, however, that ideological rhetoric did not have an influence on NKVD officers. While it was not information susceptible to verification, ideology did fit into the bureaucrat's system of ideological code and cultural symbols, enabling him to recognize the writer as "one of our own" or "an outsider.")

As a rule, vague complaints and lamentations weakly supported by evidence were forwarded to various offices without attracting much interest, and then got some kind of official stamp and were put in the files for preservation into eternity.

Ideological rhetoric had a greater effect when addressed not to state but to party organs, which were responsible for the total political situation in the country and were therefore more concerned with the mood of the population and its grievances. A complaint or denunciation forwarded from the Central Committee, especially with the magic stamp *"Kontrol'"* (check), automatically had higher status. Such a document demanded much greater attention and effort from the bureaucrats, who would use all possible verification procedures in their investigation.

If a denunciation sent from the Central Committee contained compromising material about higher officers or generals of the NKVD, and if that material interested the Cadres Division of the party's Central Committee, which was responsible for the appointment of *nomenklatura* officials, then the information was investigated by bureaucrats of the highest rank (even up to section directors in the counterespionage organ SMERSH). All documents related to higher officers of the NKVD of the USSR were classified "Top Secret." In many cases the last name of the person under investigation was written into the already typed text by hand, as an additional guarantee of secrecy, so that even the trusted clerical employees could only guess who "the cart was going to run over" this time.

The procedure for processing denunciations even depended upon the capacity in which Beria received them. In one case Beria received a denunciation at the chief military prosecutor's office that was addressed to Comrade Beria, Politburo member, and not to the People's Commissar of the NKVD. Beria did not handle the investigation within his department but immediately forwarded the denunciation to "the appropriate office," that of Central Committee secretary Malenkov, who at that time also headed the party Control Commission.[34] The latter sent the denunciation back to Beria for checking after it had been processed in the Control Commission. Malenkov was behaving in accordance with the "laws" of the party hierarchy: Beria's de facto status was higher, and Malenkov, by sending the denunciation back, was emphasizing the fact that he was carrying out instructions of the higher-level hierarch.[35]

Beria sent denunciations he received to higher-level party and state bureaucrats in the Central Committee, even if they were sent to him as People's Commissar of the NKVD.[36] This was what happened, for example, with the anonymous denunciation of the chairman of the Arts Committee of the Soviet of People's Commissars, Khrapchenko. And when Malenkov received an anonymous denunciation of the commander of the NKVD rear security troops,

[34] Komissia Partiinogo Kontrolia pri TsK VKP (b).

[35] GARF, f. 9401, op. 1, d. 4930, l. 533.

[36] Among the documents I have examined, there were also denunciations addressed to Beria as vice chairman of the Soviet of People's Commissars (Sovnarkom) of the USSR. See, e.g., GARF, f. 9401, op. 1, d. 4930, l. 533.

Second Belorussian Front—one Rogatin—he immediately forwarded the document to Beria at the NKVD.

The most common method of processing denunciations was to send them to the appropriate local NKVD jurisdiction or, if the document was not about an NKVD officer, to the Central Committee of the Communist Party, to regional or republican party committees, or to central or local state agencies.

The NKVD authorities used a special bureaucratic lexicon when submitting documents for investigation, as if to "program" into the investigating office a certain attitude toward the facts. The cover letter for an ordinary denunciation normally contained but one sentence and looked more or less like this:

From: The People's Commissariat of Internal Affairs, USSR
August, 1945
No. _____
City of Moscow
Top Secret
To: Comrade G. M. Malenkov, Central Committee of the All-Union Communist Party [Bolsheviks]
I am sending you the enclosed anonymous letter.
[Signed] People's Commissar of Internal Affairs of the USSR [Beria]

Sometimes the accompanying letter announced that the document was sent for "verification and administrative action," which indicated that the NKVD leadership had a stronger interest in the denunciatory material. Cases are known in which Beria, while forwarding the document to a party committee for "examination and administrative action," would order his own apparatus to make inquiries into the matter as well, just to be certain.

Another formula was: "Please inform us of the outcome of the investigation." Generally speaking, it was not necessary to make a special request for this. Letters signed by Beria always received answers. In the symbolic system of the Soviet bureaucracy, however, the request to be informed of the outcome indicated that higher authorities had a particular interest in the case and excluded (or practically excluded) the possibility of a purely formal answer— a form letter reply.

It was a special case when the People's Commissar or one of his deputies wrote "personal" (or, as Beria wrote on one of his covering letters to First Secretary of the Ukrainian Central Committee Khrushchev, "Please look into this" [*proshu zainteresovat'sia*]) on the address of the forwarded document (which was usually sent to someone in a high post in the party or state hierarchy—a minister, regional party secretary, or the like). In the bureaucratic shorthand of the time, a note like this was pregnant with meaning. It indicated not merely the confidentiality of the letter (all such correspondence was stamped "secret" or "top secret") but also a demand that the high authority addressed pay special attention to the course of the investigation, overseeing it personally.

So we see that the Soviet party-state system made use of a wide range of bureaucratic codes, allowing officials to signal the importance of a document or to "program" the course of the investigation by the addition of a single word or phrase to the cover letter.

Procedures for investigating denunciations on the spot might include secret operational measures; interrogation of witnesses and victims; and mailing out various inquiries to gather information about the author of the denunciation or about those whom he denounced. Sometimes an operative or even a brigade of trusted agents would be dispatched to the site. In the most important cases Special Assignment Officers of the NKVD (usually holding the rank of colonel) and their deputies would be dispatched.

The final phase of work related to the denunciation was the report to the People's Commissar (later, Minister) or his deputy on the results of the investigation and the decisions reached. The NKVD leadership could, in contravention of the law, break off further investigation on its own initiative, limit disciplinary measures taken by lower-level offices, send the denunciation on for further investigation, or forward it to the appropriate organs for final trial. And here, as will be shown below, Beria's personal attitude often decided the fate of the denunciation's victim or that of its author (if his or her accusations proved upon investigation to be slanderous).[37]

The latitude for choice in decision making; the possibility of not taking the case to court, even if it involved very serious crimes; the unlimited right (unlimited, i.e., barring the intervention of the highest state authorities) to decide questions of guilt and responsibility before trial—all these were elements of the Soviet bureaucracy's complex system of corporate self-defense against the denunciatory activities of the population.

METHODS OF BUREAUCRATIC OBSTRUCTION OF DENUNCIATIONS: THE CIRCLE OF COLLECTIVE ACCOUNTABILITY (*krugovaia poruka*)

The existence of denunciation as a specific form of political culture in traditional society and as a means of social control over the behavior of local authorities in the vast spaces of the USSR was a "sword of Damocles" hanging constantly over the heads of the bureaucrats. The population, which had no means of democratic control over officials' actions, used denunciation as a way to bring in the central power to resolve this or that conflict, to defend itself against the malfeasance of local bureaucrats, and to restore justice.

---

[37] Beria's successor at the post, Kruglov, had less latitude for action as he was not a Politburo member.

It would have been strange indeed had the bureaucracy not found ways to counteract denouncers and to defend itself against the intervention of the central power. In a situation where even potential centers of opposition were totally suppressed, especially following the "Great Terror" of the thirties, the chances that low- and middle-level bureaucrats would be able to block the denunciatory activity of the population were substantially higher. The key was not to "get into anything political," for the authorities could hope to avoid responsibility for misdeeds in other areas, such as economic crimes and malfeasance.

The most farsighted bureaucrats understood this and strove to make sure that things did not get so bad that the oppressed population would send the most dangerous form of denunciation (the "disinterested" variety) to the highest leaders of the country. Others took a riskier path. They "broke the rules of the game," by which the "people's government" was supposed to be concerned solely with the people's needs, and created in their jurisdiction, their small city or district, an atmosphere of "suppression of criticism" that made any attempt at denunciation extremely dangerous. Consider, for example, the following description: "The party committee secretaries are completely under the influence of Iosif'ian. Surrounding himself with his own people, Iosif'ian feels himself total master of the situation, he suppresses criticism without fear of reprisal, he does whatever he wants."[38] Such was the picture that many denouncers painted as they embarked on the gamble of joining battle with "the bosses."

At times the local authorities of distant regions felt that they could act with impunity. A. S. Semenova, a party member from Kursk oblast, wrote to Beria as follows:

In response to my letter and public statement at the district party meeting about the defects of the work of the district and the kolkhoz in which I live, the district leaders, Comrade Shamanin and Comrade Abrosimov, organized unprecedented harassment against me. District party representative I. A. Per'kov, together with rural soviet chairman P. A. Kostin and kolkhoz chairman A. P. Golovin, told the kolkhozniks that "Anna Semenovna sent in a denunciation because we lost interest in her" and similar insinuations.

They didn't give me the work assignment I requested. They took away my bread ration. They told Golovin: "Do everything you can to make her leave." He did it with a will.

They tried to get my landlady to evict me from my hut. . . . Life became really impossible. Anyway, the hut needed repairs and there was nothing to heat it with. The kolkhoz chairman had the nerve to say, "You're not a fine lady; you can bring some wood from the forest." He knows perfectly well that I can't walk half a kilometer without getting out of breath. . . .

One could die from this kind of life.

[38] GARF, f. 9401, op. 1, d. 4930, l. 298.

But I will not die in the hope that Moscow Bolsheviks will investigate the questions that I have raised and protect me from all these horrors.[39]

In many such cases, "the Moscow Bolsheviks" really did intervene and take measures. The central authorities, of course, had to worry about their popularity and their legitimacy in the eyes of the population: this was in the interest of the entire ruling class of Communist Russia. There is nothing more dangerous for rulers than allowing the population to lose all hope of protection and support from the government. So those who "broke the rules of the game" were actually opposing their own estate, and they could expect severe retribution.

For Russian bureaucrats the biggest risk lay not in breaking the laws themselves but in losing their "sense of proportion," their "feeling for their turf," their knowledge of what they could and could not get away with. It was precisely this simple truth that denunciation authors and the regime leaders had in mind when they referred to "out-of-control bureaucrats."

Among the permissible methods of suppressing criticism were various softer forms of pressure on subordinates and the population. Preventing the "critic's" (the denunciation author's) promotion at work, denying him use of a collective farm horse, seizing upon minor violations of formal rules and instructions, so as to put the squeeze on the actual or potential denouncer—none of these went beyond the bounds of bureaucratic propriety or put the bureaucrat in a compromising position.

It was another matter to go beyond the accepted bounds, not of the law but of community ethics. This occurred, for example, when officials were not content simply to "put the squeeze on" authors of complaints and petitions sent to central organs, but went further and actually seized their letters. Yet it was quite widely known that such things happened. People who took the road of confrontation with "the bosses" constantly feared that the local authorities were simply seizing their letters at the post office, acting just as they had in the time of Nicholas the First. (The postmaster in Gogol's play *The Inspector General* also acted in this way.)

A kolkhoznik named Khoron'ko, author of a denunciation of the malfeasance of officials in Osokarovskii district (Karaganda oblast, Kazakhstan), demonstrated that at least two of his letters had been intercepted by local authorities using the services of the military censor, who had the legal right to seize correspondence or to blank out any information of military significance. According to Khoron'ko, his enemies "were in bed with" the local NKVD and the military censor and "under the pretext of state security protect themselves from Moscow and Soviet justice. . . . I have written two letters to Comrade Stalin about the above-mentioned facts. But obviously they did not reach him,

[39] Ibid., d. 4931, l. 239.

but fell into Loshmanov's hands." (Loshmanov was a local official persecuting Khoron'ko.) Complaints of this sort were normal in letters reaching the NKVD. It is not surprising that denouncers preferred to avoid using the regular post if they could, sending their letters instead by more exotic routes: they would, for instance, drop them in the boxes set up at the entrances of NKVD or NKGB buildings, or at other offices and organizations, sometimes without an envelope.

In general, the conviction of informers and denouncers that local bureaucrats were seizing their letters, and that the country's leaders simply did not know the truth, fed the legend of the "good tsar" and his "evil servants." And indeed the "good tsar," in the person of one party hierarch or another, would, in the name of the central power, severely punish the violators of bureaucratic propriety, those who deviated from the generally accepted rules of the bureaucratic game. They would be removed from their positions and expelled from the party; some were arrested and tried. To judge from the material I have seen, sometimes there were full-scale purges of local bureaucracies or of the officials of this or that department, not only for suppression of criticism but also for serious financial malfeasance, abuse of power, corruption, and so on. In the early period such purges were referred to in bureaucratic parlance as "lancing the boil."

In short, there were both legal and illegal methods of suppressing criticism. The corporate morals of the bureaucrats censured gross and obvious violations of law that would discredit the entire bureaucracy in the eyes of the population, but they accepted, or at any rate took a neutral stance toward, more refined traditional methods of self-defense. Intercepting correspondence, using the military censor and postal workers for one's own purposes, was obviously a "shady practice." But other methods yielding analogous results did not provoke distaste even in the central authorities, much less in the lower levels of the bureaucratic estate.

The common practice of returning a denunciation to local authorities was in effect little different from the interception of correspondence. In this case the denunciation most often fell into the hands of those against whom it was written, or of their friends and associates, none of whom had any interest in "airing dirty laundry." Such an "investigation" resulted in much unpleasantness for the denouncer. This in turn strengthened the conviction of the populace that the only place to seek justice was at the very top of the pyramid of power—from the just and sinless "chiefs" (*vozhdi*).

Those bureaucrats who avoided gross violations of the "rules of the game" and did not overstep the bounds of bureaucratic morals were often saved from accountability by patrons at higher levels. Every "big boss" had his own people in local positions upon whom he depended, whom he trusted, and who were personally devoted to him. If they had good relations with higher-ups, the local "bosses" could avoid accountability for serious misbehavior and even crimes.

"Loshmanov knew of these disorders, yet he was merely transferred to another jurisdiction, without punishment." Such phrases appear often in denunciations sent to the NKVD. One common method of saving "one's own man" from accountability was to punish him for internal disciplinary infractions, even in cases of criminal misconduct. In one of the denunciations I found an egregious example: a man implicated in the rape of one of his female subordinates received as punishment twenty days of jail and a demotion. Cases that developed according to a similar scenario appear frequently in the NKVD Secretariat files: formal measures were taken and the case was filed. In one case, for example, Beria removed an acquaintance from his post as NKVD commander of rear security forces on the Second Belorussian Front for misappropriation of captured materiel, compelling female subordinates to sleep with him, and other crimes and misdemeanors. Without bringing the case to trial, Beria prevented his acquaintance from sinning further—by removing him to another post on another front.

In the bureaucrats' system of defense against denunciation, discrediting the character of the denouncer had an important place. If the denouncer frequently relied on "a few words about myself" to strengthen his case, refutation of the denunciation offered a mirror image of the same ploy. The denouncer, pointing to his services to the regime, tried to show that he was right because he was "one of our own" (*svoi*), while the bureaucrats tried to show that he was wrong because he was "an outsider" (*chuzhoi*). One distorted logic confronted another: it was the denouncer who was discredited rather than his or her information. In general the accused's defense was based on the same rhetorical tactics as the slanderous denunciation: the clear facts were not disputed but simply given another interpretation, one more favorable to the denunciation's target. The Soviet bureaucrats' system of corporate self-presentation included one very important postulate: that any "personal motive" of a denouncer who appealed to the central authorities devalued his information, bringing it into question morally and in many cases entirely obviating the necessity of seeking counterarguments or offering a defense. This was especially the case with anonymous denunciations. Refusal to sign almost automatically evoked doubt about whether the denouncer's motives were "pure," leading to suspicion that there was an element of personal interest in the results of the investigation. When an investigation concluded that an anonymous denunciation was slanderous, the revelation of the author's identity, together with some evidence of his personal interest in the results of the investigation, were the final stroke proving the complete innocence of the denunciation's victim. (And the search for an anonymous author under the pretext of seeking further information from him was an important part of any investigation.)

As noted earlier, bureaucrats who observed "the rules of the game" and knew the limits of the permissible could feel that they were relatively safe and did not need to fear denunciations: they were protected by the network of

150   *Kozlov*

"collective accountability" based on personal ties. Only the "transgressors," those who grossly violated the written and unwritten rules of behavior and bureaucratic ethics, could seriously suffer from denunciations.

However, under certain circumstances the system of bureaucratic defense against denunciations could malfunction. In the first place this could occur if the "rules of the game" were broken by those very higher authorities who had set them up. In unstable or crisis situations, or in the course of major reforms ("revolution from above"), the "chiefs" would appeal directly to the masses, calling on them to expose "enemies" and "saboteurs" and smashing the bureaucracy's congenital conservatism. In this way the stable relationships and predetermined behavior of the bureaucratic layer of society were broken up. The political symbiosis of the "chiefs," the masses, and the bureaucrats would cease to exist, one part of the bureaucracy would attack another, the denunciatory activity of the masses and of the bureaucrats themselves would reach an apogee, and the investigation of denunciations would become a mere formality. The denunciation as a "normal" instrument of administrative oversight and control, allowing the exposure and punishment of "transgressors," would be converted into a means of political struggle. The system of bureaucratic self-defense against denunciations would cease to work. The destructive potential of denunciation would be fully realized. "The people" would take their revenge upon the bureaucracy but, having smashed the complex, self-regulating equilibrium of the social system at the chiefs' call, they themselves would then become victims of still greater lawlessness.

In the second place, in certain rare cases the denunciatory activity of the population of one or another region, in combination with an influx of complaints, letters to newspapers, and so on, would reach such magnitude that it became a political rather than an administrative problem. This would force the central power to intervene to reestablish "law and order," breaking up the circle of collective accountability (*krugovaia poruka*) and the whole system of personal ties. In this situation it was no longer safe to save "one's own" people.

In the third place, local "hitches" in the bureaucrats' system of collective accountability in the localities did sometimes occur. One or another institution within the local government structure might begin a struggle for power or attempt to widen its sphere of influence. A wave of mutual denunciations and exposures would begin. The "disinterested denunciations" written "from below" would become a dangerous weapon in the internecine struggle, whether they were truth or slander. This sharply raised any given denouncer's chances of success and stimulated the composition of more and more denunciations. Intervention of the central authorities, undesirable under normal circumstances, would become the only exit from the local crisis of authority.

To use Marx's apt expression, bureaucrats treat the state as their private property. However, the paternalistic statism of the Communist regime imbued "the people," or at least its more active representatives, with the same feeling. In the resulting conflict between these two positions, neither side could gain the upper hand without smashing the system as a whole. The regime's chiefs were the arbiters of the inevitable compromise: indeed, their own power depended upon this conflict between the "masses" and the "apparatus." The denunciation in its turn was one of the instruments of control that maintained the equilibrium of the entire system of relationships that constituted Soviet society. Under certain conditions, it could become one specific factor in dynamic changes in that system, facilitating turnover in the bureaucratic elite and political transformations of the regime. The "ignition key" for these functions was always in the hands of the ruling Communist oligarchy.

IN PLACE OF A CONCLUSION

I have never been a proponent of global theoretical generalizations based on relatively limited local empirical materials. Frankly speaking, I do not believe that analysis of the denunciations from the late 1940s and early 1950s can lead to any serious changes in the traditional understanding of the nature of Soviet Communism in general or of Stalinism in particular. But such an analysis is fundamentally important for an understanding of the deep continuities between Communist governance and traditional Russian statism. In this sense, denunciations and denunciatory activity have always been an attribute of Russian governance and, in fact, have served as substitutes for many social institutions.

In modern Russia, my own observation suggests that denunciations are no longer a means of controlling the work of the governing apparatus. Fortunately, this time around denunciations have not been an instrument of political struggle in the overturn (or transformation?) of the ruling Russian elite. Yet at the same time it is hardly good that the traditional resort of the "oppressed and degraded" in their search for justice has disappeared. And the new institutions, formally established and nominally resembling the institutions of civil society, have refused to work at all effectively. This breakdown in the traditional Russian interrelationship between the central authorities, the people, and the bureaucracy is one of the salient characteristics of the present Russian crisis, producing a situation in which the populace has no place to turn and government institutions are corrupted as never before. The bureaucracy has torn itself free of all restraints; no one today exercises any control over it; the system of "Leader-bureaucracy-masses" is broken; and with it has been smashed the population's traditional view of the central authorities as higher arbiters and protectors of the people.

The fact that the institution of denunciation has ceased, or is ceasing, to play its previous role in the administrative system is a blessing, as far as any normal, thinking person is concerned. But the fact that in its place, and in place of other traditional institutions, there remains a lacuna that has yet to be filled; that through the breach has washed a wave of corruption and bureaucratic lawlessness; and that the bureaucracy has since Brezhnev's time been escaping from the control of the "chiefs" and has not yet come under the control of the institutions of civil society—all of this calls into question any hopes for the success of political and economic reforms. It is not the historian's business to prescribe remedies. But it is sad, if nonetheless necessary, to recognize that in Russia, that country of paradoxes, the disappearance of an ancient sin—mass denunciation—has been not only an obvious blessing but also a much more subtle curse.

The Uses of *Volksgemeinschaft:* Letters to the NSDAP Kreisleitung Eisenach, 1939–1940*

John Connelly
University of California, Berkeley

INTRODUCTION

"Informers," "denunciations": for students of the Third Reich these terms inevitably conjure up visions of the Gestapo and jackbooted policemen coming to arrest political opponents or the racially undesirable. Yet many denunciations in the National Socialist era had little to do with police work or internal security. Often their recipient was a person we might describe as a member of the "helping professions"—that is, a party officer in his capacity as ombudsman, welfare administrator, dispenser of patronage, or precinct captain. One such personage was the district leader (*Kreisleiter*).[1]

The district office (*Kreisleitung*) of the Nazi Party (NSDAP) was the most important party institution in the daily lives of citizens of the Third Reich. This was the place where directives from above requiring action and grievances from below requiring resolution came together. The district leaders possessed considerable powers within their districts. After 1936 they had authority over the appointment of local administrators and could intervene in any issue in the district, provided they did not oppose the interests of higher agencies and did not involve themselves in matters of a "political-police character."[2]

* I would like to thank Margaret L. Anderson, Robert Gellately, and Witold Rodkiewicz for helpful comments and Benjamin Lazier for assistance in research for this article. All translations are mine. All names have been changed except those of public officials. Historians wishing to verify sources may contact me at Department of History, University of California, Berkeley, California 94720.

[1] After 1938 denunciations became too numerous for the Gestapo and related agencies to handle, and most of them landed in the district office. Bernd Stöver, *Volksgemeinschaft im Dritten Reich: Die Konsensbereitschaft der Deutschen aus der Sicht sozialistischer Exilberichte* (Düsseldorf, 1993), pp. 335–36. See also Gisela Diewald-Kerkmann, *Politische Denunziation im NS-Regime oder Die kleine Macht der "Volksgenossen"* (Bonn, 1995), p. 89.

[2] Barbara Fait, "Die Kreisleiter der NSDAP—nach 1945," in *Von Stalingrad zur Währungsreform: Zur Sozialgeschichte des Umbruchs in Deutschland,* ed. Martin Broszat, Klaus-Dietmar Henke, and Hans Woller (Munich, 1988), p. 222. Dietrich Orlow writes, "At the end of 1939 the StdF [Stellvertreter des Führers] reiterated the party's 'sole responsibility for human relations (*Menschenführung*) functions.'. . . In essence

This essay originally appeared in *The Journal of Modern History* 68 (December 1996).

Curiously, given its crucial role in the society and politics of the Third Reich, the district office has not been a subject of concentrated historical research. Two reasons for this omission suggest themselves. The most obvious is the fact that almost all records of lower NSDAP offices were destroyed in the final days of the war.[3] But an equally important reason for historians' neglect of local party rule has been their own agendas. Early studies, informed by the totalitarian model, concentrated on central agencies like the upper reaches of the party, army, and SS. Later studies often omitted party and state as they pursued the dynamics of the National Socialist economy and the rhythms of everyday life. These revisions of the totalitarian model concentrated most insistently on social areas that were not penetrated by the National Socialist regime. Most numerous were studies of popular opinion and nonconformist behavior—and wherever historians sought nonconformist behavior, they tended to find it. Ironically, some of these historians adopted the earlier school's understanding of the basic dynamic of politics in the Third Reich: the state acted, and citizens reacted.[4]

---

it meant that there was literally no societal function in which the *Kreisleiter* could not 'legally' make his influence felt" (*The History of the Nazi Party, 1933–1945* [Pittsburgh, 1973], pp. 278–79). For the delimitation of NSDAP and Gestapo functions, see Robert Gellately, *The Gestapo and German Society: Enforcing Racial Policy, 1933–1945* (Oxford, 1989), pp. 72–75.

[3] A historian of the former West Germany maintains that only the records of two *Kreise* (Lippe and Offenbach-Main) and one *Gau* (Munich) remain (Stöver, p. 23). It is uncertain whether this calculation accounts for formerly Communist eastern and central Europe, however.

[4] In most social historical studies of Nazi Germany, the regime initiates and the population reacts. If the population seemed to act according to the regime's wishes, it still retained some "inner" integrity. Selections from the volume edited by Hans Mommsen and Susanne Willems, *Herrschaftsalltag im Dritten Reich: Studien und Texte* (Düsseldorf, 1988), are indicative of this trend. In the introduction Hans Mommsen writes that National Socialist propaganda failed to mobilize and that the "primary goal of the NSDAP, to secure the inner allegiance of Volksgenossen, was not fulfilled" (pp. 13–14, 20); Tilla Siegel examines which DAF activities elicited positive responses from workers and finds that "the mass of workers allowed themselves to be taken in by KdF activities" (pp. 133–34); Ralph Angermund writes of judges who had "inner distance" from the National Socialist regime (pp. 332–33); and see Hans Mommsen and Dieter Obst, "Reaction of the German Population to the Persecution of the Jews." See also the classical statement of Detlev Peukert, *Volksgenossen und Gemeinschaftsfremde: Anpassung, Ausmerze und Aufbegehren unter dem Nationalsozialismus* (Cologne, 1982), p. 84. In his view, the system could not have been completely rejected by the population; otherwise, it could not "jene alltäglichen Handlungen abverlangen, die zur Erfüllung routinierter Arbeit, öffentlicher Disziplin, zur Entgegennahme der NS-Propaganda." A great number of local studies have been framed as studies of resistance. A sampling: Klaus-Michael Mallmann and Gerhard Paul, *Herrschaft und Alltag: Ein Industrierevier im Dritten Reich: Widerstand und Verfolgung im Saarland, 1935–1945* (Bonn, 1991), vol. 2; Reinhard Bein, *Widerstand im Nationalsozialismus: Braunschweig, 1930 bis*

One cache of documents that has largely eluded historians' attention suggests a different picture of Nazi rule. They are the records of the district office in Eisenach, which are stored in the rare book room of the Harlan Hatcher Library at the University of Michigan, Ann Arbor.[5] Preserved are hundreds of letters from citizens of Eisenach to "their" district leader, Hermann Köhler. The letters were written in the first year of World War II, and most request assistance in resolving personal problems, especially in getting better housing. The letters reveal an interactive relation between Köhler and the citizens; both he and they use the Nazi catchword of *Volksgemeinschaft* (racial community) to pursue their own agendas.

Historical literature has tended to label *Volksgemeinschaft* as a "myth" and a "fiction."[6] Yet the term did serve important instrumental functions. First, German citizens could invoke *Volksgemeinschaft* for their personal welfare. Nazi ideology made promises to them as *Volksgenossen* (fellow countrymen), and they wrote the district leader to make sure those promises were fulfilled. The district leader, and indeed the Nazi Party, hoped that citizens in need would contact Nazi agencies because this gave the party meaning and power. The NSDAP actively solicited personal grievances from the citizenry. In the Gau (region) Düsseldorf, for example, it established "advice centers" at the local group (*Ort*) level in an attempt to "build bridges" to society. After four years,

---

1945 (Braunschweig, 1985); Peter Berger, *Gegen ein braunes Braunschweig: Skizzen zum Widerstand, 1925–1945* (Hannover, 1980); Kurt Klotzbach, *Gegen den Nationalsozialismus: Widerstand und Verfolgung in Dortmund, 1930–1945* (Hannover, 1969); Erich Matthias and Hermann Weber, eds., *Widerstand gegen den Nationalsozialismus in Mannheim* (Mannheim, 1984); Helmut Beer, *Widerstand gegen den Nationalsozialismus in Nürnberg, 1933–1945* (Nürnberg, 1976); Joseph C. Rossaint, *Widerstand gegen den Nationalsozialismus in Oberhausen* (Frankfurt am Main, 1983); Gerda Zorn, *Widerstand in Hannover* (Frankfurt am Main, 1977); and Edgar Christoffel, *Der Weg durch die Nacht: Verfolgung und Widerstand im Triererland während der Zeit des Nationalsozialismus* (Trier, 1983). For further references: Robert Gellately, "Rethinking the Nazi Terror System: A Historiographical Analysis," *German Studies Review* 14, no. 1 (February 1991): 23–38.

[5] The exception was Dietrich Orlow, who made extensive use of the Eisenach materials for his *The History of the Nazi Party, 1933–1945.* The Eisenach materials are stored in the Meyers collection; all the folders cited in this article are located there.

[6] See esp. Heinrich August Winkler, "Vom Mythos der Volksgemeinschaft," *Archiv für Sozialgeschichte* 17 (1977): 484–90: "Die VG blieb ein Mythos. Die Propaganda des Regimes konnte die Massen nicht zu jener heroischen Opferbereitschaft bewegen, die die Führung ständig beschwor. Das Bewusstsein von gegensätzlichen Klasseninteressen war durchaus präsent: Die Arbeiter vergassen nicht, dass sie 'unten' und andere 'oben' waren. Die Nationalsozialisten ihrerseits wagten nicht, die Massen durch eine radikale Minderung ihres Lebensstandards herauszufordern" (p. 489). In a study of Mannheim, Dieter Schiffmann has reached the conclusion that the *Volksgemeinschaft* was a "fiction" ("Volksopposition," in *Widerstand gegen den Nationalsozialismus in Mannheim,* ed. Erich Matthias and Hermann Weber [Mannheim, 1984], p. 461).

the party rated them a success: "The advice centers allow the party to enter all spheres of life as never before. They permit insight into people's destinies. With uninterrupted and constant contact [*Tuchfühlung*] with the people, the party has a barometer for judging the hopes, inclinations, longings, and distresses of the people and can adjust its policies according to what it finds."[7] In the district of Eisenach, the more difficult and serious problems were passed by the local group to the district. Köhler kept his door open wide to the public, holding six office hours weekly, on Tuesday and Friday mornings.[8] The letters he received show a broad awareness of Köhler's intention to become involved in the citizenry's concerns. Writer after writer cites the district leader's proclaimed "dedication to the lot of the mother" and the like.[9] One letter writer claimed that everyone in her street had urged her to write; another family referred to themselves as the district leader's "*Schützlinge*" (protégés).[10] People wrote to Köhler for every conceivable sort of aid—from having a window fixed, to drumming up business for a canteen, to having a child delivered. Party members took advantage of the ostensible intimacy of the party and often addressed Köhler as "my" district leader.[11]

The party became involved in people's problems not only to assert more power over them; it did so also out of a concern to maintain the power it already held, which required keeping a lid on social unrest. Shortly after the outbreak of war Köhler wrote his local group leaders: "I don't want to see any reports about poor morale. Whoever reports poor morale is also telling me he wants to be relieved of his duties." Eisenach's employment office failed to follow this directive; about a week later it ordered selected women to work in local factories, regardless of whether they had children. These women then threatened to write to their soldier husbands; the local office of the Security Service (Sicher-

---

[7] Heinrich Fetkötter, "Der Gau Düsseldorf," in *Das Buch der deutschen Gaue* (Bayreuth, 1938), pp. 203–11; cited in Reinhard Mann, *Protest und Kontrolle im Dritten Reich: Nationalsozialistische Herrschaft im Alltag einer rheinischen Grossstadt* (Frankfurt and New York, 1987), p. 169.

[8] See Kreisorganisationsleiter Kaeding to Anna Winckler, June 2, 1939, folder 13.

[9] For example, a woman who could not get coal and whose husband was mobilized wrote, "I knew no other way [*Rat*]." Lina Schläger to Köhler, undated, folder 1.

[10] He had helped them with an installation of AC; they claimed to want to listen to the radio in order to follow "current events." Family J. Fricke to Köhler, December 1939, folder 12. Fr. J. Lehmann wrote Köhler in November 1939: "Everyone in Saarbrückerstrasse says I should write you" (*Die ganze Saarbrückerstr. hat mir geraten mich an Ihnen [sic] zu wenden*), folder 13.

[11] For example, party member Werner to Köhler, January 1939, folder 13. On June 7, 1940, another party member requested Köhler's help in getting a transfer from a factory in Gotha to one in Eisenach in order to save several hours of train travel. He concluded: "If you want to do a favor for an old follower [*Gefolgsmann*] of the führer, then please help me, because your power can accomplish a lot [*denn mit Ihrer Macht ist viel getan*]," folder 12.

heitsdienst = SD) saw "a great danger" in this "tactless treatment of these sorely tried women."[12]

A second use of the *Volksgemeinschaft* involved attempts to rearrange the town's sociocultural hierarchy. Köhler was obsessed with achieving respectability for the "little man" in Eisenach's public places. He was the quintessential "little man" turned Nazi official, and he welcomed opportunities to advance the lot of fellow disgruntled plebians.[13] Köhler's task was more social and cultural than economic; it consisted in using all possible devices to humble what he called the "haute volée." He was not greatly exercised by the local elite's wealth and possessions; rather, it was their cultural presence—their way of dress, manner of speech, ceremonies, sensitivities—that troubled him.[14]

---

[12] Circular to Ortsgruppenleiter und alle örtlichen Hoheitsträger des Landkreises Eisenach, September 3, 1939, folder 26. Sicherheitsdienst des Reichsführers SS, Unterabschnitt Thüringen, Aussenstelle Eisenach to Kreisleitung Eisenach, September 18, 1939, folder 1. Evidence from Eisenach's files suggests that the unemployment office there was attempting to compensate for labor lost in Eisenach's factories after the start of the war. In early September it sent out orders for "obligatory work" to women in Eisenach who had been registered by the local offices of the Nazi Women's Organization (NS-Frauenschaft) as "available for work" (*abkömmlich*). They were then apportioned to factories for up to twelve-hour shifts. A letter of September 16 to Köhler from one of those affected reports the great dissatisfaction among women called up for duty, and the perception among them that the authorities had as usual "started with workers' wives," including some with school-age children. Letter of Emilie Sensenschmidt, folder 11. The Nazi regime had passed a decree on June 22, 1938 (*Dienstpflichtverordnung*), permitting the compulsory mobilization of civilian labor. Fears of worsening morale among workers in particular prevented the regime from making full use of the powers of this decree, however. Tim Mason, *Sozialpolitik im Dritten Reich: Arbeiterklasse und Volksgemeinschaft* (Opladen, 1977), pp. 289–99. Because of the availability of separation allowances, many women workers whose husbands were called to military service actually left their jobs after the outbreak of war. Demands that these women be returned to work—by, e.g., the High Command of the Armed Forces—were refused, and until 1943 Nazi leaders consistently declined to consider mobilization of women for the war effort. Tim Mason, *Nazism, Fascism, and the Working Class* (Glasgow, 1995), pp. 198–201.

[13] Karl-Dietrich Bracher describes the National Socialist elite as "rapidly rising 'revolutionary plebian' from the urban and rural lower middle class" (*The German Dictatorship* [New York, 1970], p. 275). Orlow agrees: "Since as a group the party's Kreisleiters in 1933 were typically frustrated, lower-middle-class individuals, they exhibited upon their rise to power all of the symptoms of a declining social class that suddenly sees a chance to reverse the trend of historical development." In 1935 the NSDAP had 776 district leaders, of whom 58.5 percent were either white-collar workers or civil servants (*The History of the Nazi Party, 1933–1945* [n. 2 above], p. 38).

[14] Thus Köhler's correspondence is full of slighting remarks about "lawyers," "intellectuals," people with titles of any sort, and "society." At a banquet for his political leaders he proposed "schlichtes Abendbrot" but "Es ist reichlich Vorsorge getroffen, dass jeder sich gut satt essen kann. . . .

"Zu diesen Gesellschaftsabend lade ich Sie und Ihre Gattin heute schon herzlich ein.

These agendas overlapped, of course. Köhler wanted to use welfare measures to promote the lot of the "Aryan commoner" who was down on his luck.[15] His promotion of the builder Curt Möller, whom he considered an ideal National Socialist, gives a notion of how Köhler's social and cultural agendas reinforced each other. In March 1939 the district leader supported Möller's petition for a reduction in export promotion tax (*Ausfuhrförderungsabgabe*): "Party member [*Pg. = Parteigenosse*] Möller is one of the oldest party comrades of my district. . . . He built his business up from nothing and fought desperately for the smallest contracts. He was well known as a National Socialist among all the opponents of the Party—and in Eisenach this means among just about all the possessing classes." As late as 1935 the city administration had refused to consider Möller for certain building projects, and thus "only pressure from the party could convince these gentlemen that it is their duty to give contracts to National Socialists as well, and to consider party comrades just as they do old Freemasons, who are well represented in the building trade in Eisenach."[16]

Wohlgemerkt handelt es sich nicht um eine Aufforderung, sondern um eine Einladung. . . . Ich erwarte dringend, dass jeder Eingeladene an dieser Veranstaltung teilnimmt, und ich würde es als eigenartig empfinden, wenn meiner Einladung nicht Folge geleistet wird. Es braucht nicht ein einziger von Ihnen sich dabei Gewissensbisse zu machen wegen der Kleidung, sowohl für Sie, als auch für Ihre Frau. Ich erwarte aber, dass jeder sein bestes Stück Uniform anzieht und jede Frau ihr bestes Kleid aus dem Schranke hervorholt. Besondere Gesellschaftsgarderobe brauchen sich die Frauen nicht machen zu lassen.

"Ich will Ihnen an diesem Abend zeigen, wie man eine solche Veranstaltung aufzieht. Kommen Sie mit bester Laune, vor allem aber kommen Sie nicht ohne Ihre Frau. Es wird eine Platzordnung eingerichtet, nach der sich jeder einzelne zu richten hat. Am Eingang werde ich mit meiner Frau alle Geladenen begrüssen, und dann wird jeder einzelne an Hand einer Liste feststellen, wo er placiert ist. Ich hoffe, dass keine Eifersüchteleien entstehen wegen der Placierung. Die Ehepaare sitzen selbstverständlich immer zusammen und nicht etwa, wie es bei herkömmlichen Gesellschaften üblich ist, getrennt." Circular 7-39 Kreisleitung to Ortsgruppenleiter und Kreisamtsleiter der NSDAP des Kreises Eisenach, January 24, 1939.

[15] There are several cases of Köhler going to great trouble to achieve justice for the "common" citizen who has been wronged. See, e.g., the case of the Reichsbahnrat W. Herger, who was unjustly imprisoned. Köhler took great pains to have him placed back in his profession. Köhler to Fritz Sauckel, March 16, 1939, folder 11. Köhler also devoted extraordinary efforts to secure a pension for his cleaning lady, whose husband had suddenly died. His petitions for the "little woman" went via the NSDAP *Gau* office to the Stellvertreter des Führers, but they were not successful. Köhler to deputy Gauleiter Siekmeier, February 1, 1940 (and attached correspondence), folder 13.

[16] Köhler named several Freemasons. Köhler to Schiedstelle für den Bereich Handwerk, Berlin, March 18, 1939, folder 11. Köhler's animus was directed against Jews and Freemasons, but not Communists, for whose "idealism" he had sympathy. In a letter of June 23, 1939, to the *Gau* court he took up the case of a lawyer Bohrer, who was still not permitted to practice. "Dr. Georg Bohrer is still forbidden to practice law

Petitioning was a zero-sum game. To take advantage of a resource, one had to show why someone else should be excluded. For that reason, such letters usually had a denunciatory aspect; they run the gamut from innocuous tattle to outright political denunciation. Regardless of intent, they had a political effect. Through their letters, many Eisenachers colluded with Köhler in establishing a hierarchy within the *Volksgemeinschaft* and in excluding some of Eisenach's citizens from the *Volksgemeinschaft* altogether.

THE BATTLE AGAINST "HIGH SOCIETY"

Eisenach was an unexceptional city by central German standards. Its one tourist attraction was the Wartburg, and its one large industry was the BMW factory, which had been refitted to manufacture airplane engines. But Köhler was an exceptional district leader. Dietrich Orlow describes him as a "particularly fanatical" political leader.[17] Of twenty-three district leaders in Thuringia, he was among the youngest, and only he had worked his way up from the lowly position of block leader.[18] Köhler had arrived in Eisenach in 1934, and he quickly set about re-forming public administration. By 1939 Eisenach was rivaled by only one Thuringian city (Gera) for the highest percentage of local Nazi officials in the city council. He also succeeded in packing the city gasworks with men loyal to him. By using ostensibly "illegal" methods of intimidation Köhler built up the local Nazi newspaper from nothing—at the expense

---

or even act as legal adviser. And all he did as a lawyer and member of the Democratic Party was occasionally to defend Communists in political trials. Even today the Gestapo and the party are against the reinstatement of this man as a lawyer. Let us compare him to the intellectual Häuser. Häuser may not have defended Communists, but whoever defends Jews in the fourth and fifth year after the seizure of power—as is well known the Jew is the man who makes a Communist a Communist and exploited the need of the people in order to lead the people to the brink of ruin—is worth far less than a man who once, perhaps for the sake of idealism, defended Communists in the Frankenheim trial, unlike Häuser, who does it for money," folder 12. According to information received by exiled Social Democrats from Germany, the NSDAP was more interested in enlisting Marxists than former members of the DVP, DNVP, or Stahlhelm. Success in making NSDAP members of Marxists was supposedly "not small" (*nicht gering*) (Stöver [n. 1 above], pp. 321–22). Köhler would have agreed with the district leader of Northeim, who said, "An honest Communist is more to my liking than such a *Scheiss-Akademiker*." William Sheridan Allen, *The Nazi Seizure of Power: The Experience of a Single German Town, 1922–1945* (New York, 1985), p. 301.

[17] Orlow, p. 279. Orlow also writes that "the old rural and small-town elites, consisting of independent farmers and small businessmen, was rapidly replaced by small landholders or farm laborers" (p. 38).

[18] None of the others had even been cell leader. Dienstrangliste, T-81, roll 646, National Archives, Washington, D.C. Köhler was born in 1899. NSDAP records list Köhler's profession as "engineer." He did not have a college degree.

of what he called "bourgeois" (*bürgerliche*) newspapers.[19] Local businessmen felt a need to consult or at least inform him about every conceivable issue.

Köhler's one disappointment, however, and the "greatest mistake" he made in personnel policy, involved the most important position he had to fill—namely, that of mayor. In 1937 he managed to have the venerable Dr. Janson, who had been in office since 1920, replaced by a Dr. Herbert Müller-Bowe (b. 1896), of Hanau. What recommended Müller-Bowe was his long-standing NSDAP membership, from November 1932. Köhler was soon to discover, however, that two other facts were more important: Müller-Bowe was a reserve army officer and he was a university graduate. As such he was destined to become a major impediment in Köhler's battle to humble Eisenach's "reactionary" high society.[20]

Scarcely a year after taking office, Müller-Bowe roused Köhler's ire by removing a fence surrounding a special SA (*Sturmabteilung*) burial plot, returning it to the function of a public park. Shortly thereafter the two clashed over clients for the "Aryanization" of the house of a Dr. Levi. Müller-Bowe favored the dentist Dr. Paulus, who had been received by the Führer after winning the bobsled competition at the 1936 winter Olympics. Köhler disregarded the promise of "complete support" Hitler had made to the athlete-turned-dentist. For Köhler only one thing mattered: that this dentist had belonged to a Masonic lodge. In his mind there was hardly a more nefarious organization than Freemasonry; the very word evoked for him images of racial and sexual pollution. He suspected the dentist of speculating on Jewish property and of continuing to treat Jewish patients, or, as he put it, continuing to "poke around in filthy Jew-mouths." Köhler supported the application of an "old fighter" who had served the party "for years as a plain simple block leader." In a letter to the *Gau* he wrote: "I do not know if a man who risked his life in Coburg is of greater value to the Third Reich than a man who won the sledding title and has not done anything in the party. He simply became a member in 1933." Köhler regarded this as a decision of principle. The dentist "comes marching along

[19] The *Thüringer Gauzeitung* had increased from 2,085 to 16,000 in four years. Among other things, Köhler used massive force to persuade NSDAP members to subscribe. Köhler to deputy Gauleiter Siekmeier, June 5, 1939.

[20] The Nazi system in many ways preprogramed conflict between district leaders and mayors. See Peter Diehl-Thiele, *Partei und Staat im Dritten Reich: Untersuchungen zum Verhältnis von NSDAP und allgemeiner innerer Staatsverwaltung, 1933–1945* (Munich, 1969), pp. 4–6, 160. See also Horst Matzerath, "Oberbürgermeister im Dritten Reich," in Der *"Führerstaat": Mythos und Realität: Studien zur Struktur und Politik des Dritten Reiches,* ed. Gerhard Hirschfeld and Lothar Kettenacker (Stuttgart, 1981), pp. 243–46; and Jeremy Noakes, "Oberbürgermeister and Gauleiter: City Government between Party and State," in Hirschfeld and Kettenacker, eds., pp. 206–7.

with his gracious wife to all the supposedly elegant society meetings in Eisenach. This is the reactionary society which we strictly disapprove of in Eisenach."²¹ The dentist and Dr. Müller-Bowe were "also socially very compatible."²² The decision of the *Gau* went against Köhler. Apparently, words spoken by Hitler overruled every other consideration, although Köhler suspected the dentist also had high-placed contacts in the Thuringian capital, Weimar.

Köhler's battle with Müller-Bowe and Eisenach's "reaction" only intensified. In early 1939 Köhler struck resolutely. At issue was the new directorship of the city museum. The museum's board, to which Müller-Bowe belonged, had unanimously chosen a candidate from Breslau, a Dr. Knopp, who, beyond membership in the NSDAP going back before 1933, supposedly possessed impressive professional qualifications. Yet such expertise meant nothing to Köhler. He had his own choice: Eisenach city archivist, Dr. Schläger. Schläger had also joined the party before it came to power, even though he had a family to support on RM 50–80 monthly, and "he is still today a decent, honest party member, who performs his duty to the party." The board would not even extend a trial period to this candidate. Köhler demanded that the board be dissolved. He wrote Gauleiter Sauckel that it consisted of reactionaries "of whom we have many in Eisenach." Several were Freemasons; all were old. The board's director, the septuagenarian Dr. Kitzberger, had responded with "Guten Tag" when Köhler "appeared in uniform, personally greeting him loud and audibly with the German greeting ["Heil Hitler"]." Köhler would not budge, though Müller-Bowe informed him that his "intervention in the decisions of the museum" was "not permitted." The mayor wished they could get together personally to try to reach an understanding but knew that Köhler had formed an opinion of him long ago: "Unfortunately, the experiences of these past years have taught me that you pay more heed to the statements of slanderers and denouncers than to me." Köhler suggested to the *Gau* a reorganization of the board; this time he was supported. Schläger became the museum's director.²³

Despite this victory, the influence of reaction and Freemasonry remained pervasive in Köhler's eyes. He kept close tabs on the mayor. Informers let him know of the company the mayor kept—for example, with the hotelier and

²¹ Bei allen sogenannten vornehmen Gesellschaftstreffen in Eisenach mit seiner gnädigen Frau anmarschiert. Es ist die reaktionäre Gesellschaft, die wir in Eisenach strikt ablehnen. (Köhler to Gauwirtschaftsberater Schieber, June 30, 1939, folder 4.)
²² Köhler to Kreisrichter Gimpel, November 8, 1939, folder 4.
²³ Köhler felt himself a representative of the younger generation. See his letter of March 7, 1940, to Oberstaatsanwalt Sesemann, which praises the role played by "young judges" (*blutfrische Richter*), who unfortunately now were mostly in the army (folder 12). In Köhler's view only a young district court president could make right the things older judges had spoiled.

Freemason (seventeenth degree) privy councillor (*Geheimrat*) Walther, who had invited him "with his Rolls-Roys [*sic*] for coffee from Berlin to Stettin." Disciplined party soldier Köhler claimed to make a habit of declining such invitations.[24]

The two leading Nazis of Eisenach thus lived in constant mutual suspicion, one assiduously collecting denunciations against the other. In the summer of 1939 informers told Köhler that the mayor had himself been assembling information with which to blackmail the district leader. Supposedly Müller-Bowe had requisitioned documents seized after Kristallnacht in order to find out whether Mrs. Köhler had been a patron of Jewish shops. In a letter of August 29, 1939, to Gauleiter Sauckel, Köhler demanded Müller-Bowe's dismissal. Before action could be taken, however, Müller-Bowe was called to the colors.

With the onset of war the classes of Eisenach rubbed shoulders more frequently, and disputes increased. Eisenach's citizens seemed well informed of Köhler's zeal to promote the common man. They sedulously informed him of infringements of the ostensibly lower-middle-class norms he advocated. Köhler interceded in April 1940 with district court president Spaete for a Mr. Diener, a "simple worker" who lived as a subtenant in the house of one of Spaete's administrative subordinates, county court director Zeth.[25] Diener had supplied Köhler with evidence of Dr. Zeth's socially condescending behavior toward him—referring to Diener's fiancée as "some woman or other," for example, or knocking over a pram she had been pushing while caring for a neighbor's child. Zeth wanted Diener evicted for confronting him about these insults. Köhler responded by asking Spaete to inform him that "we have more important matters to deal with in wartime than such trivialities."

The "worker" Karl Klemm carefully typed a complaint to Köhler on March 5, 1940. He reported in detail the "constant and incessant molestations, insults to honor, and hostilities" that his family had to suffer at the hands of the family of their landlord, the teacher Simon Wagenhaus:

The nasty tricks and the entirely unfounded and more than ridiculous examples of impudence increased daily, until last summer Mrs. Wagenhaus topped them off with the utterance: "Our house is not a working man's house; go look for an apartment where your own kind live!" Mrs. Wagenhaus has apparently completely forgotten that the age of such Marxist-liberalist views has for some time belonged to the past. After approximately seven years of National Socialist educational work the teachings of the Führer in regard to the *Volksgemeinschaft* should have entered the flesh and blood of every

[24] Köhler to Adjutantur des Gauleiters, June 26, 1940, folder 12. "A messenger of Mr. Walther came to me in order to invite me to a boiled-pork feast [*Wellfleischessen*]. Some prominent people attended this boiled-pork feast. . . . I indignantly declined this invitation too. . . . I have other things to do in wartime than to take part in a boiled-pork feast whose only purpose is to show me what a great man Walther is."

[25] Folder 12.

Volksgenosse or *Volksgenossin*. It is about time that the Wagenhaus family began to change its views and restrained itself from such acts of sabotage to the *Volksgemeinschaft*.[26]

Köhler invited Klemm, and then several days later Wagenhaus, to his office. The pace of production preceding the war also caused numerous disputes at the workplace. The factory representative of the DAF (German Labor Front) in an Eisenach armaments factory wrote in June 1939 that "every day and every hour disputes crop up among workers due to the fantastic pace at which they are working."[27] With the onset of war the "fantastic pace" affected hospitals as well. Workers there attempted to use Köhler's influence to replace the rigid hospital hierarchy with the norms of *Volksgemeinschaft*. In February 1940 the district office received the following report from the district women's group (*Kreisfrauenschaft*):

The two women's service assistants [*Frauenhilfsdienstmädel*], Pauline Wald and Liselotte Dietrich, employed at the city pediatric ward in Born Street, came to our office recently in order to be referred to another workplace. In the discussion that ensued the following picture emerged of the head nurse at that ward, nurse Hilde: She never uttered a word of appreciation, although Wald and Dietrich, just like [the other] nurses, have been doing three weeks of regular night [shifts] as well as mid-day shifts. . . . Besides this, never a word of appreciation was uttered about the blessed institution of the women's assistance service [*Frauenhilfsdienst*]. She does not seem to demonstrate the proper understanding of the present age in general. This was borne out by a disparaging remark at a flag raising next door. P. Wald earned the sneering epithet "National Socialist" when she insisted upon an honorable place to hang a picture of the Führer. . . . In the opinion of nurse Hilde the Führer is not the one responsible for the great progress Germany has made!

Social snobbery and poor political attitude went hand in hand. Shortly thereafter Köhler wrote Mayor Müller-Bowe—who had returned from military service in December 1939—demanding Hilde Gramsch's immediate dismissal: "A woman who describes a flag raising seven years after the seizure of power

[26] Klemm to Köhler, March 5, 1940, folder 1. The complaints of Wagenhaus range from smell of tobacco to radio noises to use of the common shack (*Schuppen*) for drying laundry. Other letter writers were careful to identify social status; like the railroad "worker" Arno Bockmann in his letter of March 17, 1940, which complains about treatment received from his boss, who had called him a "Sabateur" (*sic*) (folder 11). On October 6, 1939, an *SS-Unterscharführer* employed at BMW denounced his boss's failure to make a contribution: "Through his attitude he does not raise the *Opferfreudigkeit* and *Einsatzbereitschaft* of his co-workers. . . . I point this out not in order to seem like an informer, but rather to put a stop to the damaging influence of such elements" (*sondern um solchen Elementen rechtzeitig ihr volksschädliches Handwerk zu legen*) (folder 12).
[27] Betriebsobmann Melas to Kreisobmann der DAF, June 8, 1939, folder 1.

as 'such piss' [*so 'ne Seich*] can under no circumstances remain the head of an institution where young girls are being trained. Moreover, it is not yet customary to use the Heil Hitler greeting in this house." Within a week Gramsch had lost her job.[28]

In a second such case, the physician Busse, head doctor of the city hospital, responded to charges leveled at him by Köhler in response to denunciations:

> The assertion that I do not use the Heil Hitler greeting in principle is untrue. It is furthermore untrue that I intentionally said Heil Hitler in a room occupied by Poles. . . . My position as a doctor, both in the social and the national sense, has been well known in Eisenach for the last forty-nine years. I don't need lessons from the district leader on what greetings are appropriate or on hospital practices. . . . Ever since the brown nurses were employed in the auxiliary hospital Fürstenhof there has apparently been a supervision of admissions to the hospital by the administration. The complaint of the district leader against me gives eloquent witness to the nurses' surveillance of my person. . . . It is clear that with such goings-on the authority of a doctor—especially that of the chief doctor—in a hospital cannot be maintained.[29]

The nurse and party member Anna Mettig made a clever, if not ultimately successful, appeal to *Volksgemeinschaft* as social leveler in a letter of September 11, 1939.[30] She, along with her patients of the *Justusstift* old-age home, had been forcibly evacuated to the more plush *Waldhausstift,* since the former building had been requisitioned as a military hospital. The elderly patients were generally distressed by the move: "In these homes we are perceived as a burden, and the people in them, who mostly come from wealthier areas, try to show off their class superiority, which makes us very bitter." In her desperation to effect a return to the more homey *Justusstift,* Mettig made reference to the key nexus of the *Volksgemeinschaft*: she claimed that mothers who had borne soldier sons were being placed at a disadvantage: "We are talking of mothers who have given sons to the fatherland. . . . According to the Führer the task of the National-Socialist state is to honor such services." But there was little Köhler could do, given the circumstances. Like many contemporaries he seemed convinced the war would not last long. One of his deputies attempted

[28] Köhler to Oberbürgermeister, March 6, 1940, folder 12.

[29] Copies of letters from Busse to Mayor Hackert and Lord Mayor Müller-Bowe, September 2, 1940, folder 3. Müller-Bowe had complained to Köhler in May 1940 that the head nurse was taking her grievances to the party and not to the "command structure [*Gefolgschaft*] of the city administration" to which she belonged (Müller-Bowe to Köhler, May 9, 1940, folder 3).

[30] Folder 13. Mettig as a party member seemed better aware than the average citizen of the discrepancies between party propaganda and reality. She sent copies of this letter to deputy mayor (*Erster Bürgermeister*) Hackert (Müller-Bowe had been called up to active military duty), Köhler, and Gauleiter Fritz Sauckel.

to console Mettig, claiming that after hostilities had ceased the *Justusstift* would get a fresh coat of paint and its patients could move back in no time.[31]

Köhler revealed especial determination to assist mothers who became victims of social snobbery for taking advantage of the Nazi welfare organization's (NSV) services. A Mrs. Degenhardt wrote him on April 24, 1940, as a "soldier's wife and mother, to whom you have promised counsel and assistance": "Six families live in our house, of which five are joined in a constant, mutually helpful *Hausgemeinschaft*. Only one person (Mrs. Breithaupt) has been attempting for years to bring dissension and quarreling into the house. . . . I have to put up with her telling everyone that she is not an NSV member, because we have been clothed and fed for years by the winter aid [*Winterhilfe*]." Mrs. Degenhardt had carefully listed her services to the *Volksgemeinschaft,* including bearing children who would take leading positions in the Hitler Youth. Köhler wrote Breithaupt on May 8:

Especially you, who up to now have not found it necessary to join the NSV, have no reason to get upset about such things. First do your duty to the NSV; then you can have something to say. But even then I would not stand for reproaches to *Volksgenossen* for the support they receive from the NSV. In questioning your *Hausgenossen* here in my office, I have gained the impression that you are not really in agreement with any *Hausgenosse* and that you act in a very domineering way. I'm warning you and hope that no more than this letter will be necessary to make you stop harassing the *Hausgemeinschaft*. . . . Especially in wartime I must pay attention that not only the *Volksgemeinschaft* but above all the *Hausgemeinschaft* is observed in an exemplary manner.[32]

Köhler did not simply accept Degenhardt's word; he investigated the case himself. The district leader took reports at face value only when he received them from his subordinates. The *Hausgenossen* had found a way of dealing with a bothersome neighbor, and by contacting Köhler they had allowed him to make *Volksgemeinschaft* more than a slogan. There were those who had higher places than others in the *Volksgemeinschaft,* but there were also those who could be ostracized from it.

SOCIAL WELFARE

The Nazi regime's provisions for social welfare evolved into a method for enforcing the simple hierarchy of the *Volksgemeinschaft*.[33] The most valued

[31] Mettig ultimately sabotaged her own requests by making loud critical remarks in a streetcar: "Things are much worse than in the time of the system" (Es ist noch viel schlimmer wie in der Systemzeit [Weimar Germany]). Köhler reprimanded her.

[32] Folder 12.

[33] Nazi social welfare policies have attracted relatively little scholarly attention. The first comprehensive study of the major Nazi welfare agency is Herwart Vorländer, *Die*

member was the "German" mother, especially when she produced male off-spring. Also highly valued was anyone who could demonstrate some service to "the movement" or to "Germany," like soldiers or old party members. Party members had a special claim on the party's attention, but their personal lives were also subject to special scrutiny. The fanatical Köhler devoted great effort to assuring that party members would conform to his understanding of Nazi morality. Moreover, whether letter writers were party members or not, Köhler felt free to reject intervention or to forward requests for assistance to less competent state offices.

Köhler possessed great discretion in doling out Eisenach's social welfare resources. He kept careful control over the NSV and received reports on collections as well as disbursements.[34] The former he used as a means of establishing hierarchy within the *Volksgemeinschaft*. Those who did not contribute could not depend on his assistance. In the case of NSDAP members, Köhler even used reports on NSV contributions to maintain discipline. Those party comrades who fell behind on payments were subject to severe reprimand and could be forced to pay even more than the usual contribution. Köhler, of course, could find out precisely how much individuals earned in order to assess their abilities to pay.

Though he was a party official, Köhler could and did intervene in cases that normally the state authorities took care of—especially apartment allotments. But he decided when such interventions would take place. If he decided not to take on a case, he could easily claim that it fell under the state's jurisdiction. He gave orders to the NSV on how to respond in specific cases, and he even kept a contingent of Hitler Youth and BDM (Bund deutscher Mädel) girls in the district office to be of assistance at a moment's notice.[35]

After September 1939 the needs of Eisenachers increased dramatically. Suddenly hundreds of families had to make do without fathers. Köhler and the agencies beneath him publicly announced their desire to "assist and protect" mothers in need. Dr. Georg Ruhl, NSDAP leader in East Eisenach, addressed

---

NSV: Darstellung und Dokumentation einer nationalsozialistischen Organisation (Boppard am Rhein, 1988).

[34] In the Nazi hierarchy, local representatives of the important welfare agency NSV were directly responsible to the district leader (ibid., p. 324). An example of Köhler's determined leadership of the social welfare organization of his district is the circular of December 21, 1939, which instructs the local group leaders to get in touch with families of fallen soldiers, and then with the NSV and Nazi Women's Organization (NS-Frauenschaft) to examine the family situations and help in the "most generous way possible," folder 26.

[35] Köhler to Lotte Brödel, February 24, 1940, folder 13. In October 1939 a Mrs. Heller, whose husband was mobilized, requested a BDM girl to help take care of her children. Köhler made sure she got one. Kreisbauernschaft Eisenach to Kreisleitung, October 4, 1939, folder 1.

a letter to his "dear comrades of the *Wehrmacht*" in September 1940: "If you have any wishes at all, if you are concerned about your loved ones at home, the party and its formations are always prepared to intervene wherever possible."[36] And Köhler rejoiced in inner-party correspondence: "Thank God the woman and the mother play a different role in the Third Reich than in the time of the system. Any time a woman and mother needs protection, she will find the party in stubborn tenacity at her side."[37] Immediately after the outbreak of war he wrote to his local group leaders that "you will now prove that the party has a right to exist."[38]

Beyond a shortage of men, Eisenach experienced a shortage of housing. Immediately after the outbreak of war, hundreds of thousands of Germans were evacuated from western border areas into regions of central Germany that seemed safer from attack. Little new housing had been built in Germany after 1936, and Eisenach, like most cities, suffered grievous housing shortages.[39] Increasingly, disputes emerged in this cramped and poorly supplied Thuringian city; many of these made their way to district leader Köhler. As desperation became common, it also became common to turn to the district leader. If previously he had sought purviews, now purviews sought him.

The tendency to engage in denunciation usually stood in inverse proportion to the confidence letter writers felt about their pleas. War wives and their soldier husbands could avoid excessive politicization in their petitions, at most making reference to general nationalistic catchwords. Thus Corporal Otto Bartel wrote to Köhler on January 13, 1940: "Ever since I was called up to war service, my wife has been constantly harassed by her landlord, the railway conductor Rieber. He worries about things that are none of his business and

[36] Folder 11. Köhler himself addressed a letter to Nazi Party members in the *Wehrmacht* in January 1940, in which he offered his assistance for their wives (folder 15).

[37] Köhler ordered his subordinate party member Bauer to make sure that a Mrs. Baum stopped bothering the children of party member Kundler (folder 13).

[38] Circular to Ortsgruppenleiter und alle örtlichen Hoheitsträger des Landkreises Eisenach, September 3, 1939, folder 26.

[39] The district office organized the reception of the refugees, as well as their housing, and took measures to assure that severe shortages of consumer goods did not ensue. The Saar refugees returned home in summer 1940; from 1943 to 1945 Eisenach would give shelter to thousands of refugees from East Prussia and large cities that had been damaged by bombing. For example, three trainloads arrived from Berlin in July 1943 (letter of July 7, 1943, folder 15). On the housing shortage in German towns, see Ian Kershaw, *Popular Opinion and Political Dissent in the Third Reich: Bavaria, 1933–1945* (Oxford, 1983), p. 99; and Mason, *Sozialpolitik im Dritten Reich* (n. 12 above), pp. 172–73. In Stuttgart the building of new apartments had stopped almost completely by 1939. There was at this point a deficit of between six thousand and eight thousand apartments. As in Eisenach, this shortage was the fault not of local politicians but of "policies of the Reich," which gave "priority to armaments" (Roland Müller, *Stuttgart zur Zeit des Nationalsozialismus* [Stuttgart, 1988], pp. 232–33).

complains in the pettiest way about my wife's housekeeping. My wife, who is already very sensitive following a serious operation, suffers greatly from this coarse treatment. I request, dear district leader, that you make it possible for my wife to speak with you personally, and would be very grateful if you could put pressure on the landlord." Köhler complied promptly.[40]

In September 1939 the landlord Vollmar threatened one Emma Arnold, the second wife of his former son-in-law (very often parties to disputes were related), and her five children with eviction. Her husband, a bill collector in the city gasworks, was presently serving in the army. She wrote: "It is beyond comprehension that Mr. Vollmar has nothing better to do in this great time that we are living in now than to think of ways he can make my life unpleasant." Asking for a stay on the eviction until April, she continued: "By then our [Germany's] just struggle will be over, and my husband will be home again." Köhler replied two days later that a war statute protected her from eviction, yet if Mr. Vollmar should continue to harass her, then she should "immediately notify" him and he "would stand by her side."[41]

The district leader intervened swiftly in the pending libel case of a Mrs. Singer, who was expecting a fourth child. She had called her neighbor Mrs. Hennig a "loony" (*Klapsmale*) in response to a sneer allegedly directed at her pregnancy. Köhler practically instructed the presiding judge, Dr. Zeth, how to act: "A mother-to-be must be spared agitation. . . . In the opinion of the NSDAP there are no more pressing considerations than this. Especially in wartime, when so many young people are being lost, a high value is placed in the coming generation, and I am convinced that the court will not be deaf to this argument. I request that you instruct the arbitrator how he must act in such cases." The principle in this case was clear: "Two years ago the Führer created the cross of honor of the German mother, thus raising the mother above other *Volksgenossen* and placing her at the center of the *Volk*."[42]

Köhler consistently showed concern for the healthy upbringing of "Aryan" children. In a letter of December 1939 a Kurt Steudel—whose wife was expecting a sixth child—described his family's horrid living arrangements. The entire family slept in one room on four beds (two large, two small). The parents shared a bed with two children. "A healthy life has become impossible for the children. . . . I have already been to every possible kind of office asking for an apartment. . . . Everywhere I am told that there are no apartments, but I believe that there must be an opportunity to help a proud family that's moving ahead [proud = *und auf sich hält*]."[43] The father's ambition to work his way up from

[40] Folder 11.
[41] Letters of September 20 and 22, 1939, folder 13.
[42] Letter of June 25, 1940, to Amtsgerichtsvorstand Dr. Zeth, Eisenach, folder 1.
[43] Folder 1.

tough circumstances must have appealed to Köhler, the self-made Nazi. After intervening with the city administration, Kaeding (Köhler's district *Organisationsleiter*) was promised that Steudel would receive the first large apartment that became available, if possible, before his wife's delivery.

In December 1938 a Theresa Henke wrote Köhler that her children constantly suffered from colds because of their wretched apartment. Her husband was plagued by ulcers, and she herself by rheumatism. She concluded that "in spite of vigorous efforts I still haven't been able to find an apartment that I can afford." Köhler ordered the Nazi cell leader in Henke's street to inspect the apartment and send a brief report. The family's situation indeed appears to have been ghastly. The four Henkes shared an apartment consisting only of a kitchen and bedroom in a rear building. The bedroom received no sunlight and was damp; the kitchen walls were covered with mildew. The entire family slept in the bedroom; the twelve-year-old girl had a child's bed which was "moist and moldy," and the ten-year-old slept with her mother. Köhler took exceptional action, writing the real estate office of the city of Eisenach in February: "It is urgently desired that remedial measures be taken and this family be helped."[44]

THE PARTY

In many senses party membership implied greater claims on the services of the *Volksgemeinschaft*. There were a number of offices that Köhler insisted must be reserved for NSDAP members.[45] Party members felt a certain intimacy with Köhler; they knew that if they were in good standing they could count on his assistance, especially against those who would violate the basic norms of the racial community.[46] In particular, people who had joined the NSDAP before 1933

[44] Theresa Henke to Kreisleitung, received December 31, 1938, folder 13.

[45] See letters: Deutscher Siedlerbund e.V., Gaugruppe Thüringen, to Kreisleitung, August 10, 1938, and attached correspondence, folder 1 (Köhler refused a candidate for community leader of a housing settlement who was not an NSDAP member); Köhler to Ministerpräsident Marschler, September 30, 1939, folder 1 (Köhler explained that a Burgwart Erker may not hold an office in the Thuringian Forestry Society, because of his failure to join the NSDAP); or Köhler to Kreishandwerkerschaft, June 6, 1939, folder 1 (in which the district leader stated categorically that no non-NSDAP member may take over a guild).

[46] A party member Werner wrote "his" district leader of an impending eviction. Supposedly Werner had failed to inform his landlord that the latter's wife "was spending time with a panhandler." Werner described himself as "cell leader of the Labor Front [who did his] duty year in and year out. . . . [He] fought in the World War and received the iron cross first and second class for bravery at the front" (Kaeding to Werner, and attached correspondence, January 1940, folder 13). The Gagfah (Gemeinnützige Aktien-Gesellschaft für Angestellten-Heimstätten) in Weimar wrote a threatening note to

felt entitled to special perquisites, which extended to their families as well.[47] Letter writers carefully noted relations to party members in the belief that these would give them a better claim on services.[48]

But the party also made higher demands of its members, and no one was more determined than Hermann Köhler to see that they fulfilled these demands. He claimed to be toughest on himself, and constantly felt that he had to be the first to "give a good example."[49] Köhler considered the demands made on party members to be of a "moral" sort. In case after case he demoted party officials whose marriages fell apart, or who had perpetrated some other "moral" (*sittlich*) misdeed.[50] Köhler presided over cases in which men and women were expelled from the party for undue "affection."[51] After the war had begun, political leaders were not even supposed to sit drinking wine in a

---

one of its renters in January 1940 for not heating his apartment, appealing to his "feeling of *Volksgemeinschaft*." The renter sent this note to "my" district leader, who then instructed the Gagfah not to impede efforts to save coal (Köhler to Gagfah, February 2, 1940, and attached correspondence, folder 1).

[47] See the case of the "old party member" R. Karl of Munich, who wrote the district office in early 1940 requesting aid for his sister, Mrs. Baum. Kaeding sent the request down to the cell, to do "everything possible to help the woman." The cell leader reported having supplied Mrs. Baum with household help. Letter to Kreisorganisationsleiter Kaeding of May 29, 1940, folder 12.

[48] See the letter of Martha Kleinfuss to *Kreisleitung,* June 22, 1940, folder 11, which makes reference to having a brother-in-law "party member Hans Ziegler." Kleinfuss wanted an apartment. (See p. 921 below).

[49] Letter of July 17, 1944, folder 15. On refusal to buy Jewish property: Köhler to Kreisrichter Gimpel, November 8, 1939, folder 4. For example, Köhler had supposedly withdrawn a bid on the Levi property.

[50] Examples: the district court president Spaethe, who at age fifty-eight suddenly wanted to marry his secretary. Letter of March 3, 1940, to Oberstaatsanwalt Sesemann, Weimar, folder 12; the district propaganda speaker: "His wife isn't good enough anymore, and so he is looking for a more educated wife, with whom he can have a scholarly conversation [*mit der er sich gelehrt unterhalten kann*]" (letter of November 17, 1939, to Gauschulungsamt, folder 11); Köhler on a party member who lied about membership in a lodge: "W. is relatively young in years; he is in his mid-thirties and already married three times" (letter of August 8, 1939, folder 11); or the district organization leader of the DAF, whom Köhler wanted demoted because he was too friendly with young women (folder 1). The NSDAP *Gau* office in Weimar found his judgment severe.

[51] Examples: a legal adviser who was accused of becoming "affectionate" with a female coworker and two clients; Köhler had him removed from the party: "A man who has made use of business in an office of the NSDAP in order to satisfy his lustful desires has no place in the NSDAP" (Köhler to Walter Kramer, July 10, 1940, folder 12). A woman was removed from the party and from NS-Frauenschaft because of "moral shortcomings" (*sittliche Verfehlungen*); though they were no longer punishable, she had admitted to relationships with "older colleagues": "We in the party must find that lespian [*sic*] love is punishable" (Wir in der Partei müssen auch die lespische [*sic*] Liebe als strafbar bezeichnen) (Köhler to Deutsches Frauenwerk/Schleiz, July 15, 1940, folder 12).

restaurant after work: "We at home cannot prove ourselves as real men [*ganze Kerle*] with a weapon in our hands. For that reason we must impose a special self-discipline [*Selbstzucht*] upon ourselves."[52] Köhler summarized his morality as one of "doing one's duty," being "a decent guy" (*anständiger Kerl*) and a "real man."[53]

Average German citizens could be pressured to perform certain tasks, but party members found the pressures far greater. For example, they were expected to subscribe to the party newspaper, pay contributions on top of their dues, attend meetings, and take orders without question. Köhler's subordinates kept the district leader well informed about infractions of party norms. In May 1940 a block leader informed Köhler of party member A. Wohlgemuth's supposedly low contributions to the NSV. Köhler summoned Wohlgemuth to his office and, after yelling at him for a bit, forced him to pledge RM 20 on the spot.[54]

People not in the party reinforced this stifling regime by themselves informing Köhler of infractions of party norms. In early 1939 a party member, Oswald Förster, had planned to convert part of his house to commercial space, but the all-seeing *Volksgemeinschaft* stopped him. The space was needed for a family with three children: "The party attaches great value to making healthy living space available for families rich with children." He was given three days to comply before "administrative steps" would be taken.[55]

Women who were abused by NSDAP members took care to inform Köhler of that fact, trusting that he would hold their tormentors to party standards. Else Mehnert, whose husband was killed in the German attack on Poland, wrote in July 1940:

Since April 1, 1940, I have been living in the same hallway with party member Mr. Metzler. I lock my rooms up early every morning before I go to work in the shop. Last Saturday Mrs. Metzler bawled me out for doing this, at which point I told her she must be crazy. That evening when I returned from the shop Mr. Metzler was so mean and said that he would hit me so hard I couldn't get up again, etc. . . . I constantly feel threatened and I hardly have the nerve any more to enter the apartment with my child.

Köhler mediated on her behalf. Average *Volksgenossen* were indispensable accomplices in maintaining internal party norms.[56]

[52] Circular to Ortsgruppenleiter und alle örtlichen Hoheitsträger des Landkreises Eisenach, September 3, 1939, folder 26.
[53] Letter to the deputy Gauleiter Siekmeier, June 5, 1939, folder 11.
[54] Kaeding to Ruhl, May 25, 1940, folder 11.
[55] Ortsgruppe Eisenach-Nord to party member Oswald Förster, May 16, 1939, folder 1.
[56] Folder 1. See also Fritz Montag to Köhler (May 12, 1939, folder 11), who complained of his family's being insulted by "the party member Franz Lenger" who intimated that he and his wife were having children (five) simply in order to get money

THE DISTRICT LEADER AS GUARDIAN OF PARTY SOVEREIGNTY

District leader Köhler was at the center of a constant tension. On the one hand, he was obsessed with achieving prestige and power for his party and with upholding the norms he attached to it. Köhler saw himself as the protector of the party: nothing incensed him more than the notion that the NSDAP could be the object of ridicule.[57] His fears on this score were heightened by a thinly veiled feeling of social inferiority.[58] On the other hand, he had to ensure that the party could maintain a firm grip on the prerogatives it assumed. Once he had seized various powers to adjudicate issues of social welfare, for example, he had to struggle to make sure they did not slip away from him and become appropriated by the *Volksgemeinschaft*. The district leader would not see the party exploited and used his apparatus to keep that from happening.[59]

---

from the party. On September 14, 1939, the soldier Paul Schuster wrote Köhler of a "Max Rieber, party member" who had failed to pay him rent for three months. He claimed to have two small children and a wife who was ill (folder 12). A tailor specializing in uniforms wrote Köhler on July 26, 1939, of a party member, Stettner, who had not paid his bills. Köhler replied that Stettner would pay (folder 13). Party members were especially vulnerable to denunciation if Jews visited them; see the cases of party member Kühn (folder 11) or the alleged party member Wiese (Kreisamtsleiter NSV to Ortsgruppenleiter NSV, Eisenach West, June 7, 1940, folder 13). In the case of Wiese, neighbors concocted National Socialist membership in the hope of more easily exerting pressure upon him.

[57] In May 1940 Köhler sent an aide to one of his local groups to inspect the showing of a film and discovered that the audience, especially its younger members, took the local Nazi's speech to be a farce because he "read everything, and stuttered a lot. . . . I asked a girl sitting next to me why everyone was laughing and she said with a smile that now 'our *Gau* speaker' would speak." Köhler directed that local Nazi officials should no longer introduce films so that the party would no longer "make itself ridiculous." Circular to Ortsgruppenleiter of June 1, 1940, folder 27.

[58] Köhler's correspondence evinces constant fear that he might revert to lowly social status and that the formerly prominent in culture, politics, and the economy would reassert claims to power. In 1939 Köhler rejected a candidate for the Thuringian Forestry Society because he was not a party member. This candidate complained to state authorities that he had been discriminated against because of church membership. Köhler responded to this complaint in a letter to Thuringia's highest state official, Minister President Marschler. He might simply have written that party membership was a prerequisite for such a position, but Eisenach's district leader could not help adding: "Thuringia is governed by old party members [*alte Parteigenossen*] and not by the church." Letter of September 30, 1939, to Thuringian Ministerpräsident Marschler, folder 1. In March 1939 the DAF court of honor and discipline for Gau Thüringen reached a lenient verdict on candidate for party membership Ernst Herbst because, among other things, "further interests of the party have not been infringed." Clearly threatened by this intervention of officials farther up the political and social scale, Köhler wrote in his heavy black pencil, "Au!" (folder 1).

[59] He desired at all costs to keep Dr. Häuser, a lawyer in Eisenach, out of the party: "Why is he coming to the party? Because he needs a party pin on his lapel in order to

At the base of Köhler's concern was a tendency of the citizens of Eisenach to claim that the NSDAP stood behind them in their private disputes. They justified themselves by invoking the *Volksgemeinschaft,* and they made threats in the name of the party. This proved exceedingly difficult for Köhler to deal with. In May 1940 he received a report that a Mrs. Scholl had been making threats in his name against teachers. She told people that she often visited the district office and that they believed her. Neither Köhler nor Kaeding had ever heard of this woman. Köhler wrote back to the cell that "people often make threats in my name, but I can hardly defend myself against such abuses because I usually don't find out about [these] people."[60] In another case, the DAF factory representative at the Melas plant wrote in the summer of 1939 that "these days expressions like 'sabotage and concentration camp' are used in many situations which do not call for them."[61]

Köhler tried to keep such instances to a minimum. He gave strict instructions to subordinates to avoid political threats.[62] Presumably, this would have a cooling effect on the political atmosphere as a whole. In correspondence he warned people against careless denunciations, and he even praised one woman for phrasing her request for assistance in politically neutral language.[63]

---

do business" (letter to Gaugericht der NSDAP, June 19, 1939, folder 12). In 1940 he called a master carpenter to his office who was earning a good salary in "*aircraft construction*" (underlined by Köhler) but only gave 50 pfg. for the war aid collection of the German Red Cross. Kaeding to Schreinermeister Kluger, June 7, 1940, folder 1. See also the attempts of Hans Siemann to enter the party, and the correspondence regarding his supposedly low contributions to the winter aid work. Ortsgruppe Eisenach-Süd to Köhler, November 11, 1939; and Köhler to Siemann, November 20, 1939. The district leader was astounded at Peter's failure to join the NSV until January 1939, and at his attempt to secure the party's assistance in purchasing cheap furniture from a Jewish bank that was being driven out of business.

[60] Es wird leider oft Schindluder mit Drohungen mit dem Kreisleiter getrieben, wogegen ich mich nicht gut wehren kann, weil ich ja grösstenteils nichts davon erfahre, wenn man mit mir droht. (Zellenleiter Schellenberg of Eisenach Ost to Kreisleitung, May 27, 1940; Köhler to Schulleiter Pg. Schellenberg, May 31, 1940, folder 11.)

[61] Betriebsobmann Melas to Kreisobmann der DAF, June 8, 1939, folder 1.

[62] Köhler instructed his political leaders not to use the threat of concentration camps to achieve results. Circular to Ortsgruppenleiter und alle örtlichen Hoheitsträger des Landkreises Eisenach, September 3, 1939.

[63] A Lotte Brödel wrote Köhler on February 19, 1940, that she had attempted to have coal delivered from the company Wimmer; Wimmer told her "more people will have to freeze." She said such words did not help lighten her burden; she had three children and her husband at the "Westfront." She concluded the letter: "I know that sacrifices have to be made in time of war. But under these conditions the health of the children is in danger. The slogan of our dear Führer has always been to help people who really need it." Köhler wrote on the letter: "The woman must be helped immediately. Bring Wimmer to me." In a letter of February 24 the district leader wrote Brödel that Hitler Youths from the district office would bring her coal any time she needed it. He concluded: "By the way, I was very happy to receive your letter, which was not at all nasty,

Beyond this, he used political evaluations of the *Volksgenossen* to control the use of the *Volksgemeinschaft*. He would not act on a report against a neighbor without witnesses and used his apparatus to avoid involvement in cases in which he found the party had little interest.[64] Sometimes the process was simple. The district leader would receive a letter from a "mother" to whom he had "promised" assistance; she would come to his office hours and he would form his own impression. In the case of Mrs. Degenhardt, he questioned every member of the house individually.

In most cases, however, he relied upon his staff for political evaluations, with the goal of maintaining a balance between a citizen's service to the movement and the demands he or she could make. Mrs. Scholl, for example, was not a party member, and she overextended the credit she was due for bearing four "Aryan" children. The cell leader wrote that "as a mother of four children she deserves respect. However, she does nothing for the movement. . . . She wants to have everything and give nothing."[65] In late July 1940 a Mrs. Müller made a similar attempt to place the NSDAP on her side in a purely personal matter. She first made clear that she had five children and that her husband had been in the army for half a year. Then she gave her version of how the *Volksgemeinschaft* had been violated. One day, after discovering that her laundry hanging in the backyard was pasted with chicken droppings, she promised to "punch the person in the mouth [*Gutsche*] who let the chickens out!" The perpetrator—her landlord, Mr. Jahn—overheard this and, after calling her a "dirty pig" (*Dreckschwein*), told her to be careful that he did not "punch her in the mouth" (*Fresse*). Because of the unceasing harassment of the men in that house, Müller requested Köhler's help in getting a new apartment: "These men here in our house have no idea what the men out at the front feel like when all they ever get is mail telling them that their wives at home are being threatened with eviction. . . . It would have been very good if this man [Jahn] had been drafted." Köhler passed the letter down to Dr. Ruhl, the Nazi leader of Müller's neighborhood.[66]

The superficiality of the political evaluations Köhler received from his deputies is striking. Ideology in practice left little room for nuance; Köhler's subor-

---

and can see from it that you bear your fate [*Los*] with dignity and decency. Thank you for that" (folder 13).

[64] In 1940 a woman denounced her husband for calling the Führer an "idiot." Nothing more could be done than issue that man a warning, because only she had heard him. Oberbürgermeister, Kriminalabt. to Köhler, September 9, 1940, folder 1.

[65] Zellenleiter Schellenberg of Eisenach Ost to Kreisleitung, May 27, 1940, folder 11.

[66] Folder 11. Jahn's mother had also been present at the altercation and threatened to report Müller to the party. Apparently Müller was faster in making the denunciation. Mrs. Jahn was "jealous" of Müller: "The mother of Paul Jahn said things to me that were completely unnecessary. We [Müller and her husband] should keep quiet because we couldn't even have got married without help from the state since we got a loan from the state before our wedding." Mrs. Jahn also called Müller a "dirty pig [*Dreckzottel*]."

dinates would judge *Volksgenossen* in terms of a few stock phrases. In 1939 the NSDAP district office of Altena-Lüdenscheid issued Köhler a positive political evaluation for a businessman (not a party member) which read as follows: "He always hung out his flag, did not shop in Jewish stores, always used the German greeting, went to party meetings, never refused posters."[67] Another example of political evaluation is the case of the auditor Mr. Schuster. In 1940, Schuster (also not a party member) wrote Köhler asking for assistance in arranging an exchange of apartments. His family felt constantly molested by the landlord because of their children: "I would like to ask Mr. District Leader to help us get an apartment, perhaps by exchange, because I cannot let my pregnant wife put up with this excitement any longer, and I would like [to have] a healthy fourth child." Before acting, Köhler wanted to know about Schuster's political behavior. The NSDAP cell leader reported to Köhler: "I know *Volksgenosse* Schuster as a respectable human being. His political persuasion has been National Socialist since April 1933." The exchange was made possible.[68]

These sparing words of approval sufficed to win Köhler's advocacy, yet in many cases he chose not to intervene. Often he himself saw through the emptiness of Nazi phraseology. In January 1940 an E. Krawczyk complained of a drop in lunch attendance at her restaurant from 150–80 to 50. In ostensible selflessness, Krawczyk asked how she might still "be of service to the *Volksgemeinschaft*." Yet instead of helping her drum up more business, Köhler forwarded her letter to the unemployment office.[69]

Sometimes he stayed out of private quarrels because competing claims on the *Volksgemeinschaft* seemed equal. One Martha Kleinfuss wrote on June 22, 1940, that, after discovering that she had children, master butcher Rühle refused her an apartment that had previously been "as good as promised" to her. "In my opinion such behavior is very mean and I am amazed that nowadays, when everything is being done for our children, a landlord can get away with such a refusal." Five days later Kaeding informed Kleinfuss that her children could not have been the reason for Rühle's decision: after all, he had finally rented the apartment to a family with two children.[70] Because they were on a par in services to the *Volksgemeinschaft,* the party could not favor either side.

Köhler also refused to become involved in a dispute between the Weissbecker and the Zehm families, both of whom claimed equal ideological merit. Rather, he had them sign the following declaration: "In the present age of great historical happenings we are all linked together for better or for worse. We realize that our military strength ultimately depends on the inner community.

---

[67] Kreisleitung der NSDAP Altena-Lüdenscheid to Kreisleitung der NSDAP Eisenach, July 19, 1939, folder 1.

[68] E. Schuster to Köhler, April 18, 1940, and attached correspondence, folder 13.

[69] Kaeding to Arbeitsamt, January 26, 1940, and attached correspondence, folder 12.

[70] Martha Kleinfuss to Kreisleitung, June 22, 1940, and attached correspondence, folder 11.

We hence regard it as our honorable duty to contribute to the further building of the sturdy block of the German *Volksgemeinschaft* by living together in an exemplary fashion."[71] Rather than exploiting the party for their personal needs, these families would receive increased scrutiny. By making the political private, they had made the private political.

. Köhler could refuse requests for assistance in order to enforce his notions of morality. In the fall of 1939 a Fritz Braun was threatened with losing his license to practice a trade. The NSDAP official from Braun's place of residence sent Köhler an opinion describing Braun as a "dissolute person who left his family in the lurch and is now living with some broad" (liederlicher Mensch, der seine Famile im Stich gelassen hat und mit einem Frauenzimmer zusammenlebt). Köhler simply forwarded this negative opinion to the office responsible for the decision.[72]

One Johanna Lehmann wrote the district leader that she was threatened with eviction because her landlord did not like children. She even made an appeal to the will of Hitler, writing, "Our Führer wants us to have a lot of children and then one can't get an apartment."[73] Köhler's initial reaction was to help this woman, but then he sent NSV representatives to investigate Lehmann's social standing and political attitude. The NSV officials wrote that Lehmann's children were poorly behaved. Her fifteen-year-old daughter was reputed to spend time in the unlighted corridor with soldiers from the Eisenach garrison.[74] Worse, Lehmann herself had the makings of a political troublemaker. Her usage of *Volk*-rhetoric was clumsily self-serving; she made threats to her landlord as if the party's interests were identical with her own. She had gone so far as to instruct her landlord that his son "ought to be fighting for Adolf Hitler." Köhler proved quite sensitive to such rhetorical expropriations of his leader.

In another case of enforcing "morality," Köhler refused to intervene for a woman requesting clemency for her brother, a former party member (joined 1932) in jail for "sexually abusing apprentices who had been assigned to him." This man was a person "given to vice" and therefore he "should sit out his three years."[75]

Despite such concerns for "morality," Köhler refused to become involved in affairs between married women and soldiers. In May 1941 he wrote to his local group leaders on soldiers' "behavior toward the female population": "It is not our task to spy on women who give themselves to soldiers, just as we cannot pay attention to whether the husbands in Paris, Belgrade, or Athens behave in

---

[71] Folder 1.
[72] Letter to Handwerkskammer of October 9, 1939, folder 11.
[73] Folder 1.
[74] In other correspondence Köhler refers to the "ranks of decent German soldiers" (*Reihen anständiger deutscher Soldaten*).
[75] Letter to Gauleitung, October 11, 1939, folder 12.

such a way that they might show their faces to their wives. We cannot become involved in purely family matters."[76] In Eisenach it was Köhler who ultimately determined the boundaries of the political and of the *Volksgemeinschaft*.

EXCLUSIONS FROM THE *Volksgemeinschaft*

Köhler guarded the reputation of the *Volksgemeinschaft* as resolutely as that of the party. Just as he determined how services would be distributed within the national community, he also patrolled its borders. He determined who would belong. But he could not keep the community free of taint without the involvement of the population. Thus he was eager to learn that a Mr. Wächter had allegedly closed the door in the face of a block leader who was collecting for winter relief. Köhler directed the NSV as well as his subordinates: "In order to avoid further run-ins with this family, I order that until further notice no money be collected from them. The block leader tells me that no member of the Wächter family has attended a block evening. Wächter, who spent two years in prison in connection with the infamous BMW affair, damned well should have taken a concern for the party and for the public [hatte es verdammt notwendig, sich um die Partei bzw. um die Öffentlichkeit zu bemühen]. He has not done this, and we do not want to know anything more about him."[77]

Racism provided Köhler with criteria for far more drastic exclusion from the *Volksgemeinschaft*. The district leader's speech was thoroughly saturated with Nazi ideology and his letters drip disdain for Jews and Slavs. He also accepted "racial hygiene" and all that it implied for the handicapped. Though normally Köhler interceded for soldiers' children, he refused to help a soldier who had requested assistance in securing quieter quarters for his retarded child. He wrote the commanding officer: "I would like to tell you in complete confidence my personal opinion on this case. If a child is psychopathic (stupid), then even peace and quiet probably won't do any good."[78] In late 1939 Köhler informed a woman that she would not receive state support for her marriage to a soldier (*Ehedarlehen*) because her father had been judged "congenitally feeble-minded."[79]

More than any other group, Eisenach's handful of Jews became the targets of Köhler's efforts to cleanse the racial community. The district leader's generally deep feelings of resentment and inferiority seemed to converge in anti-Semitism. For Köhler, Jews were as much the cause of the housing shortage

---

[76] Circular of May 7, 1941, folder 28. He allowed for an exception: "Unless a civilian or even a civilian party member approaches and bothers a soldier's wife, even if she agrees to it. In all such cases I request a report."

[77] Köhler to Ruhl, March 5, 1940, folder 11.

[78] Folder 12.

[79] Köhler to E. Laufer, November 4, 1939, folder 13.

as they were of Communism, Freemasonry, and sexual vice. Eisenach's tiny community of Jews threatened culture as well as the economy; in Köhler's mind they were, literally, a biological pestilence. A hint of Jewish relations sufficed to produce an obsessive reaction. In 1939, the director of a tobacco factory—a party member, Claus—was suspected of making insulting remarks about Hermann Göring. The factory had formerly been owned by a Jew. Köhler wrote: "I always have a certain distrust of him, because I cannot get rid of the thought that until a short while ago the local cigar factory, which employs about one thousand people, was secretly run by Jews [*jüdisch getarnt*]. But no evidence could be found. . . . In the course of the last two years I have bothered every imaginable agency and office with this matter. The only thing that is certain is that Claus is a very efficient man."[80] Just as Köhler was radical in taking charge of city administration, in distributing National Socialist welfare, and in enforcing party "morality," so too he was radical in his anti-Semitism. In 1939 he even attempted to instruct Weimar's district leader about how one could "stuff" as many Jews as possible into newly designated "Jew houses."[81]

In the resolution of the "Jewish problem," as in the distribution of social welfare and the battle against high society, Köhler found many willing accomplices in Eisenach's population. Among them was his great rival, Mayor Müller-Bowe, who cooperated closely with the *Kreisleiter* in segregating Jews.[82] Decrees were passed in Berlin successively excluding Jews from the economy and from public life; the population helped to make sure these decrees were carried out to the last detail. As the housing shortage worsened in Eisenach, *Volksgenossen* saw to it that Jews would suffer most.

Given the great scarcity of housing, apartments "over-occupied" by Jews could not escape the scrutiny of the *Volksgenossen*. In April 1939 a measure had been passed allowing local authorities to terminate the leases of Jews on apartments in "Aryan" houses, provided the authorities could offer them space in "Jewish" houses. Eisenach's "Aryan" population was now guaranteed preferred access to apartment space. In October 1939 a Mrs. Fink was scheduled for immediate eviction from her apartment. Her neighbor, Mrs. Grünberg— who was Jewish—was also due for eviction from her four-room apartment, but she had secured a three-month delay of the eviction by protesting that "she can't be simply turned out on the street." Fink was incensed: "How is it possible

[80] Köhler to Kreiswirtschaftsberater, Mannheim, March 4, 1939, folder 13.

[81] Köhler had made sure that Eisenach's Jews lived "crowded together" (*zusammengepfercht*). Köhler to district leader Hofmann in Weimar, January 16, 1940, folder 12.

[82] The mayor's office, along with the city building office, police, and local *Stapo* coordinated with the district office the final measures of "Aryanization" of Jewish property in Eisenach. Müller-Bowe to Köhler, June 19, 1941, folder 5.

in the Third Reich that a Jewess is protected by law, while I as a German enjoy no protection? . . . As a German in the German Reich I should at least be able to lay claim to the same rights as the Jewess! No one demands that she be thrown out onto the street!"[83] The eighty-one-year-old Grünberg had already attracted the attention of the NSDAP and its district leader. She lived in a house owned by a Paul Mies, who had become a party member in 1937. In 1938 Mies hired the lawyer Heinrich Schlächter to help him evict Grünberg. The house had formerly belonged to Grünberg's parents, and she had spent all her life there. When the house was sold in 1924, the new owner ("the Jewish businessman Siegfried Fromm") had pledged never to break her lease. Mies had assumed this obligation when he purchased the house; now he wanted to break it. This put Mies several months ahead of the Nazi legislative apparatus, which was to permit abrogation of leases with Jews only as of May 1939. Schlächter, with the support of the district office, argued not in terms of legalities but in terms of dominant public opinion (*herrschende Volksmeinung*):

Ever since the plaintiff became a member of the NSDAP in May 1937, his obligation to get rid of the Jewess has become more urgent. . . .

It remains to be seen how the living conditions of the Jews in Germany will develop. In any case, they cannot stay here permanently. According to dominant public opinion, which forbids *Hausgemeinschaft* of Aryans and especially party members with Jews, the plaintiffs are no longer obligated to provide asylum to the Jewess. The age of the Jewess and the length of her residence cannot be factors of consideration. Such questions will not be resolved with feelings.

The old principle which says that contracts must be adhered to has always assumed that the conditions under which the contract was made do not change.[84]

[83] Anne Fink to Köhler, undated, folder 13.

[84] Seitdem der Kläger ab Mitte Mai 1937 Mitglied der NSDAP geworden ist, wurde für ihn die Verpflichtung zur Beseitigung der Jüdin aus dem Hause immer dringender. . . .

Wie sich in Zukunft die Lebensverhältnisse der Juden in Deutschland entwickeln werden, ist abzuwarten. Auf die Dauer können sie sowieso nicht mehr hier bleiben. Die Kläger sind nach der herrschenden Volksmeinung, die eine Hausgemeinschaft zwischen Ariern und insbesondere Parteigenossen mit Juden verbietet, nicht mehr verpflichtet, der Jüdin länger ein Asyl im Hause zu gewähren. Dabei muss das Alter der Jüdin und die lange Wohndauer ausser Betracht bleiben. Mit Gefühlen werden solche Fragen nicht gelöst.

Der alte Grundsatz, dass Verträge gehalten werden müssen, hat seit altersher die Voraussetzung, dass die Verhältnisse gleich bleiben, unter denen ein Vertrag abgeschlossen worden ist.

Complaint of the businessman Paul Mies and his wife Adelheid, born Korff gegen Miss Helene Sara Grünberg, Amtsgericht, Abteilung I, Eisenach, February 25, 1939, folder 12. Köhler supported Mies. He wrote the NSDAP *Gau* court later that year: "As a National Socialist, I express the feeling of the *Volk,* and don't get caught up in legal paragraphs." Letter of June 19, 1939, folder 12.

As housing shortages pushed Jews into ever smaller corners of Eisenach, there was never a shortage of "Aryans" willing to take their space and belongings. In the case of Dr. Levi, more than twenty people had made bids.[85]

Volksgenossen did not require a personal interest to inform Köhler of "over-occupied" space, however. In January 1940 a tailor of Kartausserstr. 35 wrote Köhler: "I would like to ask why the Jew Fröhlich, Kartausserstr. 31, is still able to share a six- to seven-room apartment with a woman. There must be some *Volksgenosse* worthier than a Jew who could live in this apartment."[86] Since district leader Köhler had taken a personal interest in "stuffing" together Eisenach's Jews, cases of "over-occupancy" had become rare by that time. But Eisenach's citizens were also eager to enforce *Volksgemeinschaft* in neighboring towns. The widow Korff had her eyes on an apartment in nearby Apolda, where most of her family lived. After the death of her husband, a tax inspector, she felt "completely alone" in Eisenach. She had managed to locate an apartment in Apolda shared by a Jew and his "Aryan" wife. As she wrote Köhler: "The apartment I want is still being held by a Jew from Vienna!"[87] Köhler's somewhat heavy-handed attempt at intercession with the competent district leader (Hofmann, Weimar) failed, however.

Aggrieved *Volksgenossen* could use even imagined contacts with Jews to enforce their notions of *Volksgemeinschaft*. Suspected association with Jews sufficed for full-scale denunciation. In spring 1940, a Kaspar Wiese requested support from the NSV, but "someone" (not identified in the final report) informed the district leader that "Jews are constantly coming to visit party member Wiese" (*bei Pg. W. die Juden ein- und ausgehen*). Köhler ordered his NSV subordinate to investigate and, if the allegations were true, to "take all measures that such behavior deserves." But the report revealed that, contrary to the denunciation, Wiese was not a party member. He was a "quiet, dependable man, politically unobjectionable": "he takes part in collections, and for a senior citizen gives quite generously. When asked about traffic with Jews he declared that the Jewess Berg had once visited him to ask about his wife. There can be no talk of constant visits. There are disagreements among the inhabitants of the house at Michelsbach 28 which can give rise to spitefulness and boasting (*Gehässigkeiten und Angebereien*). There is no reason to suppose that Wiese has regular traffic with Jews. He was expressly told of the consequences of such behavior, and the measures it would call forth."[88] For the small number of Jews in Eisenach, the number of denunciations for contact with Jews is

---

[85] Köhler to Gauwirtschaftsberater Schieber, June 30, 1939, folder 4.

[86] Taube to Köhler, January 29, 1940, folder 12.

[87] Folder 12.

[88] Ortsgruppenamtsleiter NSV, Eisenach West to Kreisamtsleitung, NSV, June 10, 1940, folder 13.

extraordinary.[89] Some Eisenachers may have had hidden sympathies with their Jewish neighbors, but no records of these sympathies have survived. Rather, the records reflect the intense determination of *Volksgenossen* to dissociate themselves from Jewish neighbors. Though not required to do so, an Eisenach trucking firm wrote Köhler on May 15, 1939—barely two weeks after the ordinance was proclaimed permitting leases with Jews to be broken!—asking whether it "may carry out this kind of Jew-move [*Judenumzug*]."[90] A Mr. Kleinmuth, who was not a Nazi Party member, lived in a "Jew-house." He carried out a desperate correspondence attempting to get papers proving he was not a Jew so that he would not be bothered entering and leaving the house: "The welfare office and the police know that I am a non-Jew. . . . Furthermore, the competent agencies are aware that I support the government at every opportunity."[91]

Like their district leader, *Volksgenossen* understood that even a trace of contact with Jews could be made to seem suspect. A Karl Scheglmann, scheduled for eviction, reported to Köhler on February 20, 1939, that his landlord, master butcher Georg König, already owned two houses but had now purchased a third "from the Jew Feinstein." König seemingly wanted to profit while the *Volk* suffered. Not only did he traffic with Jews but he catered to "better" society, successively pushing up rents in order to make room for wealthier tenants.[92]

The final notations in Köhler's correspondence record the last steps in the

[89] Further examples: an employee of a bank allegedly had an "animated" discussion with a Jew (Kassenleiter to Köhler, March 15, 1939, folder 11). Two Jews supposedly spend forty minutes on the property of a party member in order to buy chickens. Dr. Ruhl to party member Leonore Kühn, July 2, 1940, folder 11. Also: copy of testimony of Magda Hasel to Kreisfrauenleiterin Bernhardt of June 28, 1939 (one woman accused another's daughter of cutting Jews' hair; and then was herself accused of shopping at Jewish stores), folder 13. Jews constituted .71 percent of Eisenach's prewar population (absolute number = 360). Gary Mokotoff and Sallyann Amdur Sack, *Where Once We Walked: A Guide to the Jewish Communities Destroyed in the Holocaust* (Teaneck, N. J., 1991), p. 83; *Statistisches Jahrbuch für das Deutsche Reich, hrsg. vom Statistischen Reichsamt* (Berlin, 1940), p. 15. In her study of Lippe, Diewald-Kerkmann also expresses surprise at the relatively high number of denunciations directed at the Jews, who constituted .3 percent of the population ([n. 1 above], p. 93).

[90] Schiecke und Burgermeister, Spedition to Kreisleitung, May 15, 1939, folder 11.

[91] Dem Wohlfahrtstand sowie der Kriminalpolizei ist bekannt, dass ich Nichtjude bin. . . . Ferner ist den zuständigen Stellen bekannt, dass ich bei jeder Gelegenheit die Regierung unterstütze. H. Kleinmuth, "small pensioner," to city council, received at mayor's office November 14, 1939, transferred "for reasons of competence" to district office that same day, folder 1.

[92] Karl Scheglmann to Köhler, February 20, 1939, folder 12. No action on Scheglmann's petition was recorded, but marginal notes by Köhler suggest his appeal to the leveling notion of *Volk* did not fall upon deaf ears.

marginalization of Eisenach's Jews. In a letter of June 1941 on "miserable living conditions in Eisenach," Müller-Bowe reports assiduously moving "Aryan" renters into "Jewish houses" and says that he has arranged for the dentist Paulus to evict the former owner of his house, Dr. Levi. In September 1942 Köhler could report in his typically callous language that "very soon a large bunch of Jews will leave Eisenach. This will free up housing." [In aller Kürze kommt aus Eisenach ein grösserer Schwung Juden weg. Dadurch werden Wohnungen frei.][93]

CONCLUSION: REALLY EXISTING *Volksgemeinschaft*[94]

The National Socialist goal of *Volksgemeinschaft* was never achieved in the way the leadership intended, but neither was *Volksgemeinschaft* myth or fiction. Rather, the appeal to *Volksgemeinschaft* became an instrument with which various groups in Germany could pursue interests that were anything but communal. The context in which they acted was more or less established after 1933. Within this context state and society interacted. As of 1934, district leader Köhler was undoubtedly the driving force behind Eisenach's politics. But much of his power derived from the cooperation of *Volksgenossen*, who sought to use him and Nazi ideology for their own ends. They may not have been believers, but they were participants.

Historical scholarship has been very attentive to signs of whether Germans internalized National Socialist ideology. The consensus is that they did not. But the letters in Köhler's files show that they were at least careful to externalize this ideology. There are very few letters to Köhler in which the writers did not predictably sound all applicable Nazi catchwords, though the majority of the letter writers were not Nazi Party members.[95] This does not mean that they "inwardly" accepted all the tenets of National Socialism; yet clearly they were willing to meet at least the minimal requirements of official decrees. In fact, most letter writers offered more ideological obeisance than Köhler himself required; proof of this are the numerous letter writers he helped even though they did not bend over backward to articulate and implement Nazi ideology. A dynamic of anticipatory compliance (*vorauseilender Gehorsam*) gave National Socialism its tenacity and radicalism—a radicalism that was not de-

[93] Köhler to Gauleitung, September 9, 1942, folder 12.

[94] "Really existing socialism" became a standard self-description of Soviet Bloc regimes in the wake of the Prague Spring. Martin McCauley credits Erich Honecker of East Germany with coining the term (*Marxism-Leninism in the German Democratic Republic* [London, 1979], p. 182).

[95] As of March 1, 1939, 4,458 (9.4 percent) of 47,644 inhabitants in Eisenach's five Ortsgruppen were NSDAP members. This was over twice the German average (4.4 percent).

manded by the party. In fact, Köhler and his subordinates clearly felt uncomfortable with the overpoliticization of private matters.[96]

However, the party did depend upon *Volksgenossen* to give ideology meaning. When the Eisenachers picked up their pens and wrote to Köhler, they brought ideology to life. The more Eisenachers used *Volksgemeinschaft* in solving day-to-day problems, the more the contours of Eisenach's day-to-day reality came to approximate those of the *Volksgemeinschaft*. The result was a perversion of any *Volksgemeinschaft* Nazi Party leaders may have intended: in its innate appeal to self-interest, it turned the officially proclaimed version on its head. But this was also a working brand of *Volksgemeinschaft,* derived from broadly understood principles of National Socialism. It arranged access to scarce and vital goods according to a crude racial-biological hierarchy. Thanks to hundreds of Eisenachers well versed in National Socialist ideology, the position of "German motherhood" was indeed protected, and conditions for "Aryan" breeding were rarely endangered. Thanks to the ever watchful eyes of the *Volksgenossen,* Eisenach's Jews, and later its foreign workers, were carefully excluded from the *Volksgemeinschaft* and its resources. Decrees from above that allocated resources according to racial status meant nothing until a critical mass of citizenry became active in enforcing them. "Aryan" determination to use *Volksgemeinschaft* to secure better living arrangements literally ghettoized the remaining Jewish population. The uncoordinated efforts of diverse citizens assured that ever less room remained in Eisenach for versions of reality that could compete with the one officially sanctioned. What remained was a really existing *Volksgemeinschaft*.

This does not mean that people could do as they wished with district leader Köhler. Hermann Köhler was the ultimate arbiter of *Volksgemeinschaft* in Eisenach. He determined the meaning of the political; personal disputes attained political significance only when Eisenachers' understandings of *Volksgemeinschaft* intersected with his. His view of politics was broad. He wanted not only to fill local institutions with men loyal to him but he also desired to change Eisenach's culture. The district leader intended a deep penetration of Eisenachers' lives, yet he also wanted to shield himself and his party from "purely personal" quarrels. Displacing "high society" became an obsession for him; both within and beyond his party he attempted to enforce a new morality.

The enforcement did not require an open resort to terror, however. Contrary to cliché, the role of terror in holding together this community seems almost

---

[96] As we have seen, Köhler and his aides (see Wiese case, and DAF Melas) were at pains to avoid politicization if possible. See also folder 13 for denunciations against a family for consorting with Poles. The allegations turned out to be unfounded. Kaeding wrote the DAF on March 21, 1940: "Perhaps you will cause Mrs. Hess to be more careful with such reports [*Anzeigen*]."

negligible.[97] No doubt the latent threat of terror was constantly present, but records of Köhler summoning the political police in order to discipline wayward *Volksgenossen* are nonexistent. The consequences of being denounced to the party—if not to the Gestapo—usually amounted to a "warning" or "reprimand," or at worst the loss of a job.[98]

What is also remarkable is the feeling of impunity *Volksgenossen* exhibited in their dealings with Köhler. Petitions may have been full of self-serving ideological catchwords, but rarely were they obsequious. There were even cases in which letter writers threatened to go one step farther if they did not get what they desired. In what was in effect a threat of denunciation, the seventeen-year-old Hans-Hermann Kübel pledged to go to the *Gau* leadership if Köhler did not help him in a personal quarrel.[99] Mrs. Scholl had threatened her cell leader if she did not receive results. In a letter of mid-September 1939, the party member Sensenschmidt instructed Köhler that "in his most recent speech to the Reichstag, the Führer said that he would make every district leader . . . responsible for the morale of his district."[100] Sensenschmidt felt free to write such words because she knew that district leader Köhler determined the party line in Eisenach, as well as the structure and membership of that city's racial community. She knew that district leader Köhler—and the system he served—reserved terror for those outside the *Volksgemeinschaft*.

[97] For an example of this cliché, see Christoffel (n. 4 above), p. 108.

[98] Several reports were received about a Berlin actress's telling "bad jokes about Adolf Hitler" in Eisenach. She received a warning. Köhler to Kriminalpolizei, October 9, 1940, folder 12. In 1939 a report came from Mannheim that party member Claus, the director of a tobacco factory in Eisenach, had called Hermann Göring an "unemployed vagabound" and had referred to the DAF as a "social democratic institution." Nothing was done to him. Köhler to Kreiswirtschaftsberater Mannheim, August 9, 1939, folder 13.

[99] Köhler sent the case down to the cell, and Kübel received a reprimand (*Rüge*). Letter of July 13, 1940, folder 11.

[100] Letter of September 16, 1939, folder 11. Letter writers showed little compunction about contradicting and quarreling with Köhler. On June 30, 1937, the district leader had written the Behringer Raiffeisen Verein, Grossbehringen, on behalf of one of its former employees, party member Hermann Maas, requesting that it allow him a few months' grace period on repayment of a loan. "If you think at all in a National Socialist fashion, then this must give you greater satisfaction than to see the family bled white." The Verein responded on July 3 that the Maases still have RM 197.82 left after their monthly payments: "If Mr. Maas cannot exist on RM 197.82 and is bled white, then we cannot understand how 50 percent of the German people can still be alive" (folder 13). See also the letters of Dr. Busse (n. 29 above).

Denunciations in Twentieth-Century Germany: Aspects of Self-Policing in the Third Reich and the German Democratic Republic

Robert Gellately
Huron College, University of Western Ontario

One of the duties of the "good citizen," as constituted in modern Europe, was to inform the authorities in order to hinder the commission of crimes, track down criminals, or uphold the existing order. The surveillance societies that emerged over the past two centuries can be distinguished from their predecessors in part on the basis of their new formal policing activities, but particularly because of the role envisaged for citizens, whose duty became to watch, listen, and inform the authorities. As this participation became more systematized and became an integral part of routine policing, "panopticism" was established—the all-seeing society in which no one ever felt beyond surveillance. The theory of panopticism is identified now with the work of Michel Foucault. In a few oblique but illuminating phrases he directed attention to the development in modern Europe of a "faceless gaze"—that is, a "permanent, exhaustive, omnipresent surveillance" that "transformed the whole social body into a field of perception: thousands of eyes posted everywhere, mobile attentions ever on the alert, a long, hierarchized network" that extended into all parts of society.[1]

It is only recently that historians have begun to investigate the importance for modern political systems of denunciations, understood broadly as a variety of popular informing to the police or other authorities. This has been associated in the literature on German history with Hitler's dictatorship and, more recently, with the Communist regime of the German Democratic Republic (GDR).[2]

If denunciations have occurred in most modern political systems, historians are, nonetheless, concerned about their specificity. In what follows I shall attempt to show—on the basis of a study of their role in the operation of the Gestapo and the Stasi, the two secret police forces in Germany's two dictatorships—that denunciations vary in many important respects such as their fre-

---

[1] See Michel Foucault, *Discipline and Punish,* trans. A. Sheridan (New York, 1979), pp. 195 ff., esp. p. 214.

[2] See Gerhard Paul, "Deutschland, deine Denunzianten," *Die Zeit* (September 17, 1993), p. 16.

This essay originally appeared in *The Journal of Modern History* 68 (December 1996).

quency, effects, and significance. Although other institutions in both regimes contributed to the establishment, stabilization, and maintenance of these regimes, it was the secret police that played a decisive role in both. Denunciations were tolerated and produced on a greater scale in the Third Reich than (evidently) had been the case in German history until then, in part because the regime sought (like the GDR did later) to control and modify more areas of social life than ever before. If most denunciations flowed freely from below in Nazi Germany, they were more institutionalized, regulated, and routinized in the GDR.

It is difficult to distinguish informing—about breaches of criminal law, for example—from political denunciations of an "enemy" or "opponent" who spoke out of turn, especially in dictatorships in which the meanings of "law" and "political crimes" became so unclear that historians constantly must resort to quotation marks to underline the pseudolegal character of many measures. In this article I shall not draw a sharp distinction between informing and denunciation.

I. Denunciations in Nazi Germany

One way of assessing the nature and scope of denunciations is to examine their role in providing information to the secret police. As a number of recent studies suggest, however, denunciations were by no means restricted to the "police sphere," and they performed numerous social and political functions besides those of assisting the police and contributing to the routine operation of the terror at the grassroots level.[3] It certainly would be useful to compare the nature, extent, and consequences of denunciations to the Nazi Party and those that ended up on the desk of the Gestapo. But local and regional party headquarters destroyed most of the materials we would need as sources; and the party never kept anything like the file system of the Gestapo in the first place. The Gestapo was the final destination for all denunciations regarded by the Nazi regime as "important"—that is, those with an actual or supposed "political" content. To be sure, the concepts of "politics" and "political criminality" were given broad and arbitrary definitions. The Gestapo operated as a kind of clearinghouse for the countless denunciations it received that either streamed in directly from the people or were transmitted via the organizations and institutions of party and state. A study of Gestapo case files covering the whole period from 1933 to 1945, therefore, provides a unique opportunity for a sys-

---

[3] See the new study by Gisela Diewald-Kerkmann, *Politische Denunziation im NS-Regime oder die kleine Macht der "Volksgenossen"* (Bonn, 1995) (hereafter cited as *Politische Denunziation*); and John Connelly's article in this issue, "The Uses of *Volksgemeinschaft*."

tematic analysis of the practices of denunciation over the course of the entire Third Reich.

The mission of the Gestapo expanded steadily as, from 1933 onward, "political criminality" was given a much broader definition than ever before and most forms of dissent and criticism were gradually criminalized. The result was that more "laws" or lawlike measures were put on the books than ever. There was also a large new body of law that pertained to the private sphere and to racial and sexual questions, and the outbreak of war in 1939 brought a new stream of war measures that further strained limited police resources.[4] On top of this, the Gestapo's mission became defined as essentially a preventive one: that is, they were to arrest people and stop certain social "types" before they committed offenses.

In the context of these ever expanding tasks there arose the myth of an "all-knowing" and "ever present" Gestapo. However, the perceived omnipresence of the Gestapo was not due to large numbers of Gestapo officials. Their ranks gradually increased after 1933 until late 1938, when they thinned out as officials volunteered or were drafted for various military tasks.[5] A recent estimate by Elisabeth Kohlhaas indicates that in 1937 there was a maximum of seven thousand officials in the entire Gestapo. And even by August 1, 1941, there were no more than seventy-six hundred in all of the *alt Reich*—that is, prewar Germany.[6] In the war years, when many of the original police experts were drafted or sent to the occupied territories, the Gestapo personnel in Germany began to show signs of deprofessionalization and lowering of their police qualifications. So from the beginning to the end of the regime there was no getting around the limited personnel at the disposal of the Gestapo.[7] In view of these changes it would have been structurally impossible for the Gestapo to accomplish its expanding tasks without cooperation from other police and especially from German society.[8]

[4] For an analysis of the impact of the Gestapo on "crime," see my "Die Gestapo und die 'öffentliche Sicherheit und Ordnung,'" in *". . . Nur für die Sicherheit da?" Zur Geschichte der Polizei im 19. und 20. Jahrhundert,* ed. Herbert Reinke (Frankfurt am Main, 1993), pp. 94–115.

[5] Chef Sipo, "Die Verhütung einer Überbelastung der Staatspolizei(leit)stellen," September 6, 1938, Moscow Central State Archive, fond 500, opis 1, folder 4 (copies in U.S. Holocaust Memorial Museum).

[6] Elisabeth Kohlhaas, "Die Mitarbeiter der regionalen Staatspolizeistellen: Quantitative und qualitative Befunde zur Personalausstattung der Gestapo," in *Die Gestapo— Mythos und Realität,* ed. Gerhard Paul and Klaus-Michael Mallmann (Darmstadt, 1995), pp. 220–35.

[7] Elisabeth Kohlhaas, "Die Mitarbeiter der Gestapo," *Archiv für Polizeigeschichte* 6, no. 15/16 (1995): 2–6.

[8] See Robert Lewis Koehl, *The Black Corps: The Structure and Power Struggles of the Nazi SS* (Madison, Wis., 1983), p. 159; Koehl estimates for September 1939 a total

Some idea of the kind of cooperation that the Gestapo obtained from the population can be gathered from the case files that the Gestapo created on named individuals when they were accused or suspected of a "crime." Although nearly all of these files were destroyed at the war's end, we can deduce from the ones that survive that they reached very large proportions and that in time the regime would have had files on the political lives and opinions of nearly every citizen. The files were destroyed everywhere in Germany with the exception of seventy thousand dossiers in Düsseldorf, nineteen thousand in Würzburg, and about twelve thousand in Speyer.[9] These remaining files are invaluable sources for understanding all aspects of everyday terror, broadly defined, and denunciations in particular.

II. DENUNCIATIONS AND RACE "CRIMES"

Precisely how important were denunciations to the Gestapo? In a book published in 1990 that used as its source base the Gestapo materials in Würzburg—a Catholic area slow to support the Nazis both before and after 1933—I indicated the crucial role of denunciations there. My analysis of 175 case files involving efforts to enforce the social and sexual isolation of the Jews concluded that 57 percent began with an identifiable denunciation from the population at large. The Gestapo discovered only one case on its own. By way of interrogations it uncovered information that led to an additional twenty-six cases, or 15 percent of the total; and eight more cases, or 5 percent of this sample, resulted from tips contributed by the rest of the police network. Nazi organizations provided information that originated twenty-one cases, or about 12 percent of the total. This collaboration suggests that the party played a role in the "formal" terror system, at the very least by passing on material to the Gestapo.[10] "Informally," of course, the party tolerated, directed, and even sponsored all kinds of actions aimed at the Jews.

There is no question, however, that for the everyday activity of the Gestapo denunciations represented the single most important factor in initiating cases. Another point worth noting is that no source of information could be discov-

membership in the Gestapo of about twenty thousand. At the end of 1944, for all of the territory of the Third Reich there were approximately thirty-two thousand persons serving in the Gestapo; three thousand of these were administrative officials and 13,500 were workmen or clerks. See my *The Gestapo and German Society: Enforcing Racial Policy, 1933–1945* (Oxford, 1990), p. 44.

[9] The case files for the Rhine-Ruhr jurisdiction of the Gestapo, whose headquarters were in Düsseldorf, are located in the Nord-Rhein-Westfälisches Hauptstaatsarchiv (cited hereafter as HATA Düsseldorf). The files for Würzburg are in the Staatsarchiv-Würzburg (cited hereafter as STA-Würzburg) and pertain also to all of Lower Franconia. The case files from Neustadt an der Weinstraße are now located in the Landesarchiv-Speyer (cited hereafter as LA Speyer) and cover all of the Palatinate.

[10] For all of the above see Gellately, *The Gestapo and German Society*, pp. 130 ff.

ered in an additional twenty dossiers—11 percent of these files. Such dossiers open with a phrase like "This office has been informed" or "It has been discovered," without saying more. It is very likely that an "ordinary citizen" (a non-official or non–party member) provided the tip but that the Gestapo could not ascertain, or for some reason did not note, the identity of the informant. Given the usual attention to detail in these files, any information that had come from the regular police and/or other official or party channels almost certainly would have been acknowledged by the Gestapo. So when no source can be determined, it is fair to assume that it was either a civilian informer or merely a rumor that circulated thanks to loose tongues or idle chatter. When "agents" of the Gestapo did pass along tips, which was very rare, this information is mentioned in the file. If the cases with "no source" were included with the denunciations from the population, it would mean that nearly 70 percent of Gestapo cases enforcing Nazi racial policies aimed at isolating the Jews could be traced to the participation of denouncers. But even without adding these cases, it is clear that informing by "ordinary" Germans played a crucial role.

Since 1990 I have broadened my research beyond Würzburg and Lower Franconia to include Düsseldorf and the Rhine-Ruhr area, where I have investigated the files of Polish foreign workers, particularly the cases of those accused of "forbidden contact" with Germans.[11] The object of this ongoing investigation is to look at other minority groups regarded as "racial enemies" under Hitler's dictatorship and to study what happened in another social milieu.

If, behind the scenes, Nazi planners drew up schemes for the "extermination through labor" of the Poles, short-term contingencies made it necessary to exploit them. Some were brought to toil in Germany, and by August 1944 there were 1.6 million of them in the country.[12] A large contingent ended up in the jurisdiction of the Düsseldorf Gestapo,[13] where official policy and police instructions portrayed them as "racially foreign and inferior."[14] On arrival in

[11] Reinhard Mann's uncompleted but oft-cited study excludes such groups as the Jews and foreign workers, with dubious justification offered in a footnote. See his *Protest und Kontrolle im Dritten Reich: Nationalsozialistische Herrschaft im Alltag einer rheinischen Großstadt* (Frankfurt am Main, 1987), p. 105, n. 27.

[12] About two-thirds of the Poles were male. See Ulrich Herbert, *Fremdarbeiter: Politik und Praxis des "Ausländer-Einsatzes" in der Kriegswirtschaft des Dritten Reiches* (Berlin, 1985), p. 271, table 42, and p. 272, table 43. There were 5.7 million civilian foreign workers in Germany at that time.

[13] There were 145,946 Poles in Rhineland and Westphalia in September 1944, of a total of 558,967 foreigners there. See ibid., p. 272: Herbert's figures are for Westphalia, North and South, Essen and Düsseldorf. In all, 2,137,137 Polish men and women at one time or another were "forced workers" inside Germany. Christoph U. Schminck-Gustavus, "Zwangsarbeitsrecht und Faschismus: Zur 'Polenpolitik' im 'Dritten Reich,'" *Kritische Justiz* 13 (1980): 1.

[14] Poles were subject to German law, but on top of that they were subject to special *Justiz.* The basic study here is Diemut Majer, *"Fremdvölkische" im Dritten Reich* (Boppard

Germany Poles were told not only that any socializing with Germans was taboo but also that those found guilty of having sexual relations with a German (female or male) would be executed.[15] Marked with badges—a purple *P*—on their clothing, consigned to town, village, or farm like slaves, Poles were warned that failure to work zealously would be punished in a concentration camp. Employers were told to ensure that fraternization at the work site was kept to what was unavoidable.[16]

Threats of draconian punishment were accompanied by confinement in camps or barracks as much as possible.[17] Yet there were complications: Poles had settled in the Rhine-Ruhr area before 1914, there were religious bonds with the German residents, and some degree of popular sympathy developed for the newcomers. Also, most Poles were employed in agriculture, billeted in villages or out of public view on the farms themselves, and, as if to preserve the illusion that they had volunteered to work in Germany, they were permitted a modicum of leisure.[18]

The Gestapo in Düsseldorf created a file system that by 1945 comprised fifty-two categories, arranged according to the "enemy," "crime," or "racial" group involved. Under "foreign workers" there are thousands of dossiers. I want to focus here on just one of the subcategories under "Polish foreign civilian workers"—namely, that pertaining to "forbidden contact" (*Verbotener Umgang*) with Germans. This "crime" was similar to the one I analyzed with re-

---

am Rhein, 1981). They were also subject to "police measures." See, e.g., Reichssicherheitshauptamt to Höheren SS-und Polizeiführer usw., "Straftrechtspflege gegen Polen und Angehörige der Ostvölker," November 5, 1942, HSTA Düsseldorf, RW 36/10, 71.

[15] Indeed, numerous public hangings were carried out—arranged, like the "defamation" of the German women involved, to achieve maximum public relations effect. The exact number of *Einzeltötungen* of Poles is not known. Local and regional studies suggest that many more were killed than is usually suggested in the literature. For a brief examination of popular reactions to the executions, see Gellately, *The Gestapo and German Society,* pp. 232 ff.

[16] The phrase is "jeder gesellige Verkehr." For all of the above, see R58/1030, 28 ff. "Schnellbrief" to local Stapo, March 8, 1940, Bundesarchiv Koblenz, R58/1030, 28 ff., and 42 ff. Wages and division of labor in the workplace should reinforce the racial hierarchy of "master race" and "subhumans."

[17] Some factories had dozens of "camps," some containing over one thousand people. At one time or another there were more than twenty camps in the city of Düsseldorf with a hundred or more persons confined in them, but there were many more camps than that. See Peter Hüttenberger, *Die Industrie und Verwaltungsstadt,* vol. 3 of *Düsseldorf: Geschichte von den Ursprüngen bis ins 20. Jahrhundert* (Düsseldorf, 1989), pp. 640–41. Inside the camps the Gestapo recruited confidential informants from among the foreign workers to help with policing. For Düsseldorf, see, e.g., HSTA Düsseldorf, RW 36/12.

[18] By mid-1944 more than two-thirds of the Poles were employed in agriculture. Herbert, p. 271, table 42.

gard to isolating the Jews in Germany, and I have selected it to facilitate comparisons. Socializing with people from western Europe was not "desired" and, in fact, was specifically criminalized for Poles and others from eastern Europe lest such contacts develop into friendly or sexual relationships.[19] Having "forbidden contact" with Poles, like being "friendly to the Jews," was a vague catchall covering a multitude of sins and reflected the intention to enforce not only the letter but also the spirit of the laws. I located 165 cases of "forbidden contact" between civilian Poles and Germans for the Rhine-Ruhr jurisdiction of the Gestapo. Actually, these are the files of the Germans involved, not the Polish men and women, whose dossiers are missing. I selected eighty-six of these by a random sampling technique—half of them in all. Here I want to pay particular attention to how infringements were detected and brought to the attention of the Gestapo.

The result that stands out is that the largest single number of cases (forty of the eighty-six, or 47 percent) began with denunciations from civilians acting in nonofficial capacities. If a phrase like "it has been observed" was in a letter from the rural police to the Gestapo, I classified the case as initiated by the police rather than as a denunciation, even when there are solid grounds in the file for concluding that a citizen almost certainly had informed the police, who passed along the tip. Unless specific evidence indicated that a citizen did the informing, I gave the police or other authorities the "credit" for starting the case. Even so, denunciations from the population were responsible for more cases than all police, state, or Nazi Party authorities put together. The extent of these denunciations suggests considerable social involvement in the terror system at the grassroots level.

In this sample, thirteen of the eighty-six case files provide no evidence of the source of information, but they almost certainly derived from civilian informers. If one were to add these cases to those that were definitely identifiable as denunciations, it would mean that about 60 percent of the Gestapo files in this sample began with a denunciation. Even the more cautious minimum figure, however—about 45 percent of all these cases—shows broad social participation in the terror system.

Not a single case in this sample resulted from the observations of the Gestapo-Düsseldorf and its spies, and only four began with statements made at interrogations. Other control organizations such as the city police or rural gendarmerie informed in twelve of the eighty-six cases. No tips came from the SS, apart from one from the Secret Service (SD). Altogether, the vaunted Gestapo and police network detected only sixteen cases (19 percent of the total).

Information provided by state and communal authorities—most notably the

---

[19] See Gestapo Düsseldorf to Aussendientsstellen, November 17, 1942, HSTA Düsseldorf, RW 36/d42.

post office, which opened mail—initiated seven additional cases against the Poles. And businesses (more specifically, guards on the premises), were responsible for six more. Nazi Party organizations—or, to be more accurate, usually a member of a party organization such as the Hitler Youth—provided tips that originated four additional files.[20] Again, although there are good grounds for including denunciations from party members with all other denunciations, I wanted to single out informing from private persons. Also, it might be thought that even party members represented an institutional aspect of the terror system.

I have also completed an analysis of seventy-three randomly selected cases in the Würzburg Gestapo files on "forbidden contact" with Polish civilian workers. For reasons of space I have excluded discussion of these findings from this article. However, the results of that analysis—particularly the rate of denunciations—parallel the research findings from the Rhine-Ruhr.

III. Denunciations and Nonracial "Crimes"

As part of my continuing research I am also investigating the role of denunciations in the Nazi terror used against Germans themselves—that is, people not stigmatized as racial "outsiders." It was easy for informers to prey upon the Jews and the Poles and anyone who would help, socialize, or just sympathize with them. All were vulnerable to denunciations. But what about policing German social and "political" life in general? I hypothesized that the Gestapo, which was in charge of this task, would have had a far more difficult time getting needed cooperation when it came to dealing with the behavior of "ordinary" Germans.

To what extent were denunciations used in the enforcement of "laws" in Nazi Germany, particularly during the war, that had little or nothing to do with race? I wanted to conduct a cross-regional analysis of Lower Franconia and the Rhine-Ruhr with the only other region for which Gestapo files survive—namely, the Palatinate, whose Gestapo headquarters was in Neustadt an der Weinstraße.

In order to limit the scope of this research, since the number of potentially interesting and relevant cases is vast, I studied the enforcement of the innocuous-sounding "extraordinary radio measures" introduced during early September 1939. The radio decrees made it a serious offense—subject to the death penalty under some circumstances—to listen to foreign radio.[21] These measures were part of an effort to uphold morale in order to prevent a repeat of the col-

[20] See, e.g., HSTA Düsseldorf, Gestapo 41327.
[21] Senior officials, including some in the police, expressed all kinds of reservations and doubts about the measure, including how it could be enforced. See Reichsminister-

lapse that occurred in World War I. However, by 1939 many people had radios and there was hunger for news. Listening to the radio already had become a widespread social ritual fostered by the regime and it could take place in private. How would it be possible to stop Germans from tuning in, especially when the Allies took ingenious steps to make their broadcasts relevant to German audiences?

I studied a random sample of 226 cases drawn from the three Gestapo jurisdictions. What is remarkable is that 164 of them, or 73 percent of the total, began with an identifiable denunciation from the general population. I selected this crime for closer analysis because I wanted to study a measure that had as little as possible to do with race or political issues. It is often assumed that anti-Semitism or some other form of racism lay behind citizen collaboration with the Nazi regime. In fact, the rate of denunciation in the sphere of nonracial "crimes" was proportionally greater than that involved in enforcing racial policies aimed at the Jews and the Poles.

Other studies now under way or nearing completion that examine the role of denunciations in Gestapo enforcement of political "crimes" that had little or nothing to do with race issues are beginning to confirm this finding. For example, Gerhard Paul's analysis of Gestapo dossiers dealing with the "crime" of listening to foreign radio, now preserved in the Special Court records of Kiel, shows that just over 80 percent of the 121 cases he studied began with a denunciation.[22] Paul's and Klaus-Michael Mallmann's accounts of the Saarland suggest a similar pattern there.[23] Another analysis, which deals with Gestapo enforcement of the so-called malicious gossip law in the Rhine-Ruhr, shows that nearly 60 percent of the 261 Gestapo cases studied began on the basis of a named denouncer.[24] And Eric Johnson's analysis of records from the Special Court in Cologne (511 cases) and from the Gestapo in Krefeld (122 cases) shows that just over 60 percent of all cases dealing with matters other than the "Jewish question" began with denunciations. If the anonymous denunciations he found were added, the figure would be closer to 70 percent.[25]

---

ium für Volksaufklärung und Propaganda, Bundesarchiv Abteilungen Postdam, 630, 174.

[22] Gerhard Paul, *Die Gestapo in Schleswig-Holstein* (Hamburg, 1996).

[23] Klaus-Michael Mallmann and Gerhard Paul, *Herrschaft und Alltag: Ein Industrierevier im Dritten Reich* (Bonn, 1991), pp. 238–41, and their "Gestapo—Mythos und Realität," in *Die Ohnmacht der Allmächtigen,* ed. Bernd Florath, Armin Mitter, Stefan Wolle (Berlin, 1992), p. 105.

[24] Bernward Dörner, "Nationalsozialistische Herrschaft und 'Heimtücke': Untersuchungen zu den Auswirkungen des 'Heimtücke-Gesetzes' vom 20.12.1934 am Beispiel der Stadt Krefeld" (*Wissenschaftliche Hausarbeit,* Berlin, 1987), p. 90. This study excludes anonymous informers.

[25] Eric A. Johnson, "Gender, Race and the Gestapo" (paper presented at the conference "Gender and Crime in Britain and Europe," London, April 3, 1995), table 3.

So the assumption that the Gestapo might have a more difficult time obtaining denunciations in nonracial areas of social life does not hold up. Denunciations that were sent to the Nazi Party, at least to judge by one recent local study, show a similar preponderance of nonracial over race-oriented concerns. In her recently published analysis of 292 letters of denunciation sent to the Nazi Party in Lippe, Gisela Diewald-Kerkmann suggests that, while the largest single "offense" (just over one-quarter of the total) involved forbidden or undesired contact with Jews, virtually all the rest dealt with nonracial issues.[26] However, it is clear that care should be taken in generalizing about the nature and scope of denunciations in Nazi Germany, especially in the war years, on the basis of this sample of letters to the party, given how infrequently issues such as those stemming from "war measures" acts or those pertaining to foreign workers were mentioned by these denouncers, when in fact such matters dominated the operation of the Gestapo during the height of the terror.

Just why the rate of denunciations was proportionally greater in the nonracial sphere than it was with regard to racial issues is an important question.[27] Although further research is called for, at least four or five interrelated factors influenced the varying rates of denunciations elicited with regard to nonracial crimes compared to those that offended against anti-Semitic "laws."

1. *Opportunities for anti-Semitic denunciation.* Jews lived mainly in clusters in Germany and the general population did not have a chance to inform about possible breaches of racist measures they could claim to have witnessed directly. As the German Jews emigrated and/or were forcibly deported, such claims, and even pretexts for informing on Jews and people who offered them help or sympathy, diminished further. Of course, as is only too well known, anti-Semitism without Jews is entirely possible.

2. *Degree of direct Gestapo involvement.* The Gestapo was involved to a much greater degree when the "Jewish question" was at issue. This was the highest racial priority and to some extent the top political priority as well, so of course the Gestapo itself was more actively involved. One suspects that there was also more direct Gestapo involvement in cases against "hard-nosed" political opponents such as the Communists and in cases involving open opposition, such as the July 1944 plot to assassinate Hitler.

[26] See Diewald-Kerkmann, *Politische Denunziation* (n. 3 above), pp. 62–122, esp. p. 63, table 1, and p. 91, table 2.

[27] Johnson, "Gender, Race and the Gestapo," also found this variation. In another sample (of seventy-three Krefeld Gestapo cases that involved the persecution of Jews) he found that 47 percent began with denunciations and a further 7 percent came from anonymous tips. Johnson excludes from his analysis cases where no source of information can be established; of a total of ninety Gestapo cases on the "Jewish question," seventeen (or almost 20 percent) were of this type.

3. *Timing.* The official drive to isolate Jews in Germany took place mainly before the war, and by September 1939 most either had left or been forced out of the country. Those who remained were deported two years later. Beginning at almost the same time, the terror system—in which denunciations constituted a vital ingredient—spread as never before. With the steady criminalization of various aspects of German social life, opportunities to relay information about transgressions of all kinds also increased proportionally.

4. *Expansion of the circle of vulnerability among Germans.* While not everyone could be accused of sympathizing with the Jews or of rejecting some aspect of Nazi anti-Semitism, for example, virtually everyone had access to a radio or was vulnerable to a charge of "malicious gossip."

5. *Opportunities for denunciations against Polish workers.* Certainly the arrival of the Poles coincided with the deepening terror. However, many Poles were confined in camps of one kind or another and were therefore to some extent out of sight of many potential denouncers. There was also more official involvement in policing foreign workers. And there was even a brake on denunciations of foreign workers, since their labor was desperately needed at the time.

A final point should be made about the role of the Gestapo in policing the radio measures: the Gestapo and its mythical "spy network" were responsible for only six such cases in the three districts over the course of the war. Some of these were inquiries from other Gestapo jurisdictions or all-points bulletins. There were only two times when the Gestapo discovered cases on its own in this sample: once more or less by chance in the course of a police "roundup," and once when an official overheard a conversation on the bus on his way to work.[28]

What can be said about police-detected cases in these samples of cases dealing with the Jews, the Poles, and the nonracial radio measures? With regard to enforcing policies and various "measures" aimed at isolating the Jews and the Poles, the police network, including the Gestapo, was responsible for about 20 percent of the cases in each sample. My study of the radio measures shows that the entire police network accounted for only about 10 percent of these cases.[29] Such a relatively small amount of "active" police work in tracking nonracial crimes of ordinary citizens can also be seen in an extensive study of "malicious gossip" handled by the Gestapo in the Palatinate, which shows that

[28] Gestapo 2613, LA Speyer; Gestapo 42516 and 55490, HSTA Düsseldorf.

[29] Police other than the Gestapo found information that led to eight cases (4 percent of the total). This occurred most frequently when uniformed police saw windows improperly darkened at night and during their inquiries overheard a telling phrase or two coming from a foreign radio broadcast.

they came up with only six out of 660 of such cases, and that the police net-work as a whole was responsible for less than 8 percent of them.[30]

If these findings hold up, it would seem that at least 80 percent of all Gestapo cases resulted from sources outside the ranks of the police. If we look at all three of the samples I have investigated here in detail, the Gestapo on its own came up with information to originate forty-four cases out of a total of 560 —8 percent of the total—and in most of these—thirty-seven of the forty-four cases—the information came from interrogations of people already in custody.[31]

This relatively low rate of "active" police detection and investigation would support the hypothesis I have put forward elsewhere that the Nazi police were by and large reactive rather than active.[32] The Gestapo was important to the terror, both for the reputation it gained for mistreating men and women in its grasp and for setting a new tone for the police. Certainly its responsiveness and (generally) positive attitude toward information provided by denouncers represented a major change from the pre-1933 era, and this new attitude must have fostered denunciations. And we should not forget that the Gestapo was very active with regard to certain groups, especially the Communists in Berlin, Hamburg, and elsewhere. Nor should we overlook the fact that the Gestapo went into high gear in the wake of the July 1944 plot to assassinate Hitler, and it brought to bear all the police expertise it could muster to track down sus-pects.[33] Without underestimating the importance of this police activity, how-ever, I would argue that at least for the routine operation of the Gestapo such actions were more the exception than the rule.

These findings about the role of denunciations in the everyday operation of the police, and my characterization of the Nazi police as generally reactive and greatly reliant upon help from the outside, does put into further question at least some of our understandings of the very notion of a "police state" and all that concept implies.

What about patterns of denunciations to the Gestapo and other forms of self-policing across the Rhine-Ruhr, Lower Franconia, and the Palatinate? Much

[30] Eginhard Scharf, "Justiz und Politische Polizei," in *Justiz im Dritten Reich wäh-rend der Jahre nationalsozialistischer Herrschaft im Gebiet des heutigen Landes Rhein-land-Pfalz* (Frankfurt am Main, 1996), pp. 611–711, esp. p. 685.

[31] The total of 560 Gestapo case files includes eighty-six cases of "forbidden contact" with Poles in the Rhine-Ruhr and seventy-three cases in Lower Franconia, 175 "unde-sired contacts" with Jews, and 226 "radio measures" cases.

[32] Dr. Werner Best, one of the key Gestapo leaders behind the scenes, claimed it was mainly reactive. See Nachlaß Werner Best, Bundesarchiv Koblenz, NL 23, vol. 4, 60.

[33] For useful reminders of this aspect of the Gestapo, see the contributions in *Terror, Herrschaft und Alltag im Nationalsozialismus,* ed. Brigitte Berlekamp and Werner Röhr (Münster, 1995).

research remains to be done, but it is worth offering some tentative conclusions. These regions vary in economic structure, social milieu, religious background, and political affiliation, including levels of support for Nazism. The Palatinate was the "brownest" of the three—that is, the one that offered the most support for Nazism—and its citizens had a slightly higher propensity to denounce. However, the "blackest" (most Catholic) of the three districts—the one around Würzburg—was nearly the same. At least with regard to denunciations in the enforcement of the radio measures decree, there seem to have been remarkable parallels. With all due caution, one may conclude that the extent to which "ordinary" citizens participated in denunciations seems to have been similar in different regions, and it is a reasonable hypothesis that this was the national pattern.

How were denunciations conveyed to the Gestapo in all three of these regions with regard to the foreign radio measures? The short answer is that, just as in the samples of cases dealing with the Jews and the Poles, nearly every conceivable means was used. At one end of the scale there were letters, either signed or anonymous, sent to the Gestapo or to some institution of the party or the state, including the Ministry of Justice in Berlin and even Himmler himself. Tips were also offered less directly, to local or regional branches of the party and/or to one of its affiliates. But in many cases one or more people went personally to the offices of the Gestapo to give information. A denunciation could be aimed at one or two people or sometimes at as many as a half-dozen people at the same time.

If we look at the content of the denunciations of suspected breaches of the radio measures, additional aspects of self-policing come to light. Germans became conscious of and self-conscious about language. In conversations about the war, they not only had to guard against incautious remarks as to its cause, course, and likely outcome; they also had to watch what they said lest it betray that their source of information might be foreign radio. Again and again in the files denouncers refer to the "way people spoke," from which their listeners deduced—often incorrectly—that the speakers must have listened to forbidden broadcasts.[34]

What about the motives of the denouncers in this particular sample? It would be improbable and unrealistic to suppose that any single motive was at work. Should we at least regard the provision of denunciations as a measure of popular consensus or a sign of general agreement with the regime, as did the Socialists in exile in the 1930s?[35] Even that conclusion may be too simple, because at least some acts of informing ran directly counter to officially propagated social goals, like the "community of the people," which, at least in theory, was

[34] See Gestapo 58426, Gestapo 38569, and Gestapo 58336, HSTA Düsseldorf.
[35] Bernd Stöver, *Volksgemeinschaft im Dritten Reich* (Düsseldorf, 1993), p. 327.

supposed to be free of social conflict. In fact, the files provide less information than one might expect about the motives of the denouncers, and there are few cases in which the motive is unambiguous. And because some files contain denunciations from more than one person, there is often evidence of varying motives in the same case. When pressed by the Gestapo because of denials by an accused, some denouncers gave even more damning information, for reasons that are impossible to explain on the basis of the evidence in the dossier. One such ordeal led an accused man to commit suicide because he could not carry on in the face of mounting denunciations from neighbors.[36]

The motivation behind a denunciation was definitely of secondary interest to the Gestapo, except when the denunciation proved to be unfounded or ran up against contradictions, or when the Gestapo considered it a "knowingly false accusation." More importance was attached to obtaining information by any and every means, for without it the police could not function.

Setting aside the many files that contain no evidence of motivation one way or the other, the motives of informants in cases where there is some evidence can be divided into two groups: affective and instrumental. This distinction should not be overdrawn because motives were often mixed. Reinhard Mann's study of the Gestapo cases in Düsseldorf suggests that, of 213 denunciations he analyzed, only fifty (24 percent) were motivated by what he terms "system-loyal views (political motives)." More people (eighty of them, or 37 percent) informed for "private motives, resolving private conflicts"; and in eighty-three instances (39 percent of these cases) there was no evidence as to why information was offered. This means that for 76 percent of all these denunciations there is no evidence that the informers were motivated by Nazi ideology.[37]

---

[36] See, e.g., Gestapo 16584 and 61077, HSTA Düsseldorf. On November 12, 1941, a seamstress wrote to the neighborhood branch of the Nazi Party for Essen-Center to accuse her neighbor, Herr H., a sixty-six-year-old invalid, of listening to enemy radio. She named witnesses and said she was prepared to place her room at the disposal of the Gestapo "in order to catch H. in flagrante." The motives of one witness, Fräulein P. (a thirty-six-year-old artist), were opaque. She told the Gestapo in the presence of H. that she "was prepared to answer to her conscience and before the courts under oath." Indeed, she added new denunciations, including that H. defamed Nazi leaders, said Germany could not and should not win the war, and said the policies against the Jews were wrong. By December 10, 1941, H. was in custody. After face-to-face encounters with his accusors, and hopeless denials, H. took his own life and was found dead in his cell at three o'clock on December 11.

[37] See Mann (n. 11 above), p. 295. There is substantial agreement in the findings of Diewald-Kerkmann, *Politische Denunziation* (n. 3 above), p. 150, who suggests that "system-loyal" and/or Nazi "convictions" played a decisive role in only 30 percent of the 292 letters of denunciation to the NSDAP she analyzed, while 38 percent had a "private" or personal motive and 4 percent were anonymous (p. 136). Presumably, the rest had no discernible motive.

In the sample of cases dealing with the "radio measures," expressions of affective motives, such as belief in National Socialism or worship of Hitler, were also extremely rare. There are instances when such emotions were mentioned or when the citizen's duty to support the system was invoked, but as often as not, under scrutiny by the police, there turned out to be more instrumental and personal considerations at work—even in cases where the information was offered by Nazi officials.[38] One point is clear: denunciations were not simply an expression of rabid Nazism; nor, as I have shown with regard to the enforcement of Nazi anti-Semitism, was overt or obvious racism always the decisive factor. It does come as something of a surprise to see in these materials that relatively few people even bothered to make explicit references to the "right kinds" of motives, such as hatred of a stigmatized enemy or commitment to an endorsed or privileged "official" value, even when they were trying to take advantage of the situation for purposes of their own.

But whether or not affective motivation and/or attitudes of civic virtue as defined under Nazism may have lurked behind the acts of some informers on occasion, there is far more evidence of overt instrumental motives. Indeed, it seems safe to conclude that, in spite of the newly proclaimed social ideals, self-interest fueled the self-policing system.

In earlier studies I have suggested that many Gestapo informers played the race card to reap personal advantages of one kind or another. But this instrumental utilization of the Gestapo was at least as pronounced in the sample dealing with the nonracial crime of listening to foreign radio. Denouncers offered tips in order to get rid of enemies, rivals, and competitors. No social group and few social enclaves were entirely immune.[39] Informing tended to occur within social classes, neighborhoods, (apartment) houses, even within families. For example, informing was used extensively to gain advantages in marital conflicts,[40] especially when one party or the other was contemplating divorce.[41] Denunciations might also be made when a divorce was already under

[38] Gestapo 5043, LA Speyer. A Hassloch Blockleiterin of the Nazi Frauenschaft said it was her duty to inform (on a fifty-year-old widow), but the Gestapo concluded the allegation was baseless and "ein infolge Feinschaft entstandenes unverantwortliches Geschwätz."

[39] See Gellately, *The Gestapo and German Society* (n. 8 above), pp. 152 ff. For the view that social "inferiors" also used denunciations to the Nazi Party against their "betters," see Diewald-Kerkmann, *Politische Denunziation,* pp. 136 ff.

[40] Gestapo 53387, HSTA Düsseldorf; Gestapo 13900, STA Würzburg; LA Speyer, Gestapo 2907.

[41] For denunciations grounded also in such claims, see Gestapo 57013, HSTA Düsseldorf; and Gestapo 1341 and Gestapo 1925, LA Speyer. For a sister acting on behalf of an abused wife against the husband, see Gestapo 9395, STA Würzburg.

way, or when it recently had been granted.[42] The personal aims in such cases ran from seeking material advantage to gaining emotional revenge.[43] In spite of official guidelines from the Gestapo and Minister of Justice to do everything possible to stop these kinds of denunciations, the flood could not be held back.[44] Another example of informing within families involved a father who repeatedly denounced his son to the police not only for listening to foreign radio but also for seeking to avoid military service.[45] There were sisters who turned in siblings merely out of anger[46] or from a curious sense of idealism;[47] a nephew who informed on his widowed aunt for no apparent reason;[48] and one cousin who sought revenge on another.[49] Representative of many cases between in-laws was an instance in which a man was denounced by his father-in-law, allegedly for listening to foreign radio, but in reality because of domestic conflicts.[50] In another case a woman informed on her son-in-law in what the Gestapo tersely called an "instrumental denunciation."[51]

---

[42] Gestapo 42295, HSTA Düsseldorf; Gestapo 2240, LA Speyer.

[43] Gestapo 68352, 64749, 42407, 45907, HSTA Düsseldorf; Gestapo 1872, LA Speyer.

[44] See Chef Sipo und des SD to all Gestapo: "Betrifft: Anzeigeerstattung von Verwanten untereinander, insbesondere bei Ehegatten," February 24, 1941, Bundesarchiv Koblenz, R58/243, 317 f.; and "Richterbrief," (November 1, 1944), in *Richterbriefe: Dokumente zur Beeinflussung der deutschen Rechtsprechung, 1942–1944*, ed. Heinz Boberach (Boppard am Rhein, 1975), pp. 363–76.

[45] Gestapo 2570, LA Speyer. Investigation showed there was nothing to the charges; but the motive, according to the gendarme, was that "der Vater nun der Sohn gerne aus dem Haus haben möchte, um sich ein besseres Dasein zu verschaffen."

[46] See Gestapo 60365, HSTA Düsseldorf. The denouncer said she lived in conflict with her sister (who had nine children), who explained, "Dieser Streit entstand dadurch, weil ich meine Schwester gefragt habe, ob mein Kind ein reines Hemdschen bekommen hat."

[47] Gestapo 16582, HSTA Düsseldorf. A woman could not convince her brother that a certain station was really forbidden. Her motive: "Ich habe nur die Anzeige gegen meinen Bruder erstattet, um ihm zu beweisen, daß er nicht recht hat. Mein Bruder ist stets rechthaberisch und meint immer, was er sagt ist richtig."

[48] Gestapo 2607, STA Würzburg. The forty-nine-year-old woman was kept in jail from December 5, 1941, until early in the new year.

[49] Gestapo 1517, LA Speyer.

[50] Gestapo 2260, STA Würzburg. The original denouncer committed suicide. The police concluded he had made "unwahre Angaben über seinen Schwiegersohn."

[51] See Gestapo 11250, STA Würzburg. "Die Anzeige ist nichts anderes als eine Zweckanzeige." For an example of a man informing against his father-in-law, who was found guilty and given four years in a *Zuchthaus* by the court, see Gestapo 6524, HSTA Düsseldorf. The wife of the denouncer noted about his motives: "Die Anzeige ist nicht aus Gehässigkeit erstattet worden. Zwar sind in unserer Familie hin und wieder Streitigkeiten gewesen." For an example of a case between a woman and her brother-in-law, see Gestapo 4272, LA Speyer; for a man who informed against the stepfather of his wife, see Gestapo 2222, STA Würzburg.

Denunciations were often used to resolve frictions between neighbors.[52] One party or another might try, as one couple did, to prevail in a conflict that had begun over the rent by bringing up a "political crime" and thereby involving the Gestapo.[53] The landlord who was denounced in one such case was a member of the Nazi Party and the SS, which, however, gave him no immunity from this kind of instrumental denunciation.[54] In another case the evidence suggests that a group of people living in a house denounced a neighbor when they grew afraid that they would all end up in jail because one tenant was "crazy enough" to be listening to the radio at a volume the whole neighborhood could hear.[55] Other files merely conclude that the parties were "enemies."[56]

These dossiers strongly suggest that the denunciatory atmosphere that developed in Nazi Germany affected more than just those people who were officially stigmatized on the basis of race, or even because of their past politics. A case from Essen illustrates the tangled webs that were woven in this new atmosphere. It began on July 22, 1941, with a letter to the Gestapo in which an employee in the court system "denounced himself." He felt it was inevitable that the Gestapo would soon be at his door. The problem began with a dispute with his wife, who was also embroiled in numerous conflicts with their neighbors—so much so that she is referred to by all in the file, including the husband, as "not quite right" in the head. During one argument with her husband she called out that he was listening to forbidden news, an accusation overheard by a male neighbor. The latter decided to act on this news when he subsequently had an argument with the woman himself. "In order to get some peace and quiet," as this man explained when he was later called in by the Gestapo, he had said to the woman: "You'd better be careful; otherwise I shall turn the tables on you and make you a witness against your own husband." The implication was that the husband would be denounced and the wife would have to testify. That was meant to be only an idle threat; the man said he would never have denounced the husband, whom he and everyone else held to be a "fine and upstanding person." However, when the husband heard of this threat he denounced himself, as he told the Gestapo, because of his vulnerable and public position at the local court and because he had "no neutral witnesses" who

---

[52] See, e.g., Gestapo 58102, Gestapo 5574, Gestapo 38794, Gestapo 52146, HSTA Düsseldorf; Gestapo 8071, STA Würzburg.

[53] Gestapo 5317, LA Speyer. The landlord as the denouncer in this case passed on information given him by his wife, but he made it clear from the outset that he had been having all kinds of conflicts with these tenants. After a considerable investigation, the Gestapo decided there was insufficient evidence to proceed to court.

[54] Gestapo 4830, LA Speyer.

[55] Gestapo 58889, HSTA Düsseldorf.

[56] Gestapo 6223, LA Speyer. The Gestapo concluded that the two women here were "verfeindet."

could support his innocence. The wife soon admitted to the Gestapo that she had deliberately yelled out and spread rumors in order to damage his reputation and get rid of him.[57]

This denunciatory atmosphere also invaded the conflicts and disputes between workmates in factories,[58] and farm workers who became involved in personal strife did not shrink from bringing the most serious political allegations against comrades. One such case is illustrative of the swiftness of the terror "system" in action. A milker working on a farm near Düsseldorf was denounced on October 3, 1939, for listening to Radio Moscow and for making unflattering comments about life in Nazi Germany. He was soon interrogated and his case was sent to the Special Court, but by November 20 the court said there was too little evidence to proceed to trial, pointing out that, even if the man could be found guilty, the matter should be dropped because his "crime" fell under a führer amnesty. But the Gestapo was not content with this decision, and, in an example of "police justice," quietly ignored Hitler's amnesty and "corrected" the court's verdict by placing the accused in "protective custody" on December 2. Just over a week later he was sent ("for the duration of the war") to a concentration camp, initially to Sachsenhausen; his death was reported on November 6, 1940.[59]

Informing the Gestapo of allegations was also a temptation for fired employees seeking revenge,[60] such as one young woman who was dismissed as a servant because of petty theft.[61] Some people tried to get the boss in trouble when they wanted to cover up their own crimes or just to leave his or her service.[62] In spite of the often transparent instrumental motivations of so many of these denunciations, they were still investigated, often at great length and over a considerable period of time.[63]

Denunciations took place even among friends and acquaintances, and they

---

[57] Gestapo 63380, HSTA Düsseldorf. In spite of her selfish motives and poor reputation, and his excellent one, the case was sent to the Special Court, where it was dropped.

[58] Gestapo 9755, HSTA Düsseldorf. See also Gestapo 58353, where "hatred" between workmates was said by the Gestapo to have caused the denunciation.

[59] Gestapo 67565, HSTA Düsseldorf.

[60] Gestapo 47042, HSTA Düsseldorf. See also Gestapo 5249, LA Speyer, for a case from late 1944, fully investigated, where a fired employee denounced the employer and his wife. This case was investigated at length, even though the credibility of the denouncer should have been obvious from the fact that he was mentally disturbed and had been dismissed from the *Wehrmacht* "als geisteskrank."

[61] Gestapo 6939, LA Speyer.

[62] Gestapo 5745 and Gestapo 4032, LA Speyer.

[63] One twenty-six-year-old woman's lack of credibility over the years was summed up by the Gestapo by terming her a psychopathic liar. Her denunciation of her landlady, almost certainly to avoid paying the rent, was investigated seriously. See Gestapo 13226, STA Würzburg.

did not cease in the face of the mythical solidarity of the *Stammtisch*. One man at the evening gathering in the pub "made it evident to the five or six acquaintances by how he spoke" of events on the war front that he must have been listening to foreign news.[64]

From other studies we are beginning to see that denunciations also found their way inside the German army, long thought of as one of the social enclaves more or less resistant to this kind of informing.[65] The impression gained by historians who have studied many cases of the (vaguely defined) crime of "undermining the will to win" (*Wehrkraftzersetzung*) which often entailed little more than uttering incautious remarks—a total of thirty to forty thousand soldiers were found guilty by military courts—suggests that these soldiers were caught mainly because of investigations that began with a denunciation.[66]

Soldiers enjoyed no special immunity with the population when they returned to the "home front," either. A study of the Saarland shows, in fact, that all of the cases of "undermining the will to win" prosecuted in that region began with denunciations from the population, including neighbors, friends, and even wives and mothers. Their motives remain obscure for the most part, but they appear to have ranged from the usual instrumental ones (revenge seeking, envy, personal conflict) to political fanaticism and fear of impending defeat.[67]

The widespread use of denunciations has to be seen in the cultural and social context of an interventionist system that fostered instrumental relations between citizens and regime. The Nazi system of party and state was certainly repressive and highly invasive, but it was almost immediately "normalized" by many people as they began to accept it as part of the structure of everyday life. It is easy enough for us to overlook the many ways in which the population began to count on and even solicit the intervention of the system in their daily lives and to calculate how, by offering information or appealing to certain official values, the "authorities" could be enticed or manipulated "from below"

[64] Gestapo 6142, LA Speyer. The phrase was "ließ . . . durchblicken."

[65] See Manfred Messerschmidt, "Der 'Zersetzer' und sein Denunziant: Urteile des Zentralgerichts des Heeres—Außenstelle Wien—1944," in *Der Krieg des kleinen Mannes: Eine Militärgeschichte von unten,* ed. Wolfram Wette (Munich, 1992), pp. 255–78.

[66] Manfred Messerschmidt and Fritz Wüllner, *Die Wehrmachtjustiz im Dienste des Nationalsozialismus* (Baden-Baden, 1987), p. 143; Norbert Haase, "Aus der Praxis des Reichskriegsgerichts: Neue Dokumente zur Militärgerichtsbarkeit im Zweiten Weltkrieg," *Vierteljahrshefte für Zeitgeschichte* 39 (1991): 379–411; Bernward Dörner, "'Der Krieg ist verloren!' 'Wehrkraftzersetzung' und Denunziation in der Truppe," in *Die anderen Soldaten,* ed. Norbert Haase and Gerhard Paul (Frankfurt am Main, 1995), pp. 105–22.

[67] See the study of the Saarland, Gerhard Paul, *Ungehorsame Soldaten: Dissens, Verweigerung und Widerstand deutscher Soldaten (1939–1945)* (St. Ingert, 1994), p. 106.

into acting on their behalf. This point was brought out in a lengthy report of July 20, 1942, about "unnecessary demands on the authorities by the population."[68] From all over the country, requests, supplications, and complaints were made to the authorities (*Behörde*). Even when such entreaties to party and state proved fruitless they were repeated endlessly or redirected elsewhere. Some people denounced each other so often that only direct threats to send both parties to a concentration camp put a stop to it. Business competitors, such as one in Breslau who accused another of "incorrect" practices, brought the most serious possible charges before ten different authorities, from the city administration, magistrate, and local and regional Nazi Party headquarters to the attorney general and the Gestapo, as well as to three different professional bodies and a branch of the *Wehrmacht*. This example highlights just some of the ways in which citizens acted on the new opportunities that opened up; they were not merely passive or dependent.

Indeed, letter writing to the "authorities" became a much favored form of citizen activity in Nazi Germany, as it evidently did also in other dictatorships of the twentieth century.[69] Hitler's chancellery, for example, received at least one thousand letters and petitions every working day, and according to the postwar testimony of one official there might have been twice that many.[70] Citizens used such opportunities "to speak to the führer," free from bureaucratic and other constraints, to demonstrate their loyalty, to express some wish, or to seek some favor. People also sent letters with similar aims to other Nazi leaders, from Himmler to Goebbels. Letters to the editors of national, regional, and local newspapers were frequent, and it was not only the ones sent to the more notorious Nazi rags like *Der Stürmer* that had specific denunciatory content—highlighting how some merchant sold goods to Jews, for example, or how a particular citizen failed to accept the spirit of Nazi anti-Semitism.[71]

Further indications of citizen activity in the form of letter writing can be seen in memoranda from the Higher Command of the Armed Forces (OKW) to its regional headquarters. For example, on February 5, 1942, the OKW

[68] The phrase is "unnötige Beanspruchung der Behörden durch die Bevölkerung." See Heinz Boberach, ed., *Meldungen aus dem Reich: Die geheimen Lageberichte des Sicherheitsdienstes der SS, 1938–1945* (Herrsching, 1984), 10:3968–79.

[69] See Sheila Fitzpatrick, "Supplicants and Citizens: Public Letter Writing in Soviet Russia in the 1930s," *Slavic Review* (Spring 1996): 78–105.

[70] See Jeremy Noakes, "Philipp Bouhler und die Kanzlei des Führers der NSDAP: Beispiel einer Sonderverwaltung im Dritten Reich," in *Verwaltung contra Menschenführung im Staat Hitlers,* ed. Dieter Rebentisch and Karl Teppe (Göttingen, 1986), pp. 208–36, esp. p. 221. From 1937 to 1940, 229,101–294,568 letters per year were sent in by citizens. For the larger figure, see the evidence cited in Michael Burleigh, *Death and Deliverance: "Euthanasia" in Germany, 1900–1945* (Cambridge, 1994), p. 93.

[71] See, e.g., Fred Hahn, *Lieber Stürmer: Leserbriefe an das NS-Kampfblatt 1924 bis 1945* (Stuttgart, 1978).

wrote about the "numerous" letters it had received, signed and anonymous, addressed to the army and even to Hitler, complaining about who was or was not being drafted. Some people pointed to younger men, others to older ones, who could and should be sent to the front. The OKW complained that there were many citizens who regarded any able-bodied male who was not in uniform as a shirker and denounced them for one reason or another. However, such men might very well be essential workers, employed, for example, in a munitions factory. The OKW ordered that such denunciations, including anonymous ones, had to be investigated if for no other reason than to halt social discord.[72]

The Gestapo followed up on the flimsiest information, even though many denunciations were never substantiated enough to merit sending them on to the courts. One new study of a small sample of denunciations in Würzburg suggests that only about 20 percent of the Gestapo cases went before Nazified, and presumably receptive, courts; and of these nearly 80 percent were dropped because they were considered either trivial or without sufficient evidence.[73] Such findings have led some historians to suggest that the Gestapo was "inefficient." However, great care needs to be taken here, because any evaluation would have to take into account not only the Gestapo's "successes" in obtaining judicial verdicts but also its political successes in winning over or influencing popular opinion. A study of the Gestapo's "efficiency" also would have to deal with the multiplicity of social effects it achieved, such as the rumors and gossip that terrorized at least some sections of the population and caused anxiety in anyone faced with the prospect of having to appear at Gestapo headquarters. Police in a terror regime thrive not only on what happens to victims before the courts but as much or perhaps even more on the stories and myths that spread about what happened or could happen to anyone who had a brush with the police. So we should not conclude too readily that the Gestapo was somehow "inefficient" because it did not always get judicial convictions.[74]

The sparse direct contribution to police detection by both the Gestapo and the rest of the police network (discussed above) and their consequent reliance on sources outside police ranks, and especially on civilian denouncers, may help to account for the fact that many suspicions recorded in Gestapo files proved either totally groundless or at least dubious and may explain why a good number were dropped. False accusations and anonymous letters of denunciations were prevalent and, notwithstanding a multitude of efforts at all

[72] Bundesarchiv-Militärarchiv Freiburg, RW 21-65/13 (a).

[73] See Gerhard Paul, "Kontinuität und Radikalisierung: Die Staatspolizeistelle Würzburg," in Paul and Mallmann, eds. (n. 6 above), pp. 161–77.

[74] See Burkhard Jellonnek, *Homosexuelle unter dem Hakenkreuz* (Paderborn, 1990), pp. 308–9; and Hans Robinsohn, *Justiz als politische Verfolgung* (Stuttgart, 1977), p. 78.

levels to stop them, the problem was never solved. The country's leaders, including Hitler, expressed alarm about denunciations at various times over the course of the regime, not least because this behavior contradicted the oft-espoused ideal of the *Volksgemeinschaft.*[75]

In spite of what might appear to be the "petty" nature of so many of these denunciations, we should not lose sight of the real terror that lurked around the corner. People who were turned in could be spied upon, their mail could be watched, and their neighbors could be asked to testify against them. When enough evidence was collected, the accused could be interrogated without recourse to a lawyer, kept in a holding cell more or less indefinitely without any rights, or sent to a concentration camp. By the time of the war years, anyone who denounced someone to the Gestapo had to know of its ruthless reputation and of the uncertainty of the outcome; they must have reckoned on the eventuality that accused persons could and did pay with their lives. Death sentences and other harsh penalties were reported in the press with growing frequency as a deterrent.

Signs of the denunciatory atmosphere that was part of the new zeitgeist were in evidence also within private businesses. As Harold James has pointed out, denunciations began to arise inside the Deutsche Bank and were offered not on racial or even political grounds, nor against "obvious enemies," but as in German society more generally for entirely instrumental reasons.[76] The very example James cites—in which management tried to combat the problem by announcing that it was not interested in stories about the intimate lives of its employees—suggests by contrast that the Gestapo and the Nazi regime, insofar as they tolerated and even fostered denunciations, thereby encouraged their growth.

Policing and self-policing activities also took place under the auspices of the Nazi Party and its numerous affiliates, such as the Hitler Youth, which assumed some police-like functions—most obviously and publicly by way of uniformed patrols (*Streifendienst*) through city, town, and countryside.[77] The Nazi Party itself—in search of a role in society at large after 1933, when its major function up until that point (namely, mobilizing the voters for elections) became increasingly redundant—also took on tasks that at least bordered on policing. Of course, the Nazi Party—along with the Sturm Abteilung (SA) and SS—was denied all formal executive powers (of arrest, search, confiscation,

[75] Dieter Rebentisch, *Führerstaat und Verwaltung im Zweiten Weltkrieg* (Stuttgart, 1989), p. 126. See also Connelly (n. 3 above).

[76] Harold James, "Die Deutsche Bank und die Diktatur, 1933–1945," in *Die Deutsche Bank, 1870–1995,* by L. Gall, G. D. Feldman, H. James, C. L. Holtfrerich, and H. H. Büschgen (Munich, 1995), pp. 342–43.

[77] See Gerhard Rempel, *Hitler's Children: The Hitler Youth and the SS* (Chapel Hill, N.C., 1989), pp. 47 ff.

confinement, and so on) after the Nazi revolution was consolidated in 1933.[78] Nevertheless, evidence from city and countryside suggests that local Nazi Party bigwigs (*Ortsgruppenleiter, Kreisleiter*) continued to exercise discretionary and even (informal) police-like powers. There was some blurring of responsibilities in that some local Nazi Party leaders were granted, or took over, the office of mayor, which in German cities carried important police powers. Although it may be an exaggeration to suggest that such party leaders were the "real" repressive power over the people, at least out in the countryside, it is certainly clear that such leaders could and did exercise considerable pressure (if rarely open police terror) over the population. They did this not merely by turning people over to and/or working closely with the Gestapo—although that certainly happened also—or even by acting as extensions of the Gestapo when the police were nowhere in sight, but also in other ways, such as applying direct or indirect social and economic pressure.[79]

If we look even at the wartime activities of Nazi Party organizations in policing the "radio measures," it would seem they were not as involved in the terror as has often been assumed. They provided evidence to the Gestapo, which then opened seventeen of these cases, or 8 percent of the total. But a word of caution is in order about this "organizational" activity. Most cases in this sample began when a member of some Nazi organization denounced the crime. Only rarely did the neighborhood party hacks (*Blockwart, Zellenwart*) overhear someone listening to the radio. To judge by the instances in this sample, these officials were less omnipresent than was often assumed in the myths of contemporaries.[80] Citizens in a terroristic regime often project onto such men in uniform, even the lowly block leader, far more power and influence than they actually possess or exercise. And from the surviving documents it can be deduced that citizens almost certainly tipped them off; these officials served merely as conduits.

However, it is true that the party in rural and urban centers alike received more denunciations than it actually turned over to the police. The party operated as an institution of both conflict resolution and patronage. It was invariably asked—by state and party institutions and even private persons—about the political "reputations" of persons applying for state jobs, or promotions, and this consultative function gave the local party considerable leverage. From June 1935 this role as local information disperser was formally conferred on the party's leaders (*Hohheitsträger*), but in practice all kinds of officials in the

[78] For useful information on all these developments, see George C. Browder, *Foundations of the Nazi Police State: The Formation of Sipo and SD* (Lexington, Ky., 1990).

[79] See, e.g., Zdenek Zofka, *Die Ausbreitung des Nationalsozialismus auf dem Lande* (Munich, 1979), pp. 300 ff.

[80] See, e.g., Aryeh L. Unger, *The Totalitarian Party: Party and People in Nazi Germany and Soviet Russia* (Cambridge, 1974), pp. 99–104.

party continued to be consulted about issues like the political "reliability" of candidates for jobs, promotions, and contracts.[81] To fulfill these functions by rummaging around behind peoples' backs, the party virtually invited denunciations from the population, whether from well-meaning citizens, rivals for jobs, "true believers," or just malcontents.

IV. COMPARING THE GESTAPO AND THE STASI

The euphoria that was so marked inside Germany and abroad over the collapse of the Berlin Wall in November 1989 was soon followed by harrowing revelations about the ubiquitous Stasi and its spy system. It is not entirely surprising that these disclosures about the Stasi have led many people, including historians outside Germany and even moderate east and west German commentators, to accept the view that a "culture of denunciation" had persisted in the GDR since the days of Hitler's dictatorship.[82] This and other contentions, particularly those about similarities between the Stasi and the Gestapo, call for critical analysis.

A brief word is needed on the institutional structure of the Stasi and on the numbers of people who were formally or informally linked to it. After the initial reactions of outrage came surprise and disbelief at its sheer (numerical) size and the scope of its activities. At the end there were about one hundred thousand full-time members in the organization.[83] Perhaps the most bile was spilled over the large number of ordinary people—neighbors, colleagues at work, companions in leisure time—who, it turned out, had been involved with the Stasi though not formally part of it.[84] There have been estimates of the number of "Unofficials" (*Inoffizielle Mitarbeiter,* or IMs) active at the end of

[81] See, e.g., Gerhard Kratzsch, *Der Gauwirtschaftsapparat der NSDAP: Menschenführung, 'Arisierung,' Wehrwirtschaft im Gau Westfalen-Süd* (Münster, 1989), pp. 91 ff.

[82] Joachim Gauck endorsed the idea that there had existed a "culture of denunciation" in eastern Germany since 1933: see Daniel Benjamin, "Keeper of a Haunting Past," *Time* (February 3, 1992), p. 18. For a recent reformulation of the same point, see Jürgen Kocka, "Ein deutscher Sonderweg: Überlegungen zur Sozialgeschichte der DDR," in *Aus Politik und Zeitgeschichte,* B40/94 (October 7, 1994): 45. See also Jürgen Habermas, "Bemerkungen zu einer verworren Diskussion," *Die Zeit* (April 10, 1992), pp. 17–19; Eberhard Jäckel, "Die doppelte Vergangenheit," *Der Spiegel* (December 23, 1991), pp. 39–43.

[83] Joachim Gauck, *Die Stasi-Akten* (Reinbek, 1991), pp. 27, 61; see also Bürgerkommittee Leipzig, ed., *Stasi Intern: Macht und Banalität* (Leipzig, 1991), p. 363.

[84] Some critics said, after the wall fell and the files began to be opened, that psychologists would have to invent a new concept called *Aktenneid* (file envy)—i.e., envy of those who had found that there were files on them. The envious wanted to discover files on themselves to prove their own "resistance" retroactively. See Lutz Rathenow, "Teile zu keinem Bild oder das Puzzle von der geheimen Macht," in *Aktenkundig,* ed. Hans Joachim Schädlich (Berlin, 1992), p. 64.

the GDR that range between as few as one hundred thousand to as many as five hundred thousand individuals. On December 31, 1989, the last date for which reliable statistics appear to have survived, there were as many as 170,000 "Unofficials"—but these figures continue to be revised upward.[85]

There was enormous variety in the ranks of these "Unofficials," and the nature of their involvement changed over time.[86] Roughly 10 percent of them were "retired" each year and a new crop recruited in their place, so that within three to six years most were replaced, at least during the 1980s. This turnover indicates that a considerable number of citizens were directly involved at one time or another.[87] And although hidden devices were used to acquire information, "central to the activity [of the Stasi] stood the deployment of human beings; and the IM was the most important weapon against the enemy."[88] A former IM said that in the 1980s one in every eight persons in the country was formally involved in the effort to generate Stasi files, and that perhaps "a third of the population, more or less, had worked for the Stasi."[89] No profession, not even in the churches, appears to have been entirely immune from implication in the system.[90] One author observed that there was so much support for the Stasi that the dichotomy between victims and perpetrators did not stand up.[91]

What about the motives of the IMs? It is safe to say that a whole spectrum of factors led these people to participate in the Stasi system. Given the very large number of people who worked as IMs, a wide range of motives can be identified,[92] as well as considerable variation in the duration and enthusiasm

[85] They were controlled by some twelve thousand full-time Stasi officials, so that most Stasi members (about 85 percent of the rest) had little to do directly with the "Unofficials." See Hansjörg Geiger, *Die Inoffiziellen Mitarbeiter: Stand der gegenwärtigen Erkenntnisse* (Berlin, 1993), p. 9. About 50 percent of all IMs were controlled at the local level and the other half from the MfS-Zentrale in Berlin. See Helmut Müller-Enbergs, *IM-Statistik* (Berlin, 1993), p. 17.

[86] See, e.g., Peter Siebenmorgen, *"Staatssicherheit" der DDR* (Bonn, 1993), pp. 62–96.

[87] See Gauck, p. 64; and Geiger, p. 10.

[88] Geiger, p. 7.

[89] See Irena Kukutz and Katja Havermann, *Geschützte Quelle: Gespräche mit Monika H. alias Karin Lenz* (Berlin, 1990), p. 57.

[90] John S. Conway, "The 'Stasi' and the Churches: Between Coercion and Compromise in East German Protestantism, 1949–89," *Journal of Church and State* 36 (1994): 725–45, esp. 738, points out that it is now estimated that there were 113 IMs in the church out of about four thousand pastors in all of the GDR.

[91] Jürgen Fuchs, *". . . Und wann kommt der Hammer?" Psychologie, Opposition und Staatssicherheit* (Berlin, 1990), pp. 30–31.

[92] For more on motives, see Hans-Joachim Maaz, *Der Gefühlsstau: Ein Psychogramm der DDR* (Berlin, 1990), pp. 23 ff.; Christina Wilkening, *Staat im Staate: Auskünfte ehemaliger Stasi-Mitarbeiter* (Berlin, 1990), p. 85; Lienhard Wawrzyn, *Der Blaue: Das Spitzelsystem der DDR* (Berlin, 1990), pp. 23–24.

of their commitment, their effectiveness as informers, the size and scope of rewards they garnered, and why they did or did not break with the Stasi.[93] From cases that have come to light thus far, it seems that some people were tempted by opportunities for personal enrichment, or merely by a chance to visit the West, while at the opposite end of the spectrum others were threatened, coerced, or even blackmailed into cooperating. Some went along, perhaps sincerely or self-deceivingly, to "prevent the worst," telling themselves they could bring about improvements by "negotiating 'preventatively' with the system."[94] The Stasi itself preferred people with "positive social convictions."[95] In a number of strategically important social positions, such as those at the Humboldt University in Berlin, for example, most of those who worked as IMs appear to have done so precisely on these grounds.[96]

The broad social participation in the policing of the GDR led a member of a citizens' committee overseeing the dissolution of the Stasi to remark that "the only ones who are innocent are those who resisted, who tried to escape or were in prison."[97] These statements, along with the statistics on the rates of turnover of the IMs, suggest the extent to which the GDR had become a self-policing society. In a sense, denunciation or informing from the general population had become institutionalized. Indeed, it was the revelations about the extent of this spying among friends, neighbors, colleagues, and even husbands and wives that led many people to talk about the "obvious" similarities between the GDR and Nazi Germany.

A common comparison drawn between the Stasi and the Gestapo involves the relationship each of them had to German society. Like the Gestapo—and all other modern police forces, especially those concerned with (broadly defined) "politics" and "subversion"—the Stasi could not have operated without the participation of the broader public. It is certainly true that if we wish to

[93] Joachim Walther and Gesine von Prittwitz, *Staatssicherheit und Schriftsteller: Bericht zum Forschungsprojekt* (Berlin, 1993), p. 20. Another study of 448 IMs in Gera shows the multiplicity of motives; see Andreas Schmidt, "Auskunftspersonen," pp. 173–94. According to another writer, little pressure was exerted to win people as IMs; see Bärbel Bohley, "Die Macht wird entzaubert," pp. 38–46. Both in Schädlich, ed. (n. 84 above).

[94] Hansjörg Geiger, quoted in Jane Kramer, "Letter from Europe," *New Yorker* (May 25, 1992), p. 57. See also Kukutz and Havermann, p. 37; also Justus Werdin, ed., *Unter uns: Die Stasi: Berichte der Bürgerkommitees (Frankfurt/Oder)* (Berlin, 1990), p. 37.

[95] David Gill and Ulrich Schröter, *Das Ministerium für Staatssicherheit: Anatomie des Mielke-Imperiums* (Reinbek, 1993), p. 96.

[96] Hanna Labrenz-Weiss, "Die Beziehungen zwischen Staatssicherheit, SED und den akademischen Leitungsgremien an der Humboldt-Universität zu Berlin," *German Studies Review,* special issue (1994): 131–45, esp. 138.

[97] See Nancy Travis Wolfe, *Policing a Socialist Society: The German Democratic Republic* (New York, 1992), p. 217. But IMs were also to be found in the prisons.

understand the functioning of the secret police we have to move beyond being overwhelmed by the monumental size of the Stasi—not least because, at the moment of collapse, the system never had more resources and personnel, was never larger, and thus never looked more impressive on paper.[98]

One difference between the Gestapo and the Stasi can be revealed by looking at their attitudes toward "nonofficial" social participation by informants. The Gestapo, in spite of its ambiguous attitude toward denouncers, relied on information that was provided by such sources on a voluntary and occasional basis. Leaders of the Nazi police issued no more than a handful of guidelines and reminders in the press on the topic of denunciations, and in fact much of the concern was to warn people about offering false information or making careless charges. The Stasi, in contrast, dispensed to local leaders literally hundreds of regulations and guidelines pertaining to the unofficial informers —dealing with matters like recruitment, rewards, and duties. The regulations were renewed every ten years or so, and there was a host of follow-up directives. In 1989, for example, as the situation was growing more threatening for the regime with each passing day, there were an estimated seven hundred such regulations.[99]

The Gestapo relied on denunciations from the population both directly and indirectly—in the latter case when information was passed to other authorities. At least officially and on the record, the Stasi regarded spontaneous informers with suspicion and skepticism. From the 1950s onward, according to policy directives, such people were themselves considered to be possible enemy agents.[100] To be sure, "occasional sources" gave some information to the Stasi, but this was considered by insiders, at least, to be "often unreliable" and "too subjective"; the aggression, zeal, or "hysteria" of some such informers could lead to their providing false or useless information.[101] The rationale used by one Stasi official who was attempting to recruit an informer was as follows: "We need good people. People who can decide for themselves what is useful for this country and what is injurious. Not blind denouncers who pass along a few names. We need people who can tell us why this or that is going wrong in this country."[102]

From the late 1960s, therefore, Stasi boss Erich Mielke ordered local

[98] See Anne Worst, *Das Ende eines Geheimdienstes: Oder: Wie lebendig ist die Stasi?* (Berlin, 1991), pp. 11–17; and Manfred Schell and Werner Kalinka, *Stasi und kein Ende: Die Personen und Fakten* (Frankfurt am Main, 1991), pp. 48–49.

[99] See Geiger (n. 85 above), pp. 7–8.

[100] See Richtlinie Nr. 21 (November 20, 1952), reprinted in *Die Inoffiziellen Mitarbeiter: Richtlinien, Befehle, Direktiven,* 2 vols. (Berlin, 1992), 1:27.

[101] Reinhardt O. Hahn, ed., *Ausgedient: Ein Stasi-Major erzählt* (Halle, 1990), p. 46.

[102] F. Hendrik Melle, "I.M.," in *Machtspiele: Literatur und Staatssicherheit,* ed. Peter Böthig and Klaus Michael (Leipzig, 1993), p. 152.

branches not to sign up an "Unofficial" merely because of "favorable circumstances" (which is to say, because an opportunity presented itself); it should be clear from the beginning how that person could be used. Volunteers and zealots should be viewed with reservation. According to Stasi theory, at least, recruitment was to be carried out on the basis of the Cheka's principle: "Every recruitment [of an informer] is tied to precise, concrete, politically oriented tasks and must be designed for the solution of these tasks." Recruitment should take place when an "objective need" arose, and only then were candidates to be sought who met "the objective and subjective preconditions" required to complete precise "political-operative tasks."[103] Of course, we have to be wary of accepting these remarks at face value. Although it might be true that the GDR was to some extent faithful to the Leninist tradition of suspecting and even combating "spontaneity," scholars who have worked on Soviet history warn against accepting the Stasi's self-description as following an alleged Cheka model (in which the mythical Cheka earnestly checks and organizes its sources) because this characterization bears little relation to the Cheka's historical practices.[104]

In any case, the Stasi devoted considerable attention to recruiting IMs, spending months and on occasion even years carrying out preliminary investigations and background checks. Stasi boss Mielke often alluded to the "wisdom" of such (alleged) Cheka procedures. Various kinds of reliability tests continued throughout the career of the IM. This thorough, systematic approach represents a dramatic contrast to the practices of the National Socialist period. The Stasi not only attempted to overcome the dysfunctional aspects of the procedures used in the Nazi era, when the Gestapo and numerous other public authorities were flooded with denunciations, many of them false or frivolous and more of dubious utility; it also endeavored to obtain the best possible sources and to avoid obvious pitfalls and inefficiencies.

There were certain parallels between the GDR's "scientific socialist" aims for its planned economy and those for its political police system. In the Stasi regulations on the IMs, the words that recur (such as *planned, concrete, rational, quality control, precisely directed, effective, conspiratorial*) have a distinctly social-scientific ring to them. The intention of the Stasi seems to have

---

[103] The Cheka was the first political police agency of the Soviet Union, created under Lenin. See Richtlinie 1/68 (January 1968), in *Die Inoffiziellen Mitarbeiter,* 1:161–73; and the Mielke speech (December 1975), in ibid., 2:582.

[104] Thanks to Sheila Fitzpatrick and John Connelly for these comments. Readers are referred to Fitzpatrick's article in this volume and the literature cited there ("Signals from Below: Soviet Letters of Denunciation of the 1930s"). For the notion of Leninism fighting spontaneity, see Leszek Kolakowski, *The Main Currents of Marxism* (Oxford, 1981), 2:387.

been to create a "scientific" and thoroughly modern approach to obtaining "complete coverage" of the country. In fact, for Stasi leaders who believed they were in a hostile world, surrounded by actual or potential enemies, it was self-evident that creating a ubiquitous spying system was the only way for the GDR to survive and to save Socialism from its enemies.[105]

The "scientific" approach to informers in the GDR was to some extent grounded in law.[106] Concepts derived from the Marxist-Leninist theory of law were enshrined in the Code of Criminal Procedure. According to this theory, citizens had an important role to play in developing "the socialist state and legal consciousness" through their active participation in solving crimes. There was an implied duty to be on the alert and to report suspicions, and according to one recent study this suggested that in the GDR a citizen "had a legal obligation to aid the police."[107] The legal code of Nazi Germany also encouraged citizens to inform: indeed, it made it a legal obligation to do so, but only when suspicion pertained to the most serious crimes, such as high treason. Even after the outbreak of war in 1939, leaders of the Nazi police were unable to obtain the government's support to introduce a general duty to denounce. Reinhard Heydrich's proposal for an organized "national reporting service" (*Volksmelde-dienst*) was rejected by the highest *Reich* officials on September 18, 1939.[108] Nor does Nazi incarceration practice seem to have been as "pedagogically" oriented as that in the GDR; rather, it carried on the older tradition of emphasizing punishment and deterrence over reformation and reeducation. That is, Nazi law, infused with racial and medical theories of criminology, aimed at quarantining offenders by declaring them to be enemies or opponents and removing them from the body politic. In contrast, the Marxist-Leninist legal doctrine of the GDR described criminals as those "left behind" (*die Züruckgeblie-benen*) and thus tried to encourage informing in a socialist spirit of "rescuing" such lost souls for society.

However, given the motto that "everyone is a security risk," the Stasi was not above treating "oppositional" persons outside the law.[109] In fact, as early as the 1970s the Stasi adopted clearly extralegal measures against individuals it regarded as "enemies" and attempted to discredit them in the eyes of col-

---

[105] See Hahn, ed., p. 90.

[106] For an introduction, see Karl Wilhelm Fricke, "Kein Recht gebrochen? Das MfS und die politische Strafjustiz der DDR," *Aus Politik und Zeitgeschichte* B40/94 (October 7, 1994): 24–33.

[107] See Wolfe (n. 97 above), p. 9.

[108] For an account of the legal codes and failed efforts to change them by Heydrich, see Gisela Diewald-Kerkmann, "Denunziantentum und Gestapo: Die freiwilligen 'Helfer' aus der Bevölkerung," in Paul and Mallmann, eds. (n. 6 above), pp. 288–305.

[109] See Fuchs (n. 91 above), p. 13.

leagues, neighbors, friends, and family. Such tactics had devastating effects, particularly on writers and poets.[110] Other people considered by the Stasi as actual or potential "enemies" were also victimized in these ways. At times, agents provocateurs were employed to establish intimate relationships with the spouses of suspect persons, with the aim of destroying their marriages and thus destabilizing these "enemies."[111] The Stasi was also not above sending compromising photos and anonymous letters with false allegations to friends or neighbors, or fostering malicious gossip that the alleged "enemy" worked for the Stasi, was a counterrevolutionary, or had a "loose tongue" and could not be trusted. These operations were designed to mobilize ordinary men and women beyond the ranks of the police to put pressure on suspects and to destabilize those defined as enemies.[112] Such tactics set the Stasi apart from the Gestapo.

These kinds of Stasi campaigns amounted to nothing less than officially inspired stigmatization processes in which ordinary people were enticed or duped into playing parts. Such undertakings constituted a version of policing and self-policing not anticipated in the textbooks on modern police. No such approaches were adopted in the Nazi era. To be sure, social pressure was exerted or marshaled on occasion—for example, against spouses in mixed marriages with Jews—but such tactics were not employed quite so systematically as in the GDR. The preferred method under Nazism was the less "socialized," more "individualized" one of marking, exclusion, confinement, and destruction. Public stigmatization was aimed primarily at "race enemies": initially the Jews, and after the outbreak of war also the foreign workers from Poland and the East.

There were also similarities and differences in the nature of the victims of policing and informing in the two regimes. The full range of Gestapo activities can be divided into five main areas. With the aid of citizen denouncers and the rest of the police and Nazi Party network, the Gestapo focused on tracking down political opponents; pursuing everyday nonconformity; investigating "conventional criminality"; checking out infringements of administrative measures; and persecuting "outsiders," especially members of groups like the Jews. In the GDR, campaigns against "enemies and opponents" were carried out with much less bloodletting, and there was simply nothing that came close to

[110] Walther and Prittwitz (n. 93 above), pp. 1–2.

[111] For an exemplary case, see Ulrike Poppe and Gerd Poppe, "Ziel: Ein Intimverhältnis," *Der Spiegel* (January 13, 1992), p. 30. For a detailed interview with one of the Stasi informers on the Poppes, see Kukutz and Havermann (n. 89 above).

[112] Classic cases of such approaches have been documented from the dossiers of people like Erich Loest and Reiner Kunze. See Erich Loest, *Die Stasi war mein Eckermann,* 5th ed. (Göttingen, 1992), pp. 50–53; Reiner Kunze, *Deckname "Lyrik"* (Frankfurt, 1990), pp. 87–89; see also Werdin, ed. (n. 94 above), pp. 71–72.

the activities that defined the Nazi terror, such as the persecution and exter-mination of racial groups and other social "out-groups." So the fate in store for those informed upon was different in the two regimes; and if one wishes to characterize informing the police as complicity—literally, "partnership in wrongdoing"—it is clear nonetheless that the gravity of the consequences of collaboration with the secret police was also radically different in the two dic-tatorships.

Was there such a thing as the denouncer as "social type" in the Gestapo and Stasi systems? If one looks at the social profiles of denouncers in Nazi Ger-many, it is safe to say that they tended to originate from the same social milieu as the denounced. More of those who appear in the Gestapo files come from the lower end of the social scale. It has to be recalled, however, that the police acted with more restraint when complaints came in about the "better" classes, who also had other avenues through which they could exercise social power. And, as Johnson has suggested, men tended to be more prominent as de-nouncers than women.[113] In Diewald-Kerkmann's study, 80 percent of those who wrote letters of denunciation to the Nazi Party were male.[114] In the "radio measures" sample I analyzed there was a more even split, but men still outdid women as denouncers.[115] So, while denouncing was not always an overwhelm-ingly male proclivity, the notion that women were the "typical" informers in Nazi Germany is false.[116] As for the GDR, 90–95 percent of all IMs of the Stasi were men aged 25–40. Gabriele Stötzer remarks caustically that women were refused, among other reasons, "because they were regarded as addicted to gossip [*klatschsüchtig*] or prone to emotion [*gefühlsanfällig*]." All but one of the twenty-five IMs in her own file were men.[117]

What about denunciations inside the ruling political parties of Nazi Ger-many and the GDR (another topic in need of research)? There are hints in the primary material and in some secondary literature that informing within the Nazi Party establishment was widespread. The party's "organizations" in-cluded the SA, SS, Nazi Frauenschaft, and others, and there were a number of "affiliated associations" as well (Lawyers', Teachers', and Doctors' Leagues,

[113] Eric A. Johnson, "German Women and Nazi Terror: Their Role in the Process from Denunciation to Death" (paper presented at the International Association of the History of Crime and Criminal Justice, Paris, June 1993). He identifies about 20 percent of the denouncers as civilian females and about 60 percent as males; the rest came from officials or anonymous sources.

[114] Diewald-Kerkmann, *Politische Denunziation* (n. 3 above), p. 131.

[115] There were eighty-six male and seventy-seven female informers and ten anony-mous tips.

[116] See Helga Schubert, *Judasfrauen* (Frankfurt, 1990). For a critical analysis, see Inge Marβolek, *Die Denunziantin* (Bremen, [1993]).

[117] Gabrielle Stötzer, "Frauenszene und Frauen in der Szene," in Böthig and Michael, ed. (n. 102 above), pp. 129–37, esp. p. 134.

to mention several). All in all, the party establishment included more than a dozen such "legal entities." Many of these organizations had not only their own disciplinary bodies but also their own "courts"; and on top of this elaborate and extensive court system was the Supreme Party Court (Oberstes Partei-gericht). The party and its court system also kept a watchful eye over the entire civil service, from the Foreign Office and the massive German Labor Front (DAF) to the Propaganda Ministry and everything in between. Given the kinds of detailed aims and invasive desires expressed by the leaders of the Nazi Party, this complex internal self-policing—described in one account as a witch-hunt in search of the "disloyal," the troublemakers, and especially those sympathizing with Jews—it could scarcely have operated without internal denunciations.[118] Further investigation is needed, but it is likely that the party's internal self-policing mirrored broader social processes at work during Hitler's dictatorship.

Studies of the Socialist Unity Party (SED) in the GDR are only beginning. There were some 2 million members in the SED and, if it had followed the pattern typical of dictatorships, one would expect that party members had plenty of opportunities to report on each other's "subversive activities."[119] Members had to write regular reports—part of the *Parteiinformation*—and this represented a further dimension of the self-policing system. Indications are that the *Kreisleitungen* of the SED performed functions similar to those of the Nazi Party. Cooperation between local SED First Secretaries and the head of the Stasi was closer and more formalized in the GDR than cooperation between similar bodies in Nazi Germany: SED leaders worked hand-in-glove with the Stasi. Less clear at the moment is the precise role played by SED party members (beyond writing reports) within the *Kreisleitungen* in the policing of the country. At any rate, several writers have made the point that, notwithstanding the considerable number of full-time officials in the Stasi at the local level, cooperation of party members with all the institutions of party, state, and economy was thought by the regime to be essential, given the broad range of the Stasi's goals. Indeed, a council at the district (*Kreis*) level regularly brought together all local political and "security" leaders. It looked and spoke like a miniature war council.[120] Precisely how these local councils functioned re-

---

[118] See Donald M. McKale, *The Nazi Party Courts: Hitler's Management of Conflict in His Movement, 1921–1945* (Lawrence, Kans., 1974), esp. p. 140, for the notion of the witch-hunt for disloyal civil servants, which evidently intensified after 1936.

[119] See Schell and Kalinka (n. 98 above), pp. 61 ff. Beyond the Stasi there were other official and semiofficial policing activities, not only those carried out under the auspices of the SED. See, e.g., Dr. Wolfgang Herger, exhead of Abteilung für Sicherheitsfragen im ZK der SED, in Ariane Riecker, Annett Schwarz, and Dirk Schneider, *Stasi intim: Gespräche mit ehemaligen MfS-Angehörigen* (Leipzig, 1990), pp. 109 ff.

[120] See Gill and Schröter (n. 95 above), pp. 63–66. The *Kreiseinsatzleitung* was led by the first secretary of the SED, but included one from each of the following: the local

mains to be investigated, but the aim was a thorough and rationalized (*lück-enlos*) policing system. The Stasi developed a momentum of its own and, in spite of being formally under the leadership of the (local) SED, appears even there to have become increasingly independent by putting "security" issues above all else.

Hitler's dictatorship lasted only twelve years, half of them under exceptional wartime conditions, so there was insufficient time for denunciation to become routinized or institutionalized. However, the Nazi regime did propose a "scientifically justified" basis for the participation of citizens as informants, offering them a novel but quite systematic *völkisch* or fascist theory of the police in which they could play a part. Whereas the rationalization offered to the public early in the regime for the Gestapo and the concentration camps was the alleged threat posed by Communists and other political opponents, by the autumn of 1935 and thereafter the fascist theory of the police began to change and political opponents like the Communists, and even racial "enemies" like the Jews, were mentioned less and less as the Gestapo's mission was gradually broadened. Himmler, Heydrich, and others insisted again and again that the German people in general had to be brought to an understanding of the Gestapo's (changing) missions, and particularly of the part they themselves ought to play by cooperating with the police, keeping their eyes and ears open, and informing the authorities when their suspicions were aroused.[121]

The impression that emerges from the literature on the GDR—and other Central European states—is that the longer such regimes lasted, the more revolutionary zeal and improvisation dissipated, with numerous implications for citizen participation in the policing and security systems. Those in charge of the political police had more time to establish and improve the systems and to institutionalize denunciations, and the longer the regimes lasted, the more citizens came to terms with them. Furthermore, the Stasi and other parts of the system of domination (party and state) had more time to sink deeper roots and to spread through society in numerous ways, playing a role not only as repressor and persecutor but also as mediator of conflicts[122] and as "paternalistic sponsor and dispenser of privileges, even a substitute for usual channels of interest articulation, which were closed in that patronized society."[123]

---

head of the National People's Army (NVA); the head of the police office (*Volkspolizeiamt*); the head of the council of the district (*Rat des Kreises*); the head of the local Stasi (*Leiter der Kreisdienststelle des MfS*); the deputy secretary of the party; and the local person in charge of security of the SED.

[121] For detailed citations, see my "Allwissend und allgegenwärtig? Entstehung, Funktion und Wandel des Gestapo-Mythos," in Paul and Mallmann, eds. (n. 6 above), pp. 47–70.

[122] See Herbert Obenaus, "Stasi kommt—Nazi geht?" *Die Zeit* (August 7, 1992), p. 16.

[123] Habermas (n. 82 above), p. 18.

As long as it existed, there was a kind of Stasi image or myth not unlike that of the Gestapo. That image, perpetuated in part by rumors and gossip, was that the Stasi was ubiquitous. Everyone in the GDR had to come to grips with it.[124] Myths and the "paranoid fantasy" about its power and influence,[125] and whispers about the Stasi's technical sophistication (as earlier about the Gestapo's),[126] served in turn as informal reinforcement of its alleged omnipotence.[127] Joachim Gauck has pointed to the psychological impact of living in a world in which one might be under Stasi surveillance:[128] the possibility of being watched, and the uncertainty that accompanies that possibility, is the essence of the panoptic society.

V. Conclusions

Any essay focusing on the role of denunciations in terroristic aspects of the German dictatorships cannot end without pointing out that to a considerable extent both of these systems attained a degree of loyalty from the population. Even if both the Gestapo and the Stasi represented the most important means for the preservation of these dictatorships,[129] hardly less significant was the acceptance by most people of the legitimacy of their governments and their willingness to comply and cooperate with the terror.

The sources of legitimation of the Nazi regime changed over time; they ranged from ending the Weimar "system" and bringing about economic recovery to restoring "law and order," tearing up the hated Versailles international peace treaty system and reestablishing Germany as the dominant power on the continent. But the regime also made concessions, particularly to the working class, where they feared discontent might erupt. According to Tim Mason, it is the combination of terror, concessions to unrest, growth of legitimacy, and

[124] John Borneman, *Belonging in the Two Berlins* (Cambridge, 1992), p. 178.

[125] See Maaz (n. 92 above), p. 23.

[126] A woman reported that the Stasi not only knew her dreams but had, she said, "built in sensors in my head and they clean out my brain through the telephone. Then I experience such an empty feeling in my head." See Worst (n. 98 above), p. 109. A female medical doctor recalled of the Third Reich: "All the things one knew, that my husband told me, one kept *completely* secret, only in the family or with the most trusted people. You cannot imagine it at all. It was . . . One thought there are microphones everywhere and people listening. It was a terrible time." See Alison Owings, *Frauen: German Women Recall the Third Reich* (New Brunswick, N.J., 1993), pp. 373–74.

[127] For a contrasting insider's report on the technological backwardness of the Stasi, see Wilkening (n. 92 above), p. 203.

[128] Gauck (n. 83 above), p. 26.

[129] This point is underlined by Clemens Vollnhals, "Das Ministerium für Staatssicherheit: Ein Instrument totalitärer Herrschaftsausübung," in *Sozialgeschichte der DDR,* ed. Hartmut Kaelble et al. (Stuttgart, 1994), p. 513.

increasing divisions within the working class that is crucial to understanding how the discontent of the working class was contained and why, therefore, the regime survived to the end of the war without any mass challenge from that quarter.[130]

The sources of legitimation in the GDR, which certainly were considerable, also changed over time.[131] The relatively prosperous and more open 1960s were marked by what has been called somewhat euphemistically a "consultative authoritarianism," in which many east Germans felt that they not only had a stake in the system but also were proud of its political and ideological stance in the world.[132] But even if the balance in those years was tipped, however slightly, toward consent, Mary Fulbrook is probably right to suggest that even in the 1960s the GDR "was a place many of its citizens would not freely have chosen to live in, had they had the choice."[133] In the years that followed there was a move toward still more coercion, especially from the mid-1980s, when the economy began to unravel and the regime began to lose control of the political agenda.

Denunciations in Germany's dictatorships as a subject for historical research has only been taken up for systematic study in recent years. We are beginning to reconceptualize the relationship between the police and the people and to raise new questions. There is considerable support in the documentation on Nazi Germany, especially from the Gestapo files, that the Nazi terror constituted a radical version of a self-policing society. Thanks to denunciations from the population, it was possible for a remarkably small number of Gestapo and other officials to police not only the public but also the private spheres of social life. Above all, these denunciations made possible the myth of the Gestapo as "all-knowing" and "ever-present." The systems of policing and self-policing worked in tandem and, especially in the war years, the circle of terror spread beyond racial "enemies" like the Jews and traditional political opponents like the Communists. The Gestapo was dependent on denunciations and received them routinely at least until the system began to falter in the last year of the war, when the Gestapo compensated for the decline in denunciations by stepping up its own brutalities.

---

[130] Tim Mason, "The Containment of the Working Class in Nazi Germany," in his *Nazism, Fascism and the Working Class* (Cambridge, 1995), pp. 231–73.

[131] For a sustained analysis, albeit one mainly researched before the Berlin Wall fell, see Sigrid Meuschel, *Legitimation und Parteiherrschaft in der DDR* (Frankfurt am Main, 1992).

[132] Characterization of the GDR in the 1960s is by P. C. Ludz as cited in Mary Fulbrook, *The Two Germanies, 1945–1990: Problems of Interpretation* (London, 1992), p. 39.

[133] Mary Fulbrook, *The Divided Nation: A History of Germany, 1918–1990* (Oxford, 1992), p. 206.

In Germany's second dictatorship, although volunteered denunciations were no longer encouraged or welcomed—at least if we are to believe internal memoranda and official guidelines—many subtle forms of policing were organized on a more social-scientific basis. After the Berlin Wall came down, there was shock at the size of the Stasi and the apparently vast numbers of men and women who were formally and informally involved in its operations.[134] But many other varieties of policing and self-policing had also become prominent in the GDR. For example, subjective forms of self-policing were fueled not only by the secrecy surrounding Stasi activities and the possibility that a Stasi agent might be physically present but also by worry that party or state "authorities" might learn one way or another of information that could be considered subversive. Gauck has stated that the most frequently mentioned goal in the Stasi's plans aimed at individual suspects was to foster self-doubt.[135] These psychological aspects of self-policing—involving subjective psychological dimensions such as self-surveillance, self-discipline, and self-censorship of behavior, opinions, writings, and even thoughts—seem to play a very important role in modern dictatorships but so far have received relatively little attention.

No police force in modern European history has been able to function without the cooperation or participation of the population in its efforts. Because both the Gestapo and the Stasi sought to carry out surveillance of ever broader aspects of social and political life, and because the list of actual or potential "crimes" steadily grew, both were more dependent on denunciations, whether spontaneous or institutionalized, than any of their predecessors had been.

It is curious that the greater the degree of control that authoritarian regimes like Nazi Germany or the GDR attempted to exercise over the population, the greater the degree of participation from the population that was required. So these "police states" were not merely imposed from "above" on society at large by ruthless dictators.[136] Indeed, the concept of a "police state"—one that did not fit the self-understanding of either regime—is doubly misleading in that it puts too much emphasis on both the police and the state as entities that might exist independently of German society. Whereas the concept of a "police state" relegates the society "below" to a role of little significance, in fact policing

[134] *Zweiter Tätigkeitsbericht des Bundesbeauftragten für die Unterlagen des Staatssicherheitsdienstes der ehemaligen Deutschen Demokratischen Republik, 1995* (Berlin, 1995), p. 5.

[135] Gauck (n. 83 above), p. 25. See also Martin Walser, "Deutsche Sorgen," *Der Spiegel* (June 28, 1993), p. 41.

[136] For the notion that many citizens fell prey to a "totalitarian temptation," which entailed, among other things, a call for "law and order" and the establishment of an authoritarian system, see Detlev J. K. Peukert, *Die Weimarer Republik* (Frankfurt am Main, 1987), pp. 236–42. For a recent examination of consensus in Nazi Germany, see Ian Kershaw, *Hitler* (London, 1991), esp. pp. 87 ff.

(state) and self-policing (society) have tended to develop and to function in a complex interrelationship.

There developed in both German dictatorships a kind of denunciatory atmosphere in which people not only did not shy away from informing but also often used the system to pursue personal goals of their own. But quite apart from the subjective intentions of the men and women who offered information to the secret police, denunciations had multifarious effects. They assisted the police in enforcing both the letter and the spirit of the laws, as well as contributing greatly to other official goals, such as control of the population and suppression of opposition (broadly defined). The Gestapo, and later also the Stasi, took very seriously its preventive mission of hindering resistance, and indeed all "political criminality," before it occurred.

At the same time as they assisted the functioning of the police, denunciations also played a key role in eliminating the social enclaves that would have allowed people to gather, discuss, and organize resistance. Without denunciations in Nazi Germany, for example, there is no telling how many people might have helped Jews or members of other stigmatized groups or expressed solidarity with them. Insofar as denunciations and institutionalized informing made the Gestapo and Stasi myths come alive, they had a devastating effect on all forms of disobedience, much less resistance. Evidence of the extent and consequences of citizen informing in the German dictatorships remains a source of unease even now.

Index

A

absolutism, and denunciation, 14
abuse, see private grievances
abuse of power, denunciation of, 99–103, 108, 113, 117, 119, 121–52; and see
    bureaucracy
accountability, collective bureaucratic, 145–51
adolescents, denunciation by, 92, 104–5, 112; and see Morozov
Agier, Pierre-Jean, 27
alien classes, see class enemies
Alltagsgeschichte, 10
Ami du peuple, 30
anonymity, 31, 32, 110–12, 149, 205–6
anti-Semitism, 4, 7, 75, 118–19, 138, 160–62, 177–82, 188–94, 199, 204, 214
apartment denunciations, 109–10, 117, 166, 167, 174, 175
archives, Russian state, see GARF; Soviet, 7, 89–90
Arendt, Hannah, 10, 11, 103
army, denunciation within, 203
Austrian Committee, 37

B

Baker, Keith, 29
Barry, Etienne, 31, 32, 39
Basire, 24
Benedict XIV, 75, 76
Benedict XV, 81
Benigni, Umberto, 80
Beria, 123, 124, 138, 142–44, 146, 149
blasphemy, 40–41, 75
Bolsheviks, 10, 86, 147
Boltanski, Luc, 118
bourgeois, see class enemies
Brezhnev, 152
Brissot, Jean-Pierre, 30; Brissotins, 39
Brzezinski, Zbigniew K., 10, 11
Bund Deutscher Mädel (BDM), 11, 166
Burds, Jeffrey, 10, 103
bureaucracy, 21, 87, 99–103, 117, 120, 121–52, 124, 125, 145–51; contemporary
    Russian, 151–52

C

Catholic church, 15, 73–84
censores, 26–27
censors, see correspondence
Central Committee of Communist Party, 143–44
Central Control Commission of Communist Party, 134
Chabot, François, 36–38

Chaumette, Pierre-Gaspard, 32
Cheka, 212
children, repudiation of family by, 105
China, 2
Cicero, 27, 28
citizens as informers, see duty, civic
citizenship, see duty, civic
class discrimination, abolished, 97
class enemies, 11, 87, 95–99, 102, 104, 105, 118, 139–40
Clermont-Tonnerre, Stanislas de, 27
Cold War, 3
Comintern, 10
Commune of Paris, 24, 25, 27, 33
communism, collapse of, 3
Communist Party, archives, 7; under Nazism, 4, 196; in Soviet Union, 10, 11, 87–88, 92–94, 85–120, 121–52; in United States, 15, 18, and see Un-American Committee
community, and delation, 19; denunciation within, 35; feuding within, 59; racial, exclusion from, 177–82; and state, 20; see also religious communities
concentration camps, 11, 173
Connelly, John, 10, 11
cooperation with police, see police, secret
correspondence, and surveillance, 24, 147–48; and see surveillance
corruption, bureaucratic, 148; and ideology, 133; moral, 43–45; and see morality
cosmopolitanism, 138
court system of Nazi Germany, 216
counterrevolution, 86, 91, 133; and French Revolution, 23, 27, 31, 34, 35, 38
crime, and denunciation, 22, 25–26, 48, 69, 74, 103, 139; racial, see racism; nonracial, 192–208
criticism, suppression of, 101, 146, 148

D
DAF, see German Labor Front
Dahl, Vladimir, 121, 133
Danton, Georges, 32, 34, 37
defense of accused, in French Revolution, 32
definitions, see delation; denunciation; informing
dekulakization, see class enemies
delation, 14, 19, 31, 17–20, 26–29, 39, 85–86
del Val, Merry, 78–81
demographics of denouncers (Germany), 215
denunciation, collective nature of in French Revolution, 31; compared across countries, 13; in contemporary Russia, 152; defined, 1, 2, 17–20, 24–29, 39, 85, 91, 121, 128, 131, 135; political, 31, 91–94, 186; as right, 29
Desmoulins, 27–28
de-Stalinization, 8
Diewald-Kerkmann, Gisela, 194, 215
disciplinary nature of denunciation, 31
discipline, party, 10
disinterested denunciation, 126–33; see also motivation
divorce law, see marriage
Dreyfus affair, 2, 18, 75

Dufourny, Louis-Pierre, 36–38
Duport, Adrien, 24
duty, civic, 3, 6, 11–12, 14, 16, 17, 20–21, 85–86; communist, 92–94, 117, 126–33; in
  French Revolution, 22, 24, 26, 28–29; in GDR, 185–221; in Nazi Germany,
  185–221; religious, 73, 74, and see heresy

E
Ecclesiastical Regulation (1722), 45
education, and rhetorical strategies, 137–38
Eisenstein, Sergei, 18
elections, to Reichstag, 6
England, Restoration, 14
Evans-Pritchard, E. E., 69
everyday life, denunciation in, 86–120; see also terror, routine
exile, political, 8

F
Fainsod, Merle, 116
false accusation, 198, 205–6, 211
family, denunciation of, 11, 12, 20, 38, 54, 103–7, 119, 121–22, 200; see
  Morozov
Faure, Félix, 18
Federal Counter-Intelligence Service (FSK), 7, 9
feuding, Russian peasant, 59
Fitzpatrick, Sheila, 1, 10
Forster, E. M., 20
Foucault, Michel, 116, 185
Freemasonry, 160–62, 178
Freeze, Gregory L., 51
French Revolution, 10, 11, 13, 15, 17, 22–39, 86
Frey family, 36
Friedrich, Carl J., 10, 11
Führer, see Hitler
Fulbrook, Mary, 219

G
GARF, 9, 121–52
Gauck, Joachim, 4, 220; Gauck Authority, 4
Gellately, Robert, 1, 9, 10, 12, 116
General Will, 23
German Democratic Republic (GDR), 3, 8, 12, 185–221
German Labor Front (DAF), 163, 173
Germany, Nazi, see Nazism
Gestapo, 6–7, 11, 12, 153, 184–88; and anti-Semitism, 194; compared to Stasi,
  208–18
ghetto, Jewish, 183
Girondins, 32, 37
Gorbachev, 8, 140
governance, role of denunciation in, 121–52
graphomania, 129, 131, 139

Great Purges, see purges
Great Terror, 125, 146
Gregory XV, 75
Gregory XVI, 74
Gromyko, M. M., 58
Gross, Jan, 11
gulag, 9

H
Havel, Václav, 3
Hébert, Jacques-René, 30, 38
Helmsman, 46–47
heresy, 54, 68–72, 73–84; see also religion
Heydrich, Reinhard, 213, 217
Higher Command of the Armed Forces (OKW), 204–5
Himmler, Heinrich, 217
Hitler, Adolf, 3, 6, 10, 160–61, 176, 199, 202, 206, 208, 217; and see Nazism
Hitlerjugend, see Hitler Youth
Hitler Youth, 11, 166, 192, 206
housing, Aryanization of, 160, 167, 177–83; and see apartment denunciations
Huard, 36
Hudson, Hugh, 108
"hygiene," handicapped and racial, 177

I
ideology, as motivation, 10, 13, 15, 20, 126–33, 136–40, 149, 175, 182–84, 198–99;
    and see rhetoric
individualism, 140
informing, defined, 1, 2, 17–20, 32, 85–86, 130, 186, 191; and NKVD, 112; and
    police, 12, 14, 28; and priests, 49–52; and Stasi, 210–11
Inquisition, 15, 18–19, 74, 76
inquisition, "civil," 25–26
interpretation, and denunciation, 36–39, 197
investigations, procedures for in Nazi Germany, 205, 207
Italy, fascist, 21

J
Jacobins, 11, 15, 18, 36, 38, 86; and Terror, 23, 24, 29, 32–33, 35
James, Harold, 206
Jesuits, 82–84
Jews, restrictions on, 75–76, 160–62; in USSR, 118–19; and see anti-Semitism
Johnson, Eric, 193, 215
July 1944 plot, 194, 196
justice, denunciation as, 117–18, 120, 124, 126–27, 130–31, 145
justification for denunciation, see motivation

K
Kaganovich, 92
Kalinin, 92

Kapitsa, Petr, 108
Kazan, Elia, 18
Ketlinskaia, Vera, 92
KGB, 7, 9, 90
Khrushchev, 8, 131
Köhler, Hermann, 155–84
Kohlhaas, Elisabeth, 187
kolkhoz, denunciation within, 100–103, 107–8, 112, 115, 124, 126
Komsomol, 11, 94–95, 98, 105
Kozlov, Vladimir, 10
Krasnaia Tatariia, 105
Krest'ianskaia gazeta, 100, 107, 110, 113–16
Kreisleiter, Kreisleitung, 11–12, 153–84, 216
Kristallnacht, 162
Kruglov, 123, 135
kulak, see class enemies
Kurtz, Lester R., 81

L
labor, conditions of peasant, 43–45, 68; kolkhoz, 102; loss of, 96–97; migratory, 40–72
Lagrange, R. P., 81–82
Lambruschini, Luigi, 74
law, 25, 121, 150; see justice
Law of Suspects, 33
Lea, Henry Charles, 19
leaders, direct appeals to, 138, 176, 197, 204–5; and see Hitler, Stalin
Lease, Gary, 15
Legislative Assembly, 24
legitimation of denunciation, 218–21
Le monde, 118
Lenin, 93, 94
Leo XIII, 77
Lepeletier, Felix, 31
lettres de cachet, 14
liberty, defense of, 22, 26, 27, 32, 35
Loisy, 78, 82
Loustalot, 25, 33
loyalty denunciation, see duty, communist
loyalty, and fear, 129
Lucas, Colin, 17
Lyon, 22

M
Mallmann, Klaus-Michael, 193
manipulation, see private grievance
Mann, Reinhard, 198
Manuel, Pierre, 26, 28
Marat, Jean-Paul, 26, 27, 29–31, 38, 39

Marie-Antoinette, 36
marriage, control of, 50, 54–57, 63, 71, 106; denunciation within, 199–201, 214
Mason, Tim, 218
McCarthy period, 18, 19; see Un-American Activities
media, mass, 2
Mensheviks, 92
mental illness, and denunciation, 139
Mielke, Erich, 211
migration, peasant, 40–72
Miller, Arthur, 19
Mints, I. I., 108
Mirabeau, 27
Mironov, Boris, 58
mislabeling, see rhetoric
Modernist Movement, 74, 78
Molotov, Viacheslav, 88, 92, 96, 108
morality, denunciation for, 103–7, 125; legislated, 187; and NSDAP standing,
    170–71; sexual, 106–7, 119, 149, 176, 178, 190
Morozov, Pavlik, 8, 10, 18, 87, 103–5, 117, 119
Mortara, Edgar, 75–77
Moscow, labor in, 40–41, 48
Moscow Spiritual Consistory, 42, 56, 58, 62, 63
motherhood, in Nazi ideology, 164–68, 174, 183
motivation to denounce, 22, 93, 119–120, 123, 126–36, 139, 149, 197–200, 203,
    209–10
MVD, 9, 121–52

N
Napoleonic Penal Code, 13
National Assembly, 24, 25, 29, 33, 39
National Convention, 22, 31, 33, 34, 37
Nazi Frauenschaft, 215
Nazi Party, 7, 10, 153–84
Nazism, denunciation and, 3–7, 10, 12, 13, 21, 86, 153–84, 185–221, esp. 186–88
Nepmen, see class enemies
Newman, John Henry, 77–78
newspapers, role of, 2, 15, 87–89, 100, 118, 150, 159, 171, 204
NKVD, 9, 11, 12, 88–89, 92, 94, 100, 111–13, 121–52; archives of, 121–522;
    processing of denunciations, 140–44
nonconformism, and NSDAP, 154, 214; and politics, 70; and state, 117; see also
    religion, heresy
"normalization" of life in Nazi Germany, 203–4, 218–21
NSDAP, see Nazi Party

O
OKW, see Higher Command
Old Belief, 42–72
organizations, secret, 80–81
Orlow, Dietrich, 159

Orthodoxy, Russian, 42–72
Orwell, George, 116
outcomes for denunciations, in USSR, 113–16
Oxford Movement, 77
Ozhegov, S. I., 121

P
panopticon, 116, 185
paternalism, 140, 150, 217
patriotism, 16, 28, 37, 38; and see duty, civic
Paul, Gerhard, 193
Peter the Great, 45
petition denunciation, 135–36
Pius II, 83
Pius IX, 75–77
Pius X, 78, 81
Poels, Henry, 79–80
Poland, Soviet occupation of, 16
Poles, in Nazi Germany, 189–92, 195, 214
police, secret, 3, 9, 10, 14, 80–81, 184, 185–221, 207; cooperation with in Nazi
    Germany, 187–89, 191–93, 195, 197, 207, 215, 218–21; of papal state, 75; and
    priests, 62–65; Soviet, 121–52; Stalinist, 9, 12, 88; and see Gestapo, Stasi
police state, Nazi Germany as, 6, 9, 185–221
politics, denunciation in, 34, 133, 146, 186; and rhetoric, 137
pope, authority of, 75, 78, 80, 82, 83
Pravda, 94, 104, 119, 137
press, see newspapers, publicity
priests, and police, 62–65; Russian Orthodox, 45–53, 61–62
prisoners, 19–20
private grievance, denunciation and, 11–13, 17, 28–29, 35, 74–75, 85–86,
    104–110, 117, 134–35, 139, 172–77, 200–201, 206, 221; peasants and, 42, 65–66,
    69; see also apartment denunciations, family, professions, nonracial crime,
    Volksgemeinschaft
procedure for processing (NKVD) denunciations, 140–44
professions, denunciation within, 108–9, 117
proof/evidence, 33, 36–39
propaganda, 11
protest, denunciation as, 140
publicity, 28–31
public opinion, and French Revolution, 29–32; and NSDAP, 154
purges, 8, 10, 15, 87–88, 92–93, 97, 102–5, 112, 119, 148
Pushkin, Alexander, 121

R
racism, Nazi, 177, 188–92, 214
radio decrees, Nazi, 192–208
records, Nazi destruction of, 154, 186
religion, and migration, 40–72; and state, 45–46; and see heresy
religious communities, 13, 15, 35, 73–84, 86; Puritan, 11

reputation, 42, 67, 130, 145, 202
Revolution of 1848, 75
rhetoric and rhetorical strategies, in Nazi Germany, 167, 173, 175, 176, 182–84,
    191; Soviet, 102, 119, 123, 127–28, 135–40, 142–43, 149; and Stasi, 212–13; and
    see ideology
rituals, Russian religious, 47, 49–51
Robespierre, 35, 39
Rome as model, 14, 22, 26, 27, 33, 39
Russia, contemporary, 151; peasants in, 40–72; religion and state in, 46
Russian Revolution, 86

S
Saint-Just, 34
Sanson, Basil, 67
Sapinière, 80–81
Scott, James, 67
secrecy, bureaucratic, 143, 144; of documents, 123; see anonymity
self-criticism, 87, 101
self-defense, of bureaucracy, 145, 150; as motivation, 93–94, 133–34
self-doubt, 220
Shklar, Judith, 20
Sicherheitsdienst (SD), 156–57, 191
signal, defined, 85, 89
slander, see reputation
SMERSH, 123, 128, 135, 143
Socialist Unity Party (SED), 216
socialists, under Nazism, 4
social unrest, prevention of, 156
Soviet Union, 2, 5, 7–9, 10, 85–120; see archives
SS, 191, 201, 206, 215
Stalin and Stalinist era, 2, 3, 7–9, 11–13, 86, 88, 92, 96, 118, 120, 123, 137–39,
    140, 147
Stasi, 3, 4, 12, 185, 208–18
state, and community, 20; and enforced conformity, 117; and political repression, 101,
    125, 146, 148; as recipient of denunciations, 2; role of denunciation in, 33, 121–52
status, social, and grievance procedures, 157–58; and private grievances, 159–65, 172
Sturm Abteilung (SA), 206, 215
Stürmer, 204
Stötzer, Gabriele, 215
surveillance, 12, 116, 205–6; illusion of, 129, 218; at local level, 34, 35, 207; and
    self-policing, 185–221
suspicion, 35–37

T
Tacitus, 26
targets of denunciation, 16–17, 196; in French Revolution, 34–35; to NKVD, 124;
    and see class enemies
Terror (French Revolution), 22–24, 28–29, 31–33, 35
terror, routine, 4–5, 6, 8, 183, 188, 196; see also surveillance

theft, from kolkhozniks, 100–101
Thermidor, 33, 39
Thuriot, Jacques-Alexis, 38
totalitarianism, 2, 3, 9–13, 86, 116, 154
trials, 35
Trotsky, 93
tsar, traditional view of, 123, 138, 148
tyranny, 25–26
Tyrrell, George, 78–80

U
Un-American Activities, Committee on, 2
Unofficials (IM), 208–10, 212

V
Venetian Republic, 13, 33
Venice, 26
Verner, Andrew, 99
Volksgemeinschaft, 11, 153–84; defined, 155–56
Vichy, 16
virtue, 28–29, 39

W
"weapons of the weak," 99, 118
Weimar, 6, 218
welfare, social, in Nazism, 165–69, 178
whistle-blowing, 16, 18, 117
witch hunt, contemporary, 16; Salem, 15, 19
workers, foreign in Nazi Germany, 190–92, 195, 214; denunciations among, 202
World War I, 16, 78, 193
World War II, 14, 16, 21
writers, surveillance of, 214

Y
Young Avengers, 92, 104
Young Pioneers, 10, 87
youth movements, 11; see Bund Deutscher Mädel, Hitler Youth, Komsomol, Young
    Pioneers

Z
Zaveniagin, 123
Zhdanov, Andrei, 92, 111
Zinoviev, 94
Zola, 2, 18

CONTRIBUTORS

JEFFREY BURDS is Assistant Professor of History at the University of Rochester.

JOHN CONNELLY is Assistant Professor of History at the University of California, Berkeley.

SHEILA FITZPATRICK is Bernadotte E. Schmitt Professor of Modern Russian History at the University of Chicago.

ROBERT GELLATELY is Professor of History at Huron College, University of Western Ontario.

VLADIMIR A. KOZLOV is Deputy Director of the State Archive of the Russian Federation.

GARY LEASE is Professor of the History of Consciousness at the University of California, Santa Cruz.

COLIN LUCAS is Master of Balliol College, Oxford.